The Multichannel Retail Handbook
2016 Edition

A guide to planning, implementation, operation and enhancement

By Chris Jones

ISBN 978-1-326-47257-3

First published in November 2015
by Redsock Management Ltd

Contents

Table of Figures

Introduction

Chapter 1. Introduction to the 2016 edition

1.1 Thank you and welcome

The reason you are looking at this 2016 edition is very simple: all those who were kind enough to purchase the first edition. Judging from the feedback I received from readers, I stumbled inadvertently upon a genuine gap in the market for a practical guide-book to this complex and fascinating topic. I've had emails from a wide variety of people, including start-up entrepreneurs, training departments in large services providers, hands-on managers working day-to-day in the space, and college lecturers. Copies have sold in places as diverse as Japan, Italy and Mexico, and it been used as a set-text for a number of university modules.

Of course the big snag with publishing a book on a topical subject is that the material quickly goes out of date. Multichannel retail continues to develop rapidly worldwide and the pace of change is just as difficult to track as it was three years ago. I found it extremely instructive writing the previous edition. Both the research itself, and the process of trying to clearly explain in writing some quite complex material, have undoubtedly made me better at my day-job: that of practising consultant and sometimes also interim manager in this field.

Nevertheless, without all those readers, I'm not sure I'd have found the motivation to set about creating a new edition. So, to everyone who read the last edition, a big thank you; and to you, the reader of this edition, a bigger thank you, and welcome to the Handbook!

1.2 What's changed in the 2016 edition?

Obviously data points, charts and other statistics have been brought up to date, where possible. As observed in more depth in section *3.2 A note on data points,* this isn't the easiest subject material about which to source *reliable* data. In some places it has been necessary to make a judgment between re-using a higher-quality but older source or replacing it with a lower-quality newer one.

Secondly, and particularly interestingly, the previous edition quoted some examples of retailers making predictions or announcing future strategies to address change driven by multichannel shoppers. It has sometimes been possible to follow these up and see how they have turned out three years later. Where this is the case, I've generally left the previous material in place and then added a 2016-commentary to it.

Thirdly, material which I just felt needed improvement, or which reader feedback suggested was unclear, has of course been improved.

Fourthly, the Handbook has been restructured to better reflect its subtitle: "A Guide to Planning, Implementation, Operation and Enhancement". In particular the previous edition's *part B: fundamentals* has been removed, and its material substantially rewritten and then placed more appropriately in context elsewhere in the book.

Lastly, and most importantly, some substantial new material has been added: the chapter on stores and channel-conflict has much new material included; the chapter on international/cross-border e-Commerce has been significantly extended to provided much more insight on a highly topical (at the time of writing) subject; other chapters such as that on mobile have been fully updated. Overall the book is around 25% longer than the previous edition.

Presenting a sort of "track-changes" version of the older Handbook would be irritating to read, and particularly exasperating to those who had no interest in the previous edition. I have therefore confined such annotation to occasional explicit follow-up commentary where this may be of particular interest, plus some additional observations in the footnotes. What I can promise is that every chapter has been revisited in detail and updated as far as appropriate or possible.

Chris Jones, November 2015

Chapter 2.   Why multichannel?

2.1 It's where the money is

Many years ago, I attended a presentation given by the senior executive responsible for group strategy at a top global retailer. I was expecting rather sophisticated material, full of complex strategic concepts, probably somewhat over my head. Instead he described their strategy very simply with a famous quote: "follow the money"[1]. And that exactly sums up why multichannel is important to retailers today. If you currently operate already in a country like the UK, US, Germany or in Scandinavia, then you probably don't need persuading. But just to illustrate the point, **Figure 1** is a chart of brick-and-mortar stores versus online retail sales in the UK over the last 12 years.

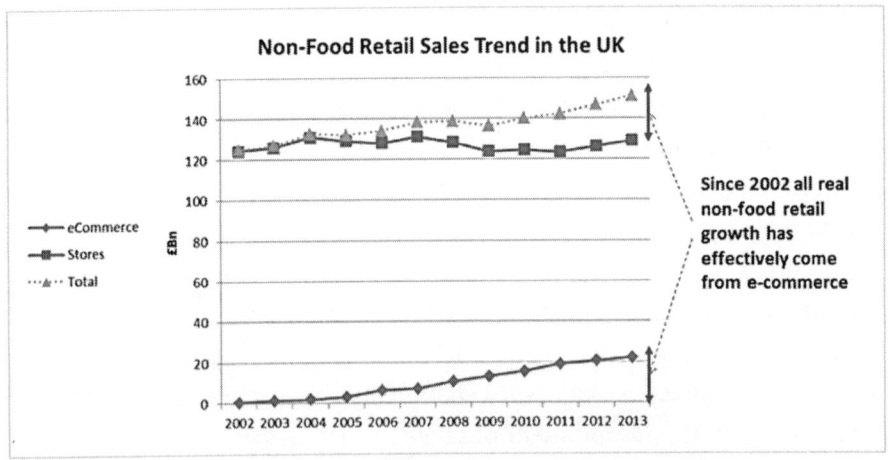

Figure 1 - Non-food UK retail sales trend[2]

There are lots of complex factors buried in the data, not least the credit crunch and the general reduction in price inflation caused by the growth of imports from China. But the overall picture is starkly clear – there a huge ongoing shift in consumer spending away from brick-and-mortar stores to online channels. In several countries this already extends as far as retailers now downsizing their stores estate in favour of investment in multichannel

---

[1] In fact this is one of those historical quotes-that-never-was; it actually comes from the movie All The President's Men
[2] Source data: UK Office of National Statistics.

(see **Chapter 20**), a trend possibly first observed in the UK and US but now extending globally. And I am aware of no (business-as-usual) country in the world where the share of online as a percentage of overall retail is declining. In most countries it is increasing rapidly.

Online penetration also varies significantly category-by-category – some categories are much easier to translate to online than others. Anecdotally, general behaviour is that a category grows online quite slowly until penetration reaches a tipping-point at about 5% penetration, at which point it accelerates significantly. An example where online penetration is already extremely high is office products in the USA. **Figure 2** illustrates of the relative importance of non-store sales to the two market leading players, Staples and Office Depot.

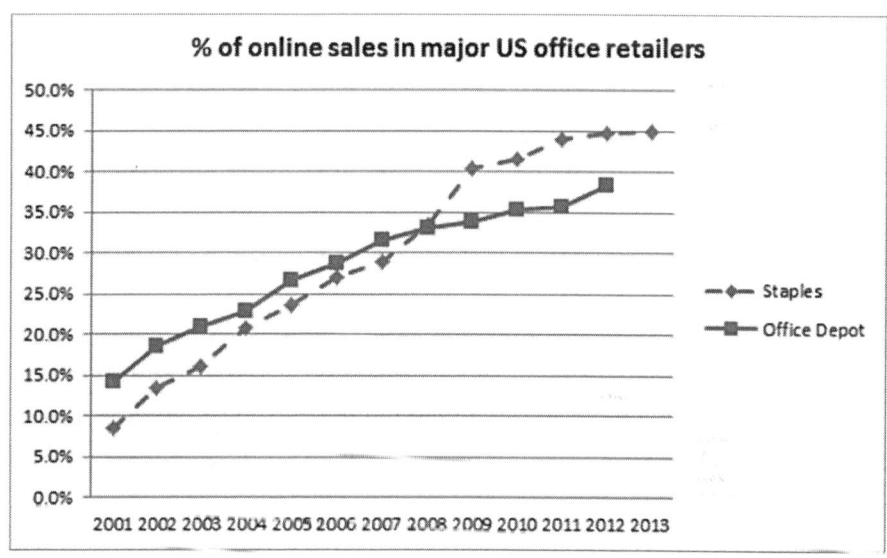

Figure 2 – Online % of sales, US Office retailers 2001-2013[3]

In the case of Staples, over 40% of all sales are now non-store sales. When this percentage of your total sales comes from non-store, you'd better take following the money seriously. In fact, very seriously, because without non-store, total sales for Staples would actually have declined sharply in the recession and kept on declining (**Figure 3**).

---

[3] As published by Staples and Home Depot in various places including annual company reports / 10K filings. Note that Office Depot merged with OfficeMax in 2013, so figures are no longer comparable.

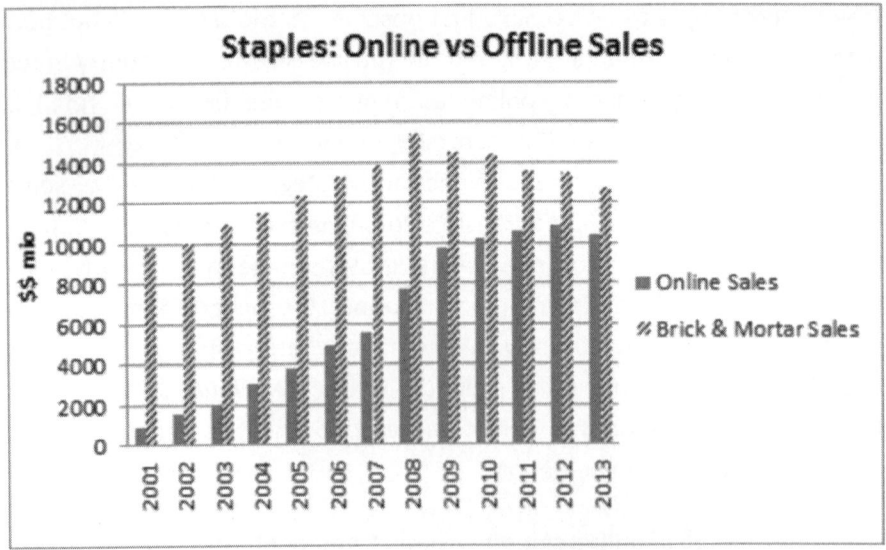

Figure 3 - Staples total sales, online vs brick-and-mortar[4]

This is not just a single retailer effect. The behaviour was replicated in almost all economies significantly impacted by the credit crunch – growth in eCommerce remained resilient despite the overall downturn.

2.2 It's where the growth is

If you are not following the money, you can be expecting to fight ongoing for a declining share of your customers' wallets. How quickly this happens will vary from country to country. Here's a look at the current trends in various geographies (*Figure 4*). Growth figures for countries like the US or UK may appear low, but they are starting from a much higher base in 2007; the average UK citizen spent more than 1700 USD online overall (i.e. not just retail) in 2011. Growth in *online* consumer spending in all countries far exceeds growth in *overall* consumer spending; globally and locally, the customer wallet is rapidly becoming an online wallet.

---

[4] Ibid. In fact Staples overall sales have eventually started to decline for a mixture of reasons, but there seems little doubt that this was staved-off by their effective adoption of eCommerce as a key sales channel.

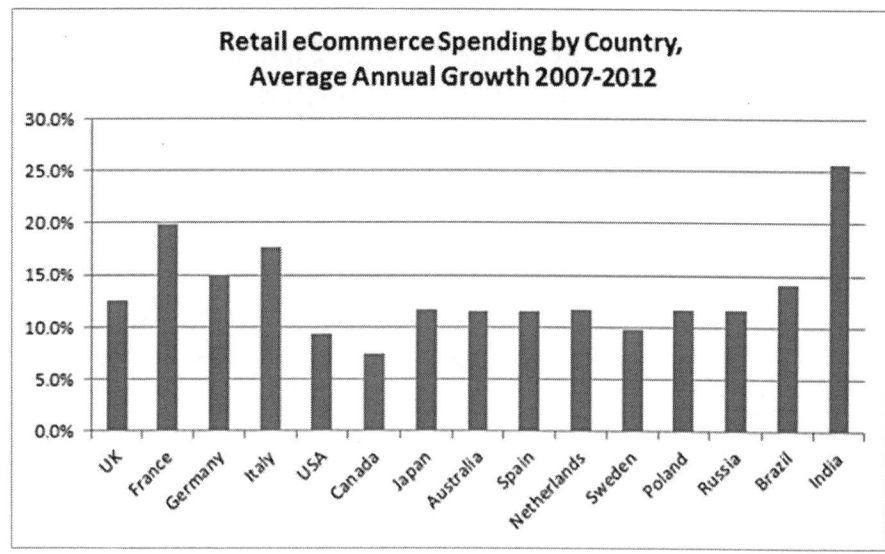

Figure 4 - Country by country growth in B2C eCommerce[5]

The trend is even more marked at category level. In most countries, online B2C begins in travel – especially airline and rail tickets - and then the first true retail categories to see a significant shift into online are consumer electronics and media/books, which are (apparently) easier categories to implement, especially for online retail start-ups. For example in the Ukraine it is estimated that over 20% of all retail sales in consumer electronics are already online, and this is in a country where a general assessment of its eCommerce-readiness would place it pretty low down the charts.

I omitted China from Figure 4 because its year-on-year growth would have distorted the chart! We can compare overall Chinese retail growth on an annual basis with the growth of B2C eCommerce (a very large percentage of eCommerce in China is currently C2C marketplace commerce, so it's necessary to exclude this from the data). *Figure 5* shows the growth curves as an index from a baseline in 2008. Yes, retail overall has grown slightly faster than Chinese GDP, reflecting the steady consumerisation of China, but much of this growth has come from online.

---

[5] Source: Cushman & Wakefield Global Perspective on Retail: Online Retailing, July 2013. Note that personal experience trying to dig out this data on a country-by-country basis suggests that it should be regarded as for guidance only: every country seems to define both retail and e-commerce differently, and collect the statistics in a different way.

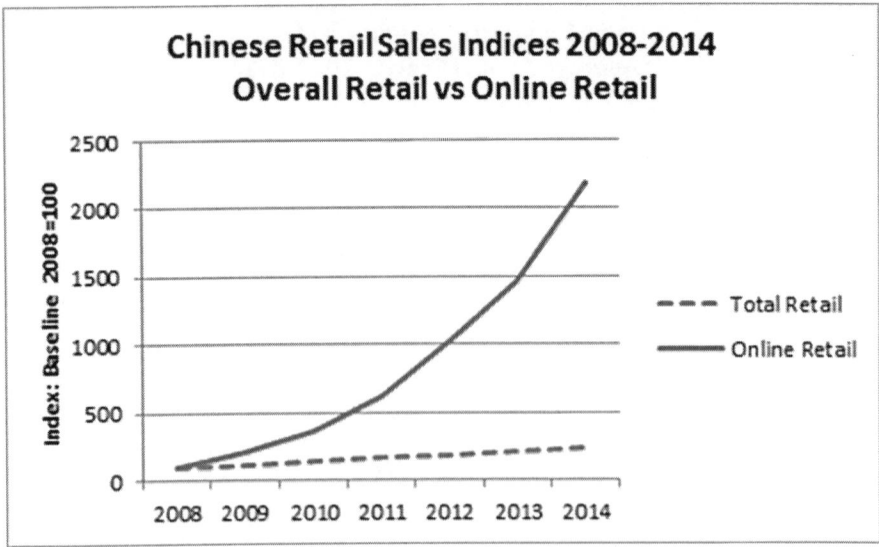

Figure 5 - Growth index for B2C online retail in China[6]

740,000,000 internet users[7] can't be wrong…

If you are an online pure-play, all this growth represents an obvious opportunity to grab your slice of the pie. If you are a brick-and-mortar retailer, why would you want to give your market share away to these upstart online pure-plays? Much better to be there already!

2.3 It's where your customers are

You may well be thinking that the above data is all very nice, but it's about online eCommerce, not really multichannel retailing – the true blending of bricks and mortar with non-store. And this is where it gets really interesting. There are two complementary headlines.

Headline #1. The more channels you offer your customers to shop your retailers, the more they spend; or the other way around – multichannel customer spend more, known as the multichannel Halo effect.

How much more is the subject of much debate, but data points anywhere from about 60% to 400%(!) have been quoted by major retailers who have attempted to measure the effect (see **Chapter 19** for a more detailed discussion). Individual studies inevitably have different figures, but

---

[6] Source: Chinese National Bureau of Statistics
[7] Source: China Internet Watch

all show the same trend; an averaged out view of some typical studies produces a picture like *Figure 6*.

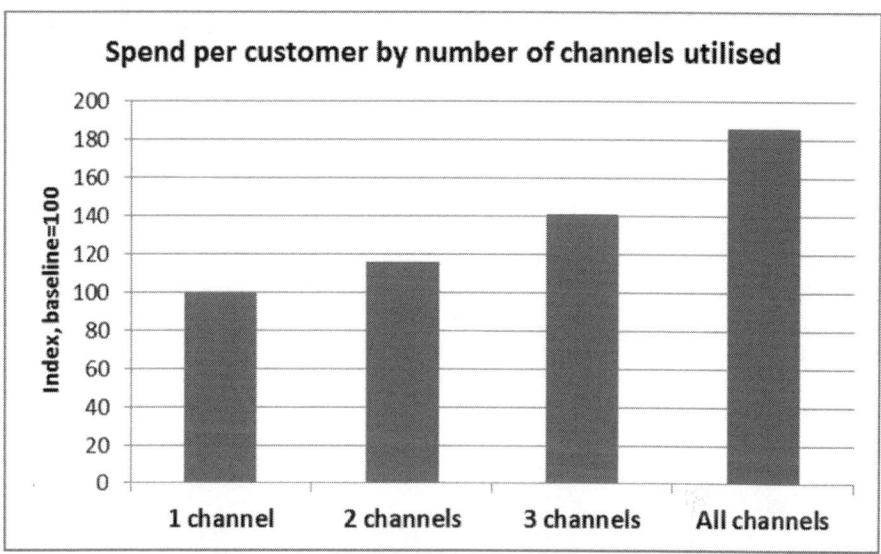

Figure 6 - Multichannel customers spend more[8]

It's important to note that not all of these channels are necessarily transactional channels. Customers don't need to be able to *make a purchase* on four or more channels for you to see this effect. They do, however, need to be able to *touch* you on four or more channels. *Figure 7* shows a typical purchase journey:

---

[8] See for example studies by IDC 2009, Accenture 2009, ORC 2010, Deloitte 2010. It's worth observing that I found it difficult to source more recent data for the 2016 edition good enough to make a graph from. My feeling is that this reflects a transition from headline#1 to #2 in the maturing markets where these studies are typically performed. However there are several more recent quotations from high profile retailers. See Chapter 19 for a much more detailed discussion.

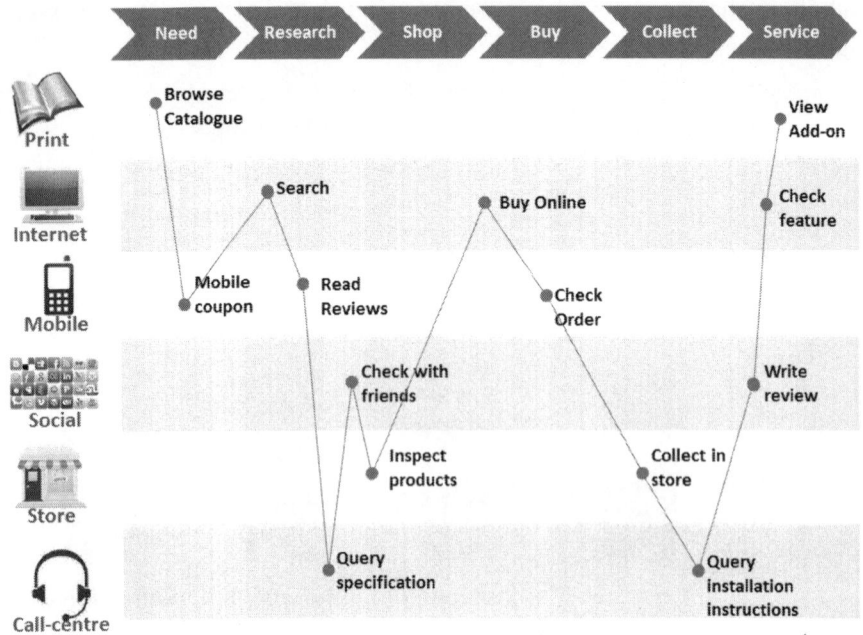

Figure 7 - An omni-channel purchase

The second, corollary, headline becomes more relevant as a category matures online and customers become educated to more omni-channel in their behaviours. Again it's easily stated:

Headline #2: Not only do consumers expect you to be on all the channels they are using, but if you are not – if there's a "break in the chain" – then they may jump to a competitor... at each step of their purchase journey.[9][10]

Multichannel is where your customers are. If you're there too, they'll spend more. If you're not, they'll more than likely go spend with a competitor. And in fact, your best customers are most likely to be the ones who will expect to be able access you via more than one channel. So your

---

[9] See for example Customer Desires Vs. Retailer Capabilities, Forrester 2014. Amongst many other data points, the 37% of customers who (say they) simply won't visit a store if they cannot pre-check inventory online is a good illustrative example.

[10] See also The New Multiscreen World, Google 2013, which shows data, for example, that although 65% of shopping journeys started on a smartphone, 61% continued on a PC

best customers are also the ones most likely to depart to a competitor if you don't meet their multichannel needs!

Losing customers to your competitors is not good, and so it is becoming more and more essential to ensure their multichannel needs are indeed met. The objective of this book is to try and help you do so.

2.4 Top Takeaways

There is a major shift in spending underway from brick-and-mortar to online channels.

In some retailers and categories online sales now represent over 40% of all sales.

Online sales have proven generally recession-proof during recent years.

Growth in consumer spending *online* has far exceeded *general* growth in all countries.

Multichannel customers spend up to 400% more than other customers (depending which study you believe…!). This effect is likely to be more pronounced during the early online growth phase for a category.

The corollary - your best customers are more likely to demand a multichannel experience. Many of them may exit to a competitor if you don't offer an option when they attempt to switch channels mid-shopping-journey – becomes a more pronounced effect as a category, and its customers, matures.

The rise of the omni-channel customer is a step-change in customer behaviour, driven by multichannel.

Online retail in China is (still) growing extraordinarily quickly!

Chapter 3.   About this book

3.1 Structure overview

This book is divided into four parts.

Part A – Planning – examines the processes involved in defining a multichannel proposition for your customers that is appropriately differentiated from your competitors.

Part B – Implementation – is essentially a guide for a currently brick-and-mortar retailer who wants to add an online channel (or wants to better understand the online channel that they already have!) It could also be a guide to creating an online pure-play eCommerce retailer, but my scope intentionally excludes those aspects of retail which are not significantly different online from offline; for example there is no "how to manage a supply chain" chapter, but there is included a discussion of how the logistics of direct-to-customer fulfilment varies from the logistics of brick-and-mortar store replenishment. Part B uses the structure of building the cost-benefit case to consider each component area in turn.

Part C – Operation – considers the challenges involved in *being* multichannel, especially organisation, measurement, finance, channel conflict, and the impact on existing stores.

Part D – Enhancement – examines major challenges faced by multichannel retailers today, including click-and-collect, personalisation, mobile, clearance, cross-border and international trading, plus a specific discussion of the specialised area of online grocery.

The material is intended to be read sequentially, so that each part, and in fact each chapter, builds on material from the previous ones. Nevertheless I have tried where possible to ensure that each chapter can also be read standalone; I recognise that my target audience may want to read only those sections relevant to their current priorities. I have also briefly summarised the key points of each chapter in its concluding section entitled Top Takeaways.

3.2 A note on data points

One of the most vexing issues in studying multichannel retail is the absence of well-founded, publicly available, quantitative data points. There is a huge amount of data. No self-respecting software or solutions vendor is without a white-paper or two, demonstrating how vital their product is to your sales curve, supported by suitable data. Retailers themselves do occasionally publish useful data or facts about their own operations or customers, but these tend to be those that present the retailer in a flattering light to its stakeholders. Other data, even if positive, is often commercially sensitive and therefore unpublished for obvious reasons. Where I have worked myself with retailers and am therefore aware of specific data, I am bound by client-confidentiality.

Quoting genuinely independent data points in support of some of the assertions in this book is thus unusually challenging. I have therefore adopted one the following approaches:

i) Where, based on my own broad experience, I believe a data point to be generally valid, I have either cited a specific representative example with a footnote reference (usually starting "see for example...") or else simply stated the data point and suggested places the interested reader might look further

ii) Where I believe a data point to be worth quoting because it feels to me valid based on experience but lacks support from other similar studies, I have stated this explicitly

iii) In a few cases I have wanted to illustrate a lack of consensus or general confusion around a topic. In these cases I have noted explicitly that the data points have been plucked somewhat at random from reasonably credible, but nevertheless conflicting or possibly self-serving, sources

iv) Where I have assembled public-domain data into a chart or graph to illustrate the point I am trying to make, I have stated the public-domain source of this data in the footnotes (typically a government statistics or trade federation websites). Be warned that even official government statistics are often in conflict, and different governments (or even departments in the same country) measure the same data-point in different ways.

Multichannel retail is a very fast moving field. This revised edition was written in the fourth quarter of 2015, building on the previous Handbook written in the fourth quarter of 2012. I have quoted recent examples or statistics where these are available.

Frequently data points are associated with monetary values in some way. I have tried where possible to use global examples, which are therefore in varying currencies. At the time of writing, exchange rates were approximately as follows (*Figure 8*):

1	GBP	British Pounds
= 1.35	EUR	Euros
= 2.15	AUD	Australian Dollars
=1.55	USD	US Dollars

Figure 8 - Exchange Rates

Many of the non-governmental data-sources used may have a commercial interest in publishing their chosen statistics. Throughout this book I am implying no endorsement or otherwise of any sources mentioned, nor on the rare occasions where I have named products or solutions are these meant to imply a recommendation or otherwise; all such examples are for illustration only.

3.3 Images & Charts

I've tried to make sure all the charts and graphs work in black-and-white as well as in colour, for example by using striped shading on bar-charts. Nevertheless, if you're reading the black-and-white print edition, or using a black-and-white Kindle, you might like to be able to see the colour versions. You can find them at www.redsock.biz/handbookpix.aspx

3.4 Feedback

Constructive feedback is always welcome, and I will endeavour to reply (once) to any received. You can contact me at this email address: handbook@redsock.biz

Reviews, good or bad, are also always welcome, so if you purchased this Handbook on a website such as Amazon, please take the time to write and post a review there.

3.5 Style

I am a practising freelance consultant, my clients expect advice as well as just information, and advice is inevitably – especially in such a young discipline – partly subjective. It seemed to me that a less formal "I talk to you" style is therefore inherently more honest for this book. I can at least promise that any recommendations or suggestions made herein are unbiased by any considerations other than my own preferences and experiences.

Therefore: I hope you find this book useful.

Part A – Proposition

Chapter 4.   Where to start?

4.1 Moscow, 1960

Moscow, March 1960, seems like a good place to start.

Figure 9 - Moscow 1960[11]

This is one of the best-known positions in the history of chess, taken from a famous world championship game. Why is a chess position relevant to multichannel retailing? Well, a strong chess player, reasonably educated in the chess-classics, will be able to recognise this position reliably after seeing it for less than a single second.[12] Not even a grandmaster, just a reasonably strong player, can digest and assess the information presented on all 64 squares on a chess board in around 0.8 seconds. Most of us, of course, are not expert chess players, but from constant practice we are expert shoppers. And once we get used to them, we are also expert users of our internet browsers, mobile phones, and tablets. Just like the expert chess player rapidly assessing a position, our expertise as shoppers and as

---

[11] Tal-Botvinnik, World Championship Match Moscow 1960, Game 6: 21. ... Nf4?!
[12] See for example Hartston & Wason, The Psychology of Chess, 1983

device-users means we can assess the content of a complex retail screen full of information in less than a second.

Take a look again at the example shopping journey presented in **Figure 7.** There are *at least* 9 basic screen-based interactions involved in this purchase, and countless actual screens. And on every single screen, the customer has a vital decision to take (**Figure 10**).

Figure 10 - Decisions decisions

And it takes them *one second* to make that decision. Because this is so important, it's worth giving a name to, for use later in this book: so henceforth, this is the One Second Rule. It is perhaps the simplest illustration of two of the biggest paradigm shifts that most traditional brick-and-mortar retailers have to come to terms with when tackling multichannel:

- The customer has much more power

- Everything happens faster; not just customer interaction, but the retailer operating cycle too

Take the simple example of a customer browsing your shop. If you've got them through the door of a brick-and-mortar store, you have all sorts of advantages: your staff can approach the customer and try to sell them something; the customer can't leave without walking through the store – which might take as long as a few minutes in a hypermarket; you can place tempting merchandise just in the customer's eye-line, like all those treats and magazines next to the checkout. By contrast, if you get a customer browsing your store online, you can't approach them, their eye-line might well be another application (possibly a competitor's) open on the same device or another device[13], and if they want to leave you it's just a matter of hand-eye coordination to reach that close-window or exit-app button. Possibly not merely the One Second Rule, but one second without ever having the customer's complete attention.

So, coming back to the title of this section: where to start? The answer is to start with the customer. Maybe this is obvious, but in practice it's often a shift in focus for many retailers who are accustomed to start all planning processes from their assortment and/or brand (or most challenging of all, from their finance department).

4.2 Starting from the customer

So who is your customer? Most successful retailers have plenty of customers, and so the answer to this question is a broad spectrum. Even if your retail business occupies a specific niche, you can usually differentiate plenty of different customer sub-segments. One of the goals of personalisation (see **Chapter 22**) is to address each of these segments in slightly different ways. If you're already at that level of sophistication, the chances are you can skip this chapter! For the rest, this spectrum presents a problem. It simply isn't practical to instantly build experiences that suit every customer, and still pass the 1-second test I described above. Equally, if your typical customer purchase involves (say) 10 steps, and each step could take place on one of only two channels (e.g. in-store versus website), then that's 2^{10} = 1024 customer journeys you need to consider. Most purchases involve more than 10 steps, and most Multichannel retailers have more than two touch-points. The numbers get completely out of hand.

The answer, and in fact well-established best practice, is to simplify the problem by resorting to stereotypes. There's some jargon: "Personas" - borrowed from advertising; and "UCD" – user centric design – because all disciplines need some three letter acronyms to confound the uninitiated. The simple idea is that if you get it right for your stereotypes, then it will probably be OK for the rest of your customers too. There's a practical side benefit to this approach too – it gets everybody talking in the same way,

---

[13] See for example The New Multiscreen World, Google 2013, which reports that 66% of people have used a PC/laptop *simultaneously* with browsing on their smartphone.

makes it easy to share priorities, and helps break down a lot of the communication barriers that might exist between, for example, your marketing and IT departments.

You could opt for a lengthy formal process to identify your personas, involving interviews with many of your employees and a large cross-section of your customers, with hopefully some very nice artwork as the output. In practice there's usually a much quicker=cheaper way: either you already know yourself (because you have good quality data available), or your store managers know (because they see these people every day). Just sit a group of store managers in a room and walk them through some basic questions about their customers – how old, what gender, what do they buy, what do they do for a living, is it the husband or wife that is making the decisions, who is paying, and so forth. It isn't particularly scientific, but the results are usually just as, if not more, valid than trawling through reams of analysis, and certainly just as useful at an early planning stage.

4.3 Creating Personas

A useful persona for the purposes of planning your multichannel proposition consists of just a few basic elements:

1. Basic demographics (age, gender, social class, income etc)

2. A "back-story" to bring them to life

3. A "mission statement" – what are they trying to do or (preferably!) buy. Clearly this should be representative of the typical reasons why your customers are usually looking to purchase

4. A relationship to your proposed channels (especially a relationship with the internet, or their mobile device)

5. A relationship to you, the retailer

Although it's a bit hypothetical without a real retail client, here's a brief, and <u>very much simplified</u> example:

Basic demographics: Chris is in his late-forties, and lives with his wife and two teenage children in a city in the English Midlands. He works as a freelance consultant, and enjoys a reasonable, if rather variable, income.

Back-story: Despite Chris's professional connections to technology and the internet in general, he never feels he knows quite as much about the topic as his teenage children appear to do! It seems like his daughter is the ultimate multi-channel shopper, while his son is permanently connected to his friends via a headset that has apparently been grafted to his skull. His wife, however, remains a determinedly reluctant user of technology.

Mission statement: As usual, Chris has failed to plan far enough ahead to buy a birthday present for his wife before an urgent client request takes him abroad on business. Over the years this has become a rather familiar scenario, and so his wife will understand that she'll get her main present later. However he would like to make sure a nice box of chocolates arrives on her actual birthday.

Relationship to your proposed channels: Chris travels extensively for his work, and is frequently away from home. Wherever he is in the world, however, he likes to stay in contact with his family on a daily basis. He is never without his smart-phone, and is an enthusiastic user of Skype. He will never stay in a hotel without a good internet connection, as online access is essential to him both personally and professionally.

Relationship to you, the retailer: Chris has never previously bought chocolates online. He has, of course, bought them on the high street, and therefore will probably start his research at a familiar name, expecting that in the UK a familiar high street store will also have a strong online offer.

While it's OK to give a single persona multiple mission-statements, you should resist the urge to create dozens of personas. In order for this technique to work effectively, everybody involved needs to be able to remember them all in meetings, and they need to come to life for everybody during discussions. Good advice is to create between 3 and 5 (maximum). Make sure you give each one an easy to remember name. Keep bringing them back to the table during discussions: they don't really exist but collectively you need to behave as though they do, and start to feel as though they are sitting in the next chair.

The next step is to take a closer look at those mission statements, and break them down step-by-step. However this is the point where the customer meets the retailer, so before we go there, we need to take a closer look at how multichannel might change your basic retail proposition.

4.4 Top Takeaways

The One Second Rule is a benchmark for customer interaction.

Two paradigm shifts for a multichannel retailer to deal with are: customers have more power; everything happens faster.

Start from the customer... not assortment, brand or finance.

Begin by considering stereotypical customers: personas. Between 3 and 5 is the optimal number for initial planning purposes. Give them a memorable name and keep reinforcing their presence.

A simple persona can be defined from five basic elements: basic demographics, back-story, mission statement, channel relationship, retailer relationship.

Personas only work if they are credible and representative, and everyone believes in them.

Chapter 5.   Introducing P.R.I.C.E. Differentiation

5.1 Introducing P.R.I.C.E.

Differentiation for the multichannel retailer is not "special" in some way. The same rules of doing business still apply, and standard models for differentiation like Porter's quadrants are still just as relevant as ever. A list of the essential factors for a multichannel retailer to consider is made memorable by the acronym P.R.I.C.E.: Price, Range, Information, Convenience and Experience. This chapter will briefly introduce each topic, before the next five chapters consider each in turn in more depth.

5.2 Price

Over the last few years there have been repeated huge protests in India by small family retailers against government plans to allow multi-national chains to invest in majority owned retail outlets. The government has understandably subsequently blown hot and cold on the issue. The family retailers not unreasonably claim that the multi-nationals will have an unfair competitive advantage. Unfortunately, they are probably protesting against the wrong thing. If they really want to succeed in their objective they need to protest against the rollout of mobile broadband or the sale of smartphones. Why? Because mobile is how the great majority of all internet access happens in India, broadband is an essential enabler for most online retail, and once you have internet retailing you have *price transparency*. In other words, you can check how much others are charging at the click of a few buttons.

Price transparency is almost always the biggest change that retailers have to come to terms with when considering their response to multichannel. Even in countries with relatively low internet penetration into retail, this is already a significant issue in some categories (especially consumer electronics).

5.3 Range

Assortment is both an opportunity and an issue.

The opportunity exists in extending your range beyond what you can physically fit into your stores. In the more sophisticated multichannel retailers, this is not merely having a big range on your website, it's about making that big range available to customers in the stores as well. The endless aisle and the long tail are both key concepts to address.

The challenge is that limited coverage in a particular category no longer cuts it. This is always a problem in limited-space retail, but is amplified by multichannel when it so easy for customers to just switch to another retailer's offer. The converse is also true however: offering a complete range drives sales, and multichannel makes it easier to offer a complete range. This is Amazon's original proposition summed up in one sentence, and look where it got them!

5.4 Information

On a very good PC/tablet retail website, only 3-5% of visits will result in a checkout. On a very good mobile site, you'll do very well indeed to convert much more than 1% of visits. In a brick-and-mortar store, only some customers actually buy anything (offline conversion rates vary enormously: a few benchmarks include 31% in fashion in the US to over 85% in luxury retail in India). What are all those other visitors doing?

Online, half of them are just having a quick glance to see if you are relevant (remember that One Second Rule again) to their needs of the moment. The other half are there to do some research. Yes, it might just be price research, but it's quite likely to also be other research – product specification for example. Becoming an information destination build visits, builds brand recognition, builds sales across all your channels. It's also very difficult (=expensive) to do well. In a brick-and-mortar store, they are probably checking how the product looks and feels before purchasing it online (a phenomenon known as showrooming). It's still important to you that they chose your store as the showroom, because they are then more likely to subsequently make the purchase from you.

5.5 Convenience

Apart from price itself (but including *researching* price), Convenience is at the heart of why customers use multichannel.

Enjoying the Moscow traffic on the evening commuter run? Check the price of that laptop you've just spotted on an advertising hoarding. Suddenly remembered you've run out of coffee? Add it to your shopping list on your mobile. Want your box of chocolates to arrive exactly on your wife's birthday? Book the premium nominated-day delivery service on the website. Not in during the weekdays to receive that parcel? Click-and-collect to the nearest store, and pick it up at the weekend after dropping your son off at his football training.

Experience is showing that once Price differentials between upstart pureplays and established retailers are ironed out, the next battleground in a country/category tends to become Convenience.

5.6 Experience

Also known as Everything Else.

Obviously giving your customers a great experience goes without saying. What is important in multichannel retailing is that you also give your customers a *consistent* experience across all your touch-points. Internally you might be more or less organised into channels (see the discussion of organisation in **Chapter 18**), but the customer is not going to understand this; they see you as one brand.

Just to pick a single, classic issue – you cannot refuse to accept returns from your website in your stores. Customers will return the stuff there anyway, whether you like it or not. Don't fight it, make it work seamlessly for them. Here's a quote from a top multichannel executive:

"It is not unusual for customers to view a product in-store and then to order it online for home delivery. But if they want to return it, they prefer to do so at the store because customers enjoy the physical experience of getting their money back." [14]

5.7 Top Takeaways

Multichannel retail differentiation can be described by the factors forming the acronym P.R.I.C.E.: price, range, information, convenience, experience.

Price transparency must be addressed by retailers in their response to multichannel.

Assortment (range) completeness is enabled by the endless aisle/long tail.

---

[14] Laura Wade-Gery, executive director multichannel & eCommerce at Marks and Spencer, speaking the world retail congress, London, September 2012

97% of desktop site, 99% of mobile site, and a sizeable proportion of store visits do not lead directly to the checkout. Many of these customers are there for research (information) reasons.

Convenience is at the heart of why many customers choose multichannel.

Multichannel retailing experiences need to be consistent for the customer across all channels.

Chapter 6. Price

6.1 Introduction: A Salzburg Nightmare

As an introduction to this topic, here's a case-study of a major retailer demonstrating how to get this issue extremely wrong:

ACER
ASPIRE 7740G-434G64MN 03...

Gerätetyp: Notebook, Prozessortyp: Core i5 2.26 GHz I5-430M, Prozessor-Marke: Intel, Prozessor-Modell: Core i5, Prozessor-Nummer: I5-430M, Prozessor-Taktfrequenz: 2.26 GHz, Festplattenkapazität: 640 GB, Festplatten Typ: SATA

Q Zoomen & weitere Detailansichten

Media Markt Onlinepreis

€**739,-**

+ Versand: € 9,90
Sofort lieferbar

🛒 In den Warenkorb

Marktpreis *i*
Salzburg

€**699,-**

Figure 11 - One Product, Two Prices! [15]

Two prices in *Figure 11*: an online price of €739 plus a further €9.90 for delivery; a store price *in Salzburg store only* of €699.

It's worth breaking this down step-by-step, just to illustrate some of the issues.

---

[15] Media Markt Austria website, screenshot taken in May 2010

6.1.1 Branding.

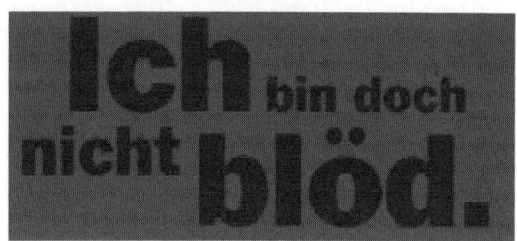

Figure 12 - Media Markt motto

Media Markt's slogan, emblazoned across their website, throughout their stores, and in all their advertising is approximately translated as "I'm not stupid". In other words, I know I'm getting a great deal from Media Markt. In the pre-internet days, before price transparency became commonplace, this might well have been true. Post internet, it still might be true, except that they went out of their way to carefully inform the customer that it was not true.

Firstly, the website appears to show two prices. So which is the "not stupid" price? Secondly, actually the website allowed you to change your designated store. And lo and behold, the prices in Salzburg are different to the prices in Vienna... or Innsbruck... or Graz... or you get the idea. So there could be 30+ prices for the same product? Which one is the stupid price now then?

6.1.2 Channel Conflict

Channel conflict is a topic we'll return to later (*Chapter 19*), but it's at the heart of what's gone wrong here. Media Markt stores are partially franchises, and the franchisees have made significant investment in their stores. They do *not* want to see themselves being undercut by the (head-office operated) website. Hence the excruciating attempts to have the website price higher than the store price.

6.1.3 Price comparison and transparency

Branded consumer electronics are particularly easy products to include in a price comparison website, or to price compare generally. Displaying a high online price means you'll have a high price on any price comparison site. Having a high price on a price comparison site means your customers will draw the obvious conclusion: you are expensive. It is particularly unfortunate if your slogan is "I'm not stupid" and you then demonstrate quite so explicitly to your customers that, if they were buying from you in the past, they probably were stupid. Reputational damage to your brand is not so easy to repair.

6.1.4   The world has changed

An alternative option, presumably rejected for the reasons mentioned the Channel Conflict point, would have been to have a lower price online, competitively positioned if not necessarily the lowest. The consequence would have been well-informed customers marching into stores and demanding the online price. The reality, of course, was that well-informed customers were already researching prices online. In the single currency zone of the EU, they could even easily extend their researches outside Austria if they so wished. These customers could already march into stores and demand an online price, or simply vote with their wallets and purchase from another retailer. Based on data published by Media Markt, it seems quite likely that the stores were quietly discounting their prices in a small way (2 -3% on average) when customers did so.[16]

But it cost them a CEO and a CFO to accept that the world really has changed, power has moved from the retailer to the customer, and it would be better to change than to die.

6.2 Strategic Options

Forewarned by this cautionary tale, we can explore some of the strategic options available.

6.2.1   Retreat from the high street

This is not quite as bizarre as it might sound. There are several credible instances of retailers simply deciding that retaining brick-and-mortar stores in the multichannel age was not going to work for them. Here's a quote from a fairly successful example, Shop Direct, a GBP 1.7 Bn business

---

[16]http://www.metrogroup.de/internet/site/metrogroup/get/documents/metrogroup_international/corpsite/05_inrel/presentations/events-2011-07-26-MSH-Field-Trip.pdf

annually (around USD 2.5 Bn) with over 5M customers including the 3rd largest clothing and 5th largest non-food retailing brands in the UK:

"A 21st century business: Since 2005, we have transformed and modernised the entire business. We have <u>sold our stores</u> and merged the home shopping businesses to create the UK's leading online and home shopping retailer." [17] *[my underlining].*

Effectively they have turned themselves into a catalogue/phone-order/online pure-play, and done so fairly effectively. It has allowed them to strip costs out, and either compete on price or sell products where direct price competition is less of an issue. If you are pure-play in the first place, you probably already got there. If you are a successful mail-order or catalogue-based business, this is maybe not a good time to be opening stores.

6.2.2   Channel-based pricing

In the long run – and "long" here might be a matter of months, depending on the multichannel maturity stage of your country market – this is not sustainable. In a highly developed market like the UK or US, it's already not an option anyway. But there are plenty of examples of retailers who have managed to sustain pricing differently online versus offline for at least a short while, giving them a bit of breathing space to resolve the wider business model issues. A higher price online, as Media Markt chose to try, is at best unorthodox, but a higher store price might be doable for a period, at least until consumers in your country get the hang of show-rooming.

Sooner-or-later customers will demand "One Retailer, One Price"[18]. Once this starts to happen, you have little option but to follow the money. However there are still ways to obfuscate the issue, which are generally accepted by consumers:

Channel specific promotions: Channel-based Promotions are usually considered acceptable, simply because customers get the concept

---

[17] http://www.shopdirect.com/shop-direct/
[18] An interesting recent example of this operating in reverse is Amazon's opening of a brick-and-mortar bookstore in Seattle. Pricing is achieved by customer's scanning shelf-edge barcodes and reading the price from the website.

rationally. In fact they may well be essential, particularly when choosing NOT to reflect store-based loss-leader promotions online. Put a stellar price for a highly desirable item up on a popular website, word will quickly go round the forums and social networks, and you'll get raped. And on a website, it won't generate as much in terms of cross-sell or beneficial incidental footfall that you might see in brick-and-mortar. People will just buy the cheap item that you're losing money on.

Shipping Fees: Recover some of the lost margin via fees, especially Delivery Fees. Delivery fees are a difficult option because unfortunately they're also the biggest barrier to online customer-conversion; the reality is that most online retailers subsidise them. Other fees are more dubious, and although that doesn't seem to stop budget airlines, I can't think of an example where it's been successfully sustained in retail.

Just to reiterate, this is probably only a temporarily viable strategy, but if you are operating in a less developed market, then it may well work for you for a short period. Once mobile broadband and smartphones are a reality for a significant proportion of your customers, then the showrooming factor comes into play. Customers in your stores will check online *while they are in your stores* and validate the prices. There have been some desperate attempts to prevent this behaviour – Best Buy in the US for example, tried proprietary barcodes for some of their higher ticket items to stop customers scanning generic bar-codes with their smartphone – but they are destined to fail. More sensible retailers are taking the route of accepting they can't beat this behaviour, and offering their customers free in-store Wi-Fi as a service instead (see **Chapter 20**).

6.2.3   Be the cheapest!

If you had a price advantage before the days of price transparency, then now you have a PRICE ADVANTAGE: great news, stop reading this book now, and get out there marketing yourself like crazy. Otherwise, take a hard look at what this option would mean for your business. If you are fortunate enough to have the buying power, then you have been given the ammunition to squeeze the life out of your suppliers (sometimes literally, unfortunately). Otherwise, of course it means reduced gross margins. This is a fairly horrible thought, but it's much more horrible if you are forced into it reactively by your customers and competitors than if you plan for it, and take all your stakeholders with you on the journey.

Our useful Media Markt case study also illustrates a retailer that (eventually) decided to address this challenge proactively. *Figure 13* summarises the plan in their published investor relations presentation. In summary, they believed their stores were already discounting in practice due to online price pressure, and therefore that they had already absorbed some of this in reduced effective margins. They then planned to reduce margins by a further 2-3% to retain price perception compared to larger/credible online brands, which they would compensate for via various cost savings. Separately they would also continue a two brand strategy for now. At least the issue had been tackled explicitly head-on and a strategic plan put into action: we can see in the retrospective section below that it has apparently worked to a reasonable extent.

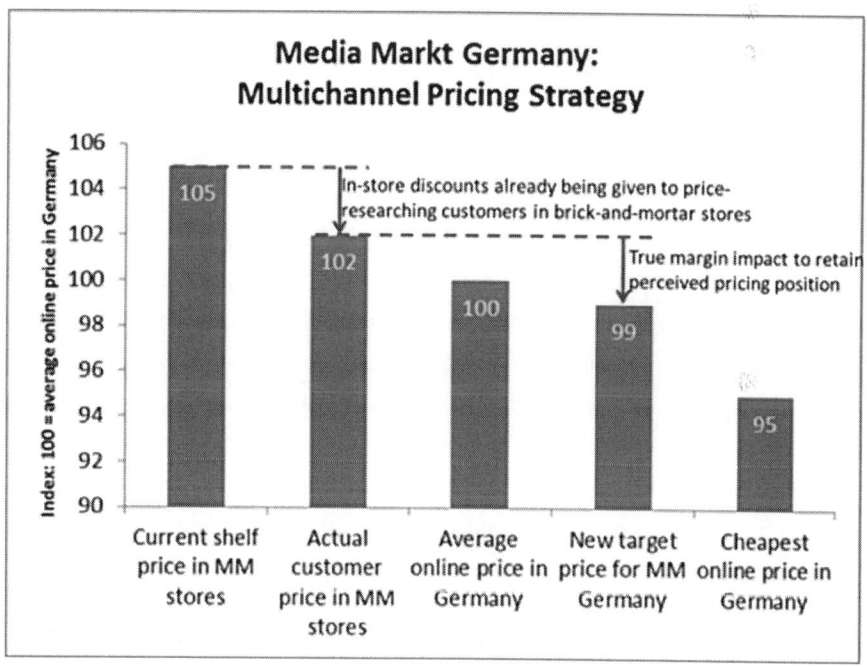

Figure 13 - Planning for reduced gross margins[19]

---

[19]http://www.metrogroup.de/internet/site/metrogroup/get/documents/metrogroup_international/corpsite/05_inrel/presentations/events-2011-07-26-MSH-Field-Trip.pdf

6.2.4   Don't sell products that customers can price-compare

Simple? Well not necessarily. If you have non-comparable products, especially something like own-branded fashion, then it probably is simple. But even in some of the war-zones like consumer electronics there are various options being explored by multichannel retailers. The reason consumer electronics is a war-zone in the first place is that, in any country with reasonable consumer-protection legislation, a customer can always be certain that if they purchase a Widget 2013GTi, that's exactly what they are going to get, no matter who they purchase it from. So they may as well buy from the cheapest outlet. The retailer is merely acting as a supply-conduit from brand manufacturer to end-customer, retaining a service-fee for the transaction, and getting no more long-term value from the transaction than the credit-card provider who processes the customer's payment. The challenge for the retailer is to transform the transaction in some way.

One option is to completely change the concept of the transaction in the first place – to stop it being just a supply-conduit/service-fee transaction – by adding value along the way, for example by providing set-up, configuration, knowledge, support or other services. This is an element of the strategy being pursued, for example, by Dixons Retail (PC World) in the UK. Japan's Yamada Denki offers the same idea in a different flavour.

Another option is to change the Widget so that you have an exclusive Widget 2016GTk while everybody else only has the 2016GTi. Basically the same product, slightly different specification, no longer price comparable (in theory anyway). Many branded goods manufacturers are rapidly waking up to this issue and supporting their retailer clients in these endeavours. If you are a retailer in an even slightly vulnerable category, then putting in place such a long-term strategic co-operation with your brands is strongly recommended, even if you yourselves have no immediate Multichannel plans. (Other brands try to avoid supplying in the first place to retailers who might discount, especially luxury brands. I once did an engagement with a luxury jewellery retailer planning to go online who found their plans seriously hampered by non-cooperative brands. Adidas/Reebok have recently announced that authorised dealers will be banned from selling their products on Amazon or eBay marketplaces, citing brand-devaluation arguments[20]). Even the most basic steps like offering the 6Gb of memory option while everybody else has the 4Gb or 8Gb are a start.

Creating or developing own-brands is a variant of the same idea that retailers are increasingly adopting. Nobody else stocks them, so they can't be price-compared directly, and just as important you have full control over their price-positioning and gross margin. Our central case-study MediaMarkt is just such an example (see below).

Still another possibility is to take a lead from mobile phone service providers, and group products into bundles that prevent the customer directly comparing prices, for example as a product + extended warranty option.

One last choice is of course some kind of price maintenance collaboration, either official or unofficial, within your market. These come with a high risk even where legal. You may well be able to obstruct legislation preventing this kind of behaviour. You are unlikely to be able to stop customers remembering that it's not called the World Wide Web for no reason, and just switching to purchasing from overseas websites. A current high-profile example is Australia, where the issue is exacerbated by sales tax that does not apply to goods shipped in from overseas until they are of significant value (A$1000 at the time of writing). In 2012 UK government moved this threshold right down virtually nil partly as a result of tax-haven pure-plays undercutting local retailers (and reducing the government tax-take as a consequence), but it hasn't really eased the price competition, just moved the bar a bit.

6.2.5   Two Brands

Not every customer is an internet-loving, comparison-trawling, price-obsessed shopper. And even in countries where this appears to be the case, it doesn't happen overnight. Yes, your younger customers may well live online, but younger customers don't necessarily have much buying power on average. The Rise of the Silver Surfer (i.e. older people becoming heavy internet users) is a phenomenon that takes some time to happen in every country.

---

[20]   See for example http://www.e-commercefacts.com/news/2012/06/adidas-dislikes-ebay-and-/index.xml

Russia is a reasonable semi-developed example. Multichannel in Russia could reasonably be described as relatively immature. Only around 1% of retail sales are non-store in Russia (compared to over 10% in the UK[21]), but internet and broadband penetration is rising rapidly in the major cities, to almost 70% in Moscow and St Petersburg.[22] How is this 70% divided?

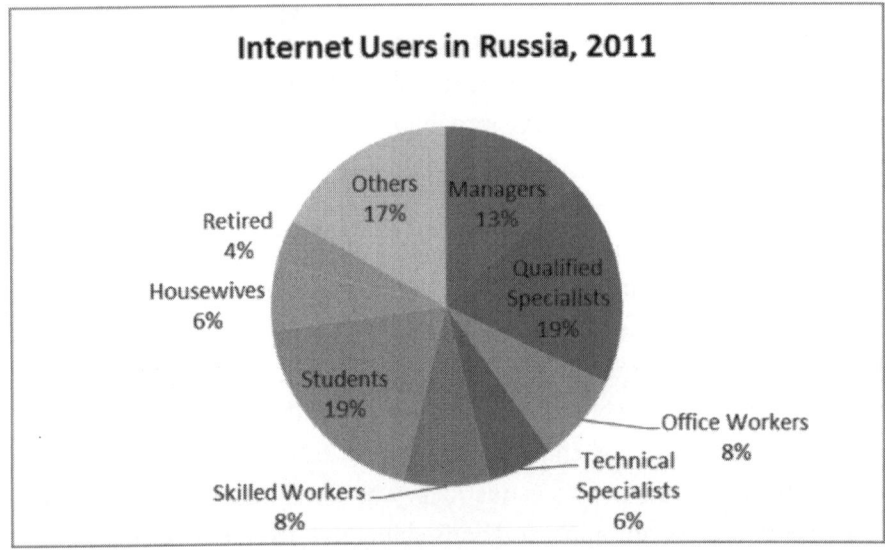

Figure 14 - Distribution of internet users (aged > 12) in Russia[23]

As **Figure 14** shows, only 4% of internet users (aged > 12) are retired, and yet 15% of the population (aged > 12) are over 65.[24] There remains a significant segment for whom the internet is still a rumour.

In a market like Russia, a two brand strategy might well be a reasonable option. One online pure-play brand for the young price-comparers, another multichannel brand with the emphasis on stores and service for the rest. Once again our Media Markt case-study illustrates the point. Even in a market as developed as Germany, the company still believes a two brand strategy is feasible, and purchased an online pure-play Redcoon.de (let's hope they don't try roll out this brand-name in any English speaking markets!) as part of its Multichannel strategy.

---

[21] UK Office of National Statistics.
[22] TNS Web Index, Russia
[23] TNS Web Index, 2011
[24] CIA World Factbook, www.cia.gov

If this is an appropriate option in your local market, then the important thing is to plan your exit strategy at the same time. Eventually your customers will become more multichannel aware, the Silver Surfers will come floating in, and you'll have to converge the brands (as Dixons Retail plc are now doing in the UK for example).

6.2.6   Don't Compete on Price

As I hope this chapter has illustrated, competing on price in a price-transparent world is challenging at best. If possible, make plans to shift into less price-driven product ranges. If you can't avoid selling products that customers can price compare, you can always choose not to worry too much if you lose a few sales due to price comparison, and focus on those customers for whom price is not the biggest issue.

Don't let this happen by drifting into it. Price transparency is coming to a country near you right now, so if your strategy is not to compete on price while remaining active in price-sensitive categories, plan strategically for it. Expect to see sales volumes reduce, aim to see profitability increase. Consider what this means for your stores estate. And if price is not your differentiator, then make sure something else is!

6.2.7   Hope the issue will go away[25]

In a section devoted to strategic options, you might expect that this particular possibility would not feature. To be fair, it does so less and less: the cautionary tales are just too blatant to ignore. A particularly high profile example was the consumer electronics retailer Comet in the UK, which ceased trading at the end of 2012. As the BBC News website described it at the time:

Comet "was an accident waiting to happen" because successive managements had failed to understand the online world.[26]

6.3 MediaMarkt retrospective

Having used Media Markt as a case-study when writing this chapter in 2012, and in particular focussed on their explicit decision to invest in

---

[25] If you have a spare moment, google for "we need to rethink our strategy of hoping the internet will just go away"

[26] http://www.bbc.co.uk/news/business-20164228

pricing specifically in response to pressure caused by online competition and price-transparency, it's already interesting 3 years later to take a look back and see how this has gone (*Figure 15*). (Unlike US retailers, German retailers aren't obliged to publish gross-margin figures, and unfortunately Media Markt is part of a larger parent group[27], which taken together somewhat obscures the story due to consolidation of data in the reporting.)

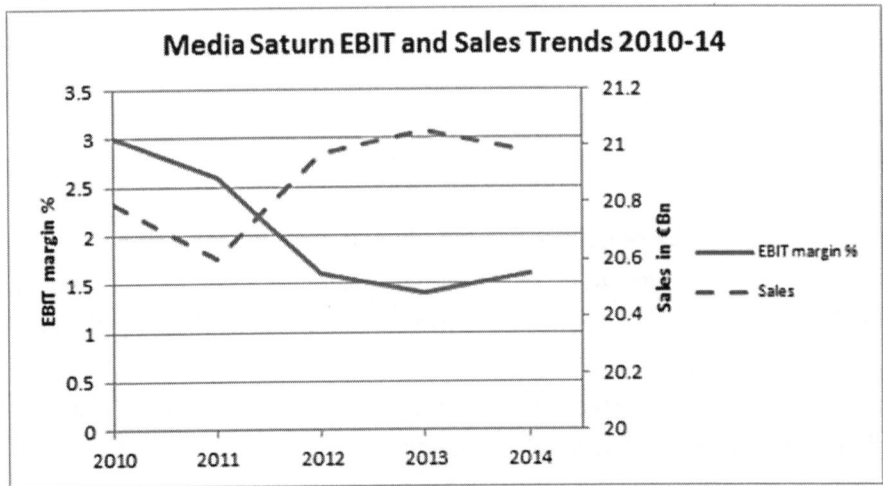

Figure 15 - Trends at Media Saturn

If this were a school report, the headline would probably be a sort of B+: maybe A for effort and B for achievement so far. Perhaps the most impressive result is that, despite a fairly lethal trading environment with Amazon and other pureplays challenging in almost every important country, sales have generally grown and they remain profitable. Moreover there's little doubt that deliberate investment in pricing was a significant contributor, and they explicitly acknowledge this:

"This decline [in EBIT] is largely due to price investments ... More efficient cost structures had a positive effect."[28]

---

[27] Media Markt is part of the Media Saturn division of METROGROUP (METRO AG). Wading through the English translation of their annual reports does at least permit some headlines to be extracted.

[28] METROGROUP annual report 2011/12

In other words, they did in fact manage to execute their declared strategy, although cost-reductions did not (or have not yet), as they had hoped, fully offset the investment in price.

It's also interesting to note that their latest strategy summary headlines the development of own brands as one of its pillars, especially since this is via collaboration with manufacturers who are evidently prepared to "compete with themselves" to support it:

"Media Markt... began to offer exclusive own brands in Europe... There are currently about 400 own-brand items available for sale... To assure the highest possible product quality, the sales line works closely with well-known manufacturers"[29]

6.4 Top Takeaways

The challenge of price transparency requires a planned strategic response. It won't go away, ignoring it is unacceptable (and sometime fatal), and artificial workarounds are unsustainable. Price investment may be required.

The benefits of a price advantage will be magnified by multichannel.

Showrooming – customers using stores as a place to inspect products before then buying them via the cheapest channel (often online) – cannot be prevented. It is futile to try. It is an example of how power has shifted to the customer and away from the retailer.

The world-wide web means that customers can also shop across borders for standardised products; single country cartels are easily bypassed.

Channel based pricing may be a temporary option, but is unsustainable in the long term, because it is inconsistent with offering customers a seamless multichannel experience. Channel based promotions, however, are generally acceptable.

Unique specification products increase in relative importance: own brands, distinct specifications, product bundles. Supplier/manufacturer partners can, and should, be engaged to help.

---

[29] METROGROUP annual report 2013/14

A two brand strategy is possible in countries/markets which divide sharply into internet literate and illiterate customer segments, especially where buying power remains significantly offline and Silver Surfers are not yet common.

A few retailers have elected to simply retreat from brick-and-mortar completely.

Chapter 7.   Range

7.1 Kompetenz

Run this nice German word through Google Translate, and you'll get four very relevant words as the English definition: "capability, authority, competence, jurisdiction."

"Jurisdiction" is the odd man out, but still worth some quick discussion. This is the World-Wide Web: put a product up for sale on a website, and in principle anybody from anywhere can try to buy it. They may fail for two basic hygiene reasons: a) you don't offer a delivery service to their location; b) you block payments from methods registered in their country (probably for fraud-prevention reasons – see **Chapter 15**). Otherwise, you can theoretically sell to them. (**Chapter 26** is an extended discussion of using e-commerce to sell cross-border).

The important question is then: do you have contractual permission from your supplier to sell this product in that location? If your products are music or film or similar, then the answer is almost certainly no. If your products are premium branded items, then the answer is maybe still no. Even if your products are "standard" products, it is extremely sensible to take the precaution of changing your supplier Terms & Conditions to explicitly give you permission to sell these products via non-store channels. This should be a basic first step for any brick-and-mortar retailer planning to add virtual channels or considering the increasingly attractive option of using eCommerce to expand overseas – review all your supplier contracts, and change them if needed. In fact if you are brick-and-mortar retailer who is even thinking about possibly going multichannel sometime in the distant future, this is a very useful foundation to address now. Changing contracts or terms and conditions is much more easily done gradually over time as contracts naturally come up for renewal.

Basic legal issues being safely taken care of, let's return to "capability, authority, competence." Bookshops are usually nice places. You can get a coffee and a cake, browse through hundreds or thousands of books to your heart's content. The staff are generally a world-away from the typical supermarket checkout clerk, helpfully passionate about books and reading. And yet, even in its pre-Kindle, books-only days, Amazon started to vacuum up their market. The most basic reason: on Amazon you can find every book currently in print, and with the arrival of the Amazon Marketplace, almost every book that has ever been in print. When it comes to books, Amazon has capability, authority, competence. In fact, in combination with aggressive pricing, this pretty much sums up their strategy. As they say themselves:

"We design our websites to enable millions of unique products to be sold... We strive to offer our customers the lowest prices possible"[30]

The Amazon/books story is an extreme case of a well-documented phenomenon when multichannel hits a category. Kompetenz has always been a relevant consideration for retailers. Those secondary categories have always been slightly unconvincing to customers, but worthwhile sticking with either because they're reasonably profitable in their own right, or because they help complete your assortment overall. Multichannel simply moves the bar up: secondary categories are no longer slightly unconvincing, they're now completely unconvincing. And many retailers are seeing their secondary category sales drop off dramatically as a consequence. It's part of the shift in power away from the retailer towards the customer.

I don't want to bombard this section with evidential data points in support of the above assertions, but just take a look at the annual results for almost any retailer in a market with significant multichannel players, and it will include phrases like "focussing on our core categories". A telling quote from the CEO of one of the biggest players:

"As we look forward, I think our larger stores will have a bit more food space, a little bit less general merchandise space, a bit more clothing space."[31]

This quote nicely highlights the secondary category decisions that most multichannel players face, or that other retailers have to tackle in the face of multichannel competitors. Get out of the category, reinforce the category, move the category to a more appropriate channel? Just don't do nothing and hope the problem will go away – the problem won't, but you probably will (see Woolworths UK or Neckermann Germany as a few of

---

[30] Amazon Inc 10K SEC filing, 2014
[31] Tesco former CEO Philip Clarke, interview 3rd October 2012

many examples). So how do you reinforce the category, or move it to a more appropriate channel, within the reasonable constraints of store space? The answer lies in the Endless Aisle.

7.2 The Endless Aisle

At its simplest, the Endless Aisle just means offering a fully complete range in a particular category. Amazon and books is the obvious example again. Once you step outside the boundaries of store space-planning constraints, the only limits lie in your supply chain and buying; for now let's just assume that you can plan a category unconstrained by anything except overall coherence and margin.

The outcome of such a category plan is inevitable: you just range everything your customers might ever want. This chapter is about differentiation, so from a customer perspective, what you aim to become is a go-to destination for the category. For the online pure-play retailers this is so easy to do that customers now come to expect it. If you can't offer a complete range, your sales will suffer badly. There is a slightly bizarre corollary to exploit as well: many retailers find that increasing the size of their range in a category drives sales, not of the extended range, but of the core items. It's a bit like those corner-stores that display five cheap brands of blended whisky on the shelves plus a ridiculously expensive premium single malt in a locked glass cabinet. No-one buys the premium malt, but people feel better about buying the cheap brands because it's there.

For the true multichannel retailer, with both brick-and-mortar stores and online sales channels, there are now some nice options. In your stores, you can focus on core categories, on take-away categories, and on categories which don't work well online (e.g. light-bulbs is a nice example of a category that is tricky online for a whole host of reasons). The big opportunity then lies in those secondary, space-constrained, potentially threatened categories. Suddenly they are no longer space-constrained. To make this work well, of course, your customers have to be able to order that extended range in store, and they also have to be able to pick it up in store.

Enabling this kind of elastic store is what drives basics like click-and-collect, but also drives the development of in-store ordering points and kiosks. NB in most categories, standalone kiosks unsupported by staff do

NOT work; I've been involved in a few failed pilots. This is another thing Apple currently gets right – the staff assist you to order. There is a challenging implication to all this: your store-staff have to be familiar with your non-store range and able to explain and sell it to customers (see **Chapter 20**).

In the UK and US, it's already starting to drive another strategic shift: shrinking the average size of stores and the overall store estate. An extreme version of this concept is now being piloted by some retailers in the UK, although it's probably going to take a few iterations to get it right: the stock-less store..[32]

In some markets the availability of decent quality retail space is an issue (Ukraine for example). As/when customers become educated to understand this kind of elastic-store type offer, and/or store staff can be given good enough tools to explain it to customers, there may be less challenges in finding quality locations, hopefully reducing overall costs significantly while allowing greater overall coverage of the country.

7.3 Top Takeaways

Kompetenz - capability, authority, competence, jurisdiction – is essential to demonstrate in a multichannel category.

Multichannel can have the effect of making primary categories relatively stronger, secondary categories relatively weaker.

Endless Aisles allow retailers to plan assortments unconstrained by store space.

The Long Tail of the range must be available on all channels, including stores. However it's not expected to be actually stocked in the store.

Elastic Stores offer additional options: reduced space or stock-less stores. However customers must be able to order and/or collect non-stock products in the store.

Supplier contracts should be amended as soon as possible to permit products to be sold via non-store channels, especially if you plan to use eCommerce to trade internationally

---

[32] See for example http://www.bbc.co.uk/news/uk-scotland-scotland-business-15411541 covering House of Fraser Aberdeen pilot store

Chapter 8.   Information

8.1 A two-way trade

99% of smart-phone visitors, 97% of PC or tablet visitors, and most likely well over 50% of brick-and-mortar store visitors don't buy anything when they visit you. So what use are they to you? Well the chances are they're there to gather information. For at least half of them, that information is probably just price.[33] For the other half they're looking for something more. Seeking alternative products, ratings & reviews, detailed specifications, inspiration, how-to, are a few amongst a multitude of possible objectives. The question when considering your differentiation approach is whether to service any of these objectives, and if so, whether you can extract any value from the customer for doing so.

Here's just one basic dilemma (although caveat emptor here: the current deluge of mobile-related statistics, mainly from those with a vested interest, can be used to "prove" just about any plausible argument). In a survey of smart-phone owners in France, Sweden and Germany[34], 71% had used their smart-phone to research products, and 32% had done so in the previous week. Great, better get a mobile site then. But 90% of smart-phone owners who used their mobile *while in a store* to research products were looking at *somebody else's site*.[35] Scrap the mobile site again.

Speaking personally, for me the ultimate nightmare customer experience is that of buying a used-car from a showroom forecourt. It seems like every word I utter gives the salesman more and more information about me that allows him to exploit my ignorance of motoring matters in general, and then use it sell me something that I probably don't really need for more than I ought to be paying. A key reason why customers do so much research online in the first place is to avoid being put at the same information disadvantage as me looking at used-cars. In a

---

[33] Tesco former CEO Philip Clarke at the World Retail Congress, September 2012: "Over half of visits to our Tesco.com website are to check prices - and this is our food site, not our general merchandise site"

[34] http://www.tradedoubler.com/pagefiles/25098/tradedoubler_shopping_on_mobile_oct2012_uk.pdf

[35] See for example http://www.slideshare.net/kkrossing/2011-mobile-retail-infographics

less malign way, deciding to service your customers' information needs is similar to that second-hand car salesman's patter. Everything your customer does tells you something about them. Even the simple act looking at a product tells you the customer is interested in that product, and possibly in other similar products, related items, accessories etc.

There is a two-way trade. The customer tells you something about themselves. You then have the opportunity to use this information to tell the customer something about yourself which will be "beneficial" to the customer. There are a series of potential investment decisions to consider:

Reference data: should you invest in providing detailed factual information, in the expectation of some knock-on benefit: short-term such as rapidly converting that customer or gathering data about them; longer-term, such as customer brand-loyalty or even simply returning to us a bit later to make a purchase?

Active data: should you invest in actively seeking to exploit customers' use of this reference information, which in turn causes them to disclose information about themselves which you can exploit to advantage?

Personalisation: can you take this one step further and change your proposition or behaviour on a customer-by-customer basis, based on the information each customer discloses?

Multichannel reuse: can you carry the information provided by customers on one channel across to our other channels (especially from online into brick-and-mortar)?

Customer participation: should your customers contribute to the information, for example via ratings and reviews, or social networks?

Destination information: should you invest in providing information over-and-above the merely factual, for example in how-to guides?

8.2 Reference data

In the later chapter on Product Data Management (**Chapter 12**), I'll develop this argument much further. Let's just assert here that basic reference data about your products is a wonderful thing. It's the foundation of your online channels – every website needs to display its products! It can also be the foundation of many other competitive advantages in brick-and-mortar operations: better informed sales staff, better wrap-rates in call-centres, lower returns rates (it's surprising how many fully-functioning electrical items are returned because neither customers nor staff knew how to switch them on), to name just a few.

But reference data is also very expensive to capture. The industry benchmark figure is that capturing even basic good quality product information plus a reasonable quality image requires an average of 25 man-minutes per SKU. Or put another way, 4000 SKUs requires one *FTE-year* of work. And it's quite a skilled job, so that FTE-year is probably an expensive graduate FTE-year (product data maintenance is a typical first-job-after-college type of role, so watch out if you're reading this as part of your course – you have been warned!).

In less developed online markets, many online pure-plays do fairly well without ever really tackling this task properly. They have a buying-price/cost-base advantage, they exploit this price advantage for all it's worth, and that is sufficient for now. Sustaining this advantage as the market around them catches up, however, usually requires them to bite the bullet and make the effort.[36] In very developed markets, other online-pureplays still don't make a great job of it.[37] Amazon's data about many consumer electronics items could best be described as average. Amazon in the US, however, has found another way to provide this data, and it's called Best Buy.

Some basic data is unavoidable. It's pretty difficult to sell apparel without telling the customer what size the garment is, and if you want to sell it online, showing high quality imagery is a must (some displaying the item on a real model: cut out pictures alone don't cut it). If your product is

---

[36] Just as one typical example, see www.rozetka.com.ua; before you object that you don't read Russian, auto-translate is the main plus point of using Google Chrome as a web-browser. Actually I'm hoping that you do read Russian, as Russia and other CIS countries are a big potential new market for the services of people like me!

[37] Compare these two pages for the same product, one from the US and one from the Ukraine, on these two website. For example:
http://www.amazon.com/Panasonic-DMC-FZ150K-Digital-Camera-Optical/dp/B005HQ50SO and
http://rozetka.com.ua/panasonic_lumix_dmc_fz150_black/p169041/. Which is better?

an Own Brand, then you have no choice but to be the reference data source for it. For the rest, there is a serious commercial decision to take: are you the right player to be the reference data source for this category of data online? If you are, can you translate this into sales, or would it be better to leave this to the competition, or better still, the manufacturer? How much data is sufficient to be the reference? Do you really need to capture every item from the back-of-label data (*Figure 16*) in order to give the customer the experience they require? It comes back to your customers and personas again: what do they need for the missions you've defined for them? Never forget that multichannel retail is customer-centric first, product-centric second.

Incidentally also don't forget that online retail is increasingly being regulated, and the display of product data is one area in which regulations may apply, especially if your products are edible (and this includes theoretically edible such as pet-food). The FIR regulations in the EU are especially onerous in this context.[38]

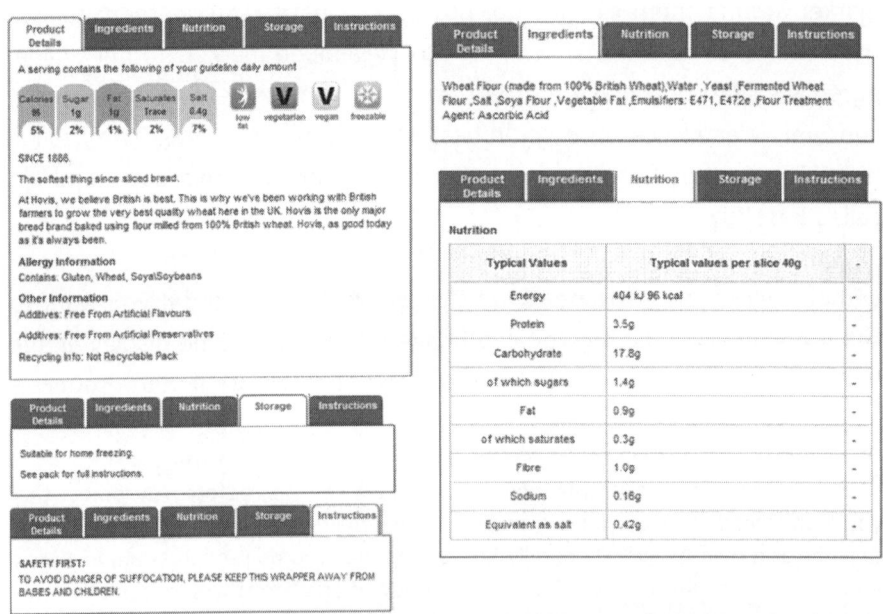

Figure 16 – For one loaf of bread, 43 data points are needed?[39]

---

[38] See for example www.legislation.gov.uk/uksi/2014/1855/contents/made for an English-language example

[39] Tesco.com, collage of screenshots, January 2011

There's not much of that two-way trade-off in basic passive reference data. OK, the customer has told you they are interested, you've responded by asserting your authority as a source in this area. Hopefully the customer responds to this assertion in the same way as they respond to Kompetenz in assortment.

8.3 Active Data

By looking at the reference information, the customer has told you they are interested in one of your products. How do you actively respond? By trying to sell them something else. To an extent, that statement is just about as logical as it sounds, and it's notable that there has been an increasing focus in the last few years on techniques that simply remind the customer what they were looking at if they didn't buy it first time around, especially re-targeting and abandoned-cart, but also simply browsing history. Here's Amazon, for example, helpfully sending me an email reminding me about the previous edition of my own book (*Figure 17*).

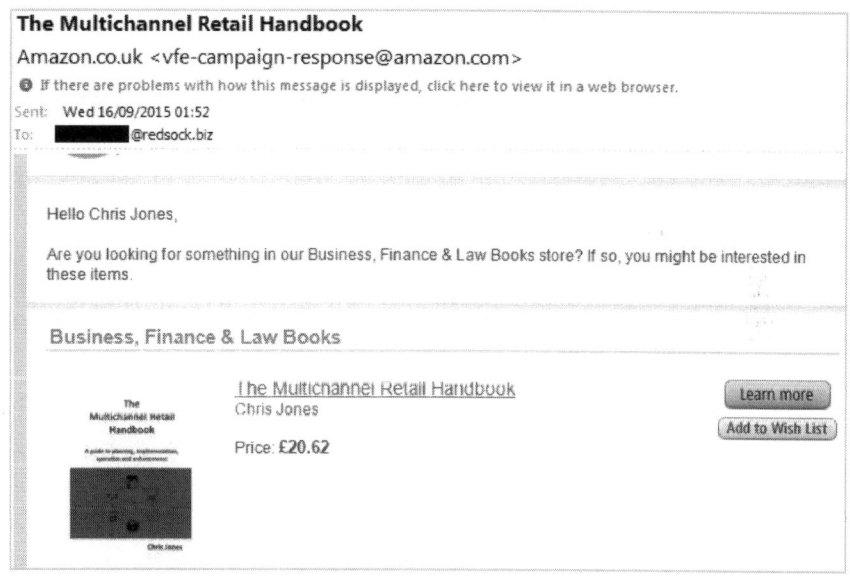

Figure 17 - Amazon reminds me what I browsed

8.3.1 Cross-selling

Amazon allegedly shared the statistic that in 2006, cross-sells accounted for 35% of all their sales, resulting in lots of enthusiasm for cross-selling. Google for this statistic and you'll find it endlessly repeated, but you may well struggle to find the original source. And in any case, Amazon represents a special case, particularly in books and music. Amazon also has something else that most retailers don't have: the data on a huge number of very similar shopping visits for highly homogeneous products to analyse statistically to construct their cross-sells.

This isn't to say that cross-selling doesn't work. Most studies imply a sales uplift of somewhere in the 3-5% range. But once again there's an investment to make. Either you've got to analyse the data if you've got it and then maintain it for re-presentation to your customers, or you'll need to invest in suitable automation software. Automation doesn't necessarily work even for Amazon. Take this example, which only took me a couple of minutes to find on their US site (*Figure 18*):

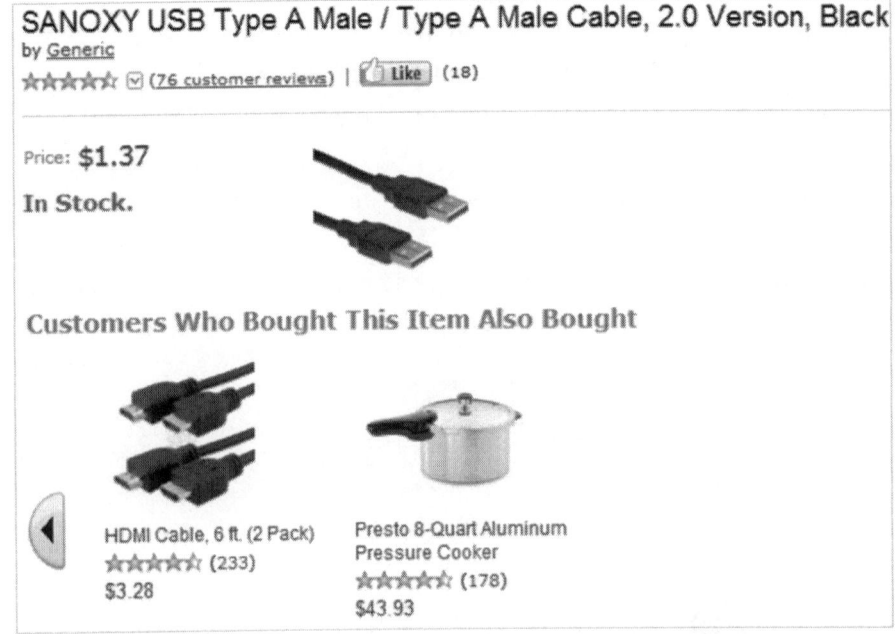

Figure 18 – The USB connected pressure cooker?[40]

How has this error occurred? It has happened because Amazon is actively exploiting information provided by customers. When a lot of customers do something, the inferences drawn will be statistically valid. When a very small number of customers do something, the inferences can end up being bizarre. Amazon doesn't make too many mistakes like this

---

[40] Collated screen-shot from Amazon.com, October 2012

because their huge data volumes of fairly similar carts help prevent it. Many other retailers end up with an unattractive choice between software tools performing non-valid automation over small datasets or maintaining/cleaning this data semi-manually. If you sell smaller volumes of bigger ticket items you may have no other option but the latter, albeit it is one of the areas where multichannel retailers have an advantage over their pure-play cousins: the skills and knowledge already exist in the merchandising teams. A good percentage of the "customers who bought this also bought that" data you see online is probably partially faked, while the majority of alleged "best sellers" should be regarded with deep suspicion, especially on smaller sites whose traffic volumes don't provide enough data to really fire automation tools up.

It probably is worth doing, but do make the business-case explicitly first, based on some reasonable estimated upside. There's a lot of data maintenance required and/or some expensive software needed, for an upside which in one recent study might be as low as 0.2% of profits.[41] I'd suggest you use 3% as a planning/business-case benchmark, but beware that the effectiveness is notoriously difficult to actually measure, especially in true multichannel where the customer might see the cross-sell on a website, but then go buy it in store later. (Note to analytics enthusiasts: it's not enough to measure A/B-tested click-through rates or even conversions, you need to measure whether these clicks result in overall more *net profitable* customer shopping carts).

There is also a huge cross-over with the topic of personalisation (see below), and in many cases the tools which do one also do the other, making the business case potentially a lot easier to justify.

8.3.2 Multichannel reuse

Surprisingly few multichannel retailers seem to take this customer/data-based learning back into their stores. Cross-sells which work online, also work in store. Do put the top cross-selling online items next to each other on your shelf planograms. Do make this information available to your store staff if you operate the kind of stores where staff are actively selling to

---

[41]See for example http://econsultancy.com/uk/blog/8632-up-selling-is-20-times-more-effective-than-cross-selling-online

customers on the shop-floor; tell your staff what works online, because it will work offline too – your customers have told you so.

8.3.3   Personalisation

This topic is covered in detail in ***Chapter 22***. It's the next logical step on the journey from cross-selling. In the "customers who looked at X finally bought Y" offers described above, every customer who looks at X will be suggested Y. Personalisation considers information gleaned about the individual customer to decide whether it would be better to suggest Z to that particular individual instead.

The standard formula "customers who bought this also bought" is worth further inspection. There is a reason why retailers don't say "we suggest you also think about." Customers trust other customers much more than they trust retailers. Which is why the next section is…

8.4 Ratings & Reviews

8.4.1   Overview

Ratings and reviews drive sales. In 2005.

OK, that isn't really fair, ratings and reviews still drive sales, and back in the happy days of 2005-6, when it was possible to make presentations about Web 2.0 being the future, some quite credible, reasonably well controlled studies were published, showing plausible average sales uplifts in the 12-30% range. Ignore any hype about reviews driving 300% increases. Yes, they maybe could drive a 300% increase for a well-reviewed top-selling line. But reviews aren't all good, not every product is a top-seller, and 12-30% is still a great average. The market leaders in this space currently claim average uplifts in the 15-25% range.[42]

But… the internet is full of reviews. By the time most customers come to buy it, every branded product has already been reviewed, multiple times on multiple sites. Customers shopping on any channel, including brick-and-mortar, will have read at least one review[43], probably several, or if they

---

[42] For example, see www.reevoo.com, who claim an uplift of +18%; no endorsement or otherwise implied
[43] For example see this study by PWC claiming that 88% of all US shoppers research online first, and still 73% even in more challenging categories like fashion,

haven't already, will read a review on their smart-phone whilst standing in your store checking out the product. (One minor mystery, actually, is why so few brick-and-mortar stores seem to acknowledge this reality and display highlights of positive ratings and reviews on their shelf-edges.)

If you have own-branded products that won't get reviewed elsewhere, if your target customers generally don't have access to other review sites, if your customers' native language and education is likely to make it difficult for them go elsewhere for the information, if internet penetration is still quite low in your country or region so it's still relatively new for customers, then implement them.

Otherwise, yes, your online channels undoubtedly need to display reviews and ratings. But have a serious look at whether or not you have to manage them, or whether to just syndicate them in. If you are going to do them yourself, you really have to drive your customers to post them. There needs to be sufficient critical mass of them to make it worthwhile for customers to stay on your site and read them in preference to looking someplace else. You have to follow up with your customers to get them to rate and post reviews. You have to moderate them (check them for appropriateness). Soliciting them may be great reactivation email marketing campaigns, or it may be a costly pain in the neck. Generating sufficient critical mass needs to be a KPI in its own right. There is a real cost to operating and managing them, potentially with very little readership. That's not to say don't do it, just take a proper look at the options and the business case first and seriously consider outsourcing. Do it very well, like Amazon, and you immediately become an information destination, the go-to place for customers considering your categories. Do it poorly and you look limp, and it will actually cost you sales: it damages that Kompetenz differentiation you've worked so hard to demonstrate.

Operationally, by the way, don't omit the other side of the story. One negative review doesn't matter. Multiple negative reviews are telling you something (usually. There are instances of coordinated bad reviews, one example being teenage PC gamers protesting at effective software copy protection techniques, which – gasp – meant they might actually have to

---

footwear and health (http://www.pwc.com/en_US/us/retail-consumer/publications/assets/pwc-us-multichannel-shopping-survey.pdf)

pay for the software, coordinating negative ratings and reviews on Amazon). Monitor reviews of your assortment. If it's an own-brand product, do something to fix it, and tell your customers you did so; listening-to-you messages are generally good marketing. If it isn't, get it on clearance before everybody else does. I realise this is an isolated data point, but the suggestion in one study that 80% of people changed purchase decision after seeing negative reviews seems intuitively reasonable, and should be a real call-to-action.[44]

Customers trust each other more than they trust you the retailer, but they trust their friends even more. Informal reviews via social networks are very strong influencers, but of course they are pretty difficult for retailers to do much about. There's no point in trying to fight it, so you may as well make it easy (hence all those "share this" buttons – which reduce on-page conversion by the way), monitor where you can, respond if possible.

8.4.2   Ratings & Reviews good practice

So, assuming that you've considered all such context and still decide to go ahead with reviews, what does good practice look like?

Seek coverage: products without a rating displayed on a page, or site, with many rated and reviews products are screaming "nobody else bought me, so why should you?" So if you bought this book on Amazon, please review it, even if you hated it!

This is another reason why you might consider syndicating rather than going it alone – it helps ensure critical mass.

Moderate all reviews, against a well-defined policy: all reviews need to be checked, by a human being in whose native tongue the review is written, before posting them on the site. The policy needs to include obvious things (no spam, no political statements and so forth), but much more importantly it needs to make clear that the review should be specifically about the product. Ideally pricing should be treated separately.

Verify purchase: all reviews really should be written by someone who has actually purchased the product. This means organising follow-up email from your orders, not simply allowing anyone to post a review on the site, which is open to abuse (*Figure 19*):

---

[44] See for example at http://www.marketingpilgrim.com/2011/08/80-percent-of-shoppers-change-purchase-decision-based-on-negative-reviews-research.html

Figure 19 - Anyone can review[45]

A legitimate consequence of a verified purchase policy is that you can eliminate customers who return the product from reviewing, simply by waiting a week or two before sending the follow-up. This is reasonable behaviour when you think that really they should have taken the time to use the product before reviewing it (well maybe...).

Make the customer describe themselves: customers want to read reviews written by someone "like them". So insist on some colour by asking for some descriptive information such as age, gender and ideally some relationship to the category: a review by a "serious hobby photographer" versus a "point-and-shoot holidaymaker" has a completely different impact on the reader. Post the descriptive alongside the review.

Bad reviews drive sales. True, if applied with care. Firstly, if you have followed the previous recommendation, customers react by thinking "well, she's not like me, and she sounds like a complete idiot, I'll prove she's wrong"; strange but true. Secondly, a few bad reviews mixed into a large profile of positive ones add weight and credibility.

But pay attention to lots of bad reviews. However... a lot of bad reviews mean the product is bad, or worse still, that you are bad. Pay attention to an obvious pattern like this. Establish a monitoring process.

---

[45] Animalstore.ru, translate by Google

Allow brands to respond. Some brands will, some brands won't, but you should offer the opportunity for them to respond to consumers. Once again, it adds credibility and also is good customer service.

Respond yourself. Some bad reviews will be about the product. Some, however, are really a proxy customer-service complaint. Follow these up *and* post your follow up on the review.

Don't fiddle. Your reviews will lose all credibility if you seem to be gaming the system. Customers are not stupid. If a customer posts a legitimate review, post it up, good or bad.

Don't let others fiddle. If you suspect a review is not legitimate, follow it up. Don't just reject it out of hand: blocking legitimate reviewers will damage your reputation. But as anyone who followed the scandal over "paid for" reviews on Amazon will be aware[46], allowing faked reviews will damage your reputation even worse.

8.5 Help and Advice

One of my favourite websites of all time is Blue Nile[47], although sorry, Blue Nile, I've never actually bought anything from you; as they reported profits of $14.6M in 2015 on sales of $473M[48], it doesn't look like they've suffered too badly from the lack of my personal custom. As you might guess from the name, they sell jewellery with a particular focus on diamonds. Not something that most people, even those who (unlike me!) can afford it, buy every day, or in general know too much about. Recognising that this ignorance is an opportunity to attract customers who might be intimidated by displaying their lack of knowledge face-to-face in an expensive store, their customer experience successfully focusses on educating the customer throughout the journey (*Figure 20*).

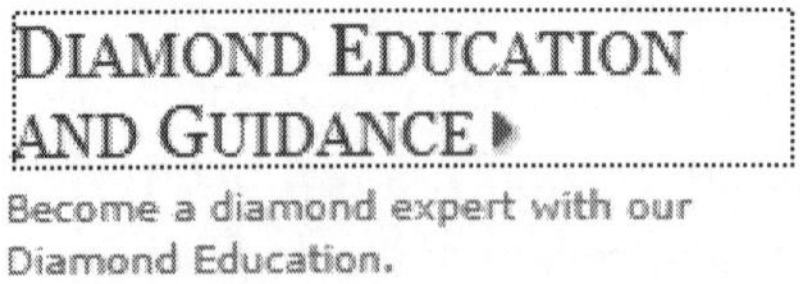

DIAMOND EDUCATION
AND GUIDANCE ▶

Become a diamond expert with our
Diamond Education.

Figure 20 - Education at Blue Nile

---

[46] See for example Sunday Times, 11th October 2015
[47] www.bluenile.com
[48] Blue Nile Inc SEC 10K filing 2015

This is an example of one company which has focussed on help and advice as a differentiator. OK it's an online pure-play, and yes diamonds are a slightly special category. But Blue Nile have evidently succeeded in translating education into (profitable) sales.

The same concept can be translated into a true multichannel retailer too. Anglo-French DIY retailer Kingfisher (Castorama / B&Q core brands, with 1178 stores in 9 countries) has invested heavily in "how to do the job" videos (and other content) which are a key feature of its websites (*Figure 21*).

Figure 21 - Advice from Castorama[49]

The roll-out of advice and help was a key reporting target, tracked in its annual shareholder report for 2011/12, and associated with a stated KPI measure of like-for-like sales growth.[50] More than a hundred multi-lingual videos represent a serious investment, and nobody does that (and tracks in their annual report) without a solid business case. The expectation is not that it will drive specifically *online* sales (DIY is a category with relatively low online penetration) but that it will drive *overall* sales growth.

Last words go to another pure-play, Asos, now a star of branded fashion online (although even they are increasingly developing own-brands – see previous chapter):

"2011/12 has been a stellar year for ASOS Magazine… and the December 2011 cover shoot with Jessica Chastain achieved 50 million global viewers."[51]

and more recently

---

[49] Collage from castorama.pl, castorama.fr, diy.com
[50] See Kingfisher plc annual report and accounts 2011/12. It is, however, noticeable that this KPI disappeared subsequently.
[51] Asos plc, annual reports for FY11/21

"We publish daily fashion and lifestyle content, and the monthly ASOS magazine is sent for free to around 500,000 customers."[52]

8.6 Top Takeaways

Multichannel customers visit all sales-channels first for information/research and only second to make purchases.

Customer research activity via online channels is also a source of data about the customer which can be exploited by the retailer.

There are a series of investment decisions to make in: reference data, active data, personalisation, multichannel reuse, customer participation, destination information.

Product reference data is a key enabler, but is expensive to capture. It is important to make a business case for becoming an information reference source over and above the minimum basic data necessary to sell products online.

Be aware of regulatory compliance issues with the display of product data online, such as FIR regulations in the EU.

Cross-selling is a proven sales driver on online channels, but the benefit is more difficult to measure for multichannel retailers where the ultimate sale might take place in brick-and-mortar store.

"Customers who did X also did Y" merchandising is highly sensitive to data volumes. With low volumes, significant manual maintenance may be required.

For online channels, there is a big overlap between exploiting customer research activity, cross-selling, and personalisation.

Ratings and reviews are also proven sales drivers. A decision is required whether it is appropriate to collect and moderate them yourself, or whether to syndicate this task to save costs and exploit a wider pool.

Ratings and reviews best practices include: ensuring coverage, clear policy, strong moderation against that policy, verified purchasers only, customer

---

[52] Asos plc annual report for FY13/14

descriptors, allowing bad reviews, enabling brand response, replying to proxy complaints, monitoring for genuinely poor products or situations.

Information on online channels, such as how-to guides and interest-magazines, can drive sales across all channels, including brick-and-mortar. Similarly offline activities (such as magazine distribution) can drive online sales.

Feedback from customers online, such as ratings and reviews, can be reused in brick-and-mortar.

Chapter 9.   Convenience

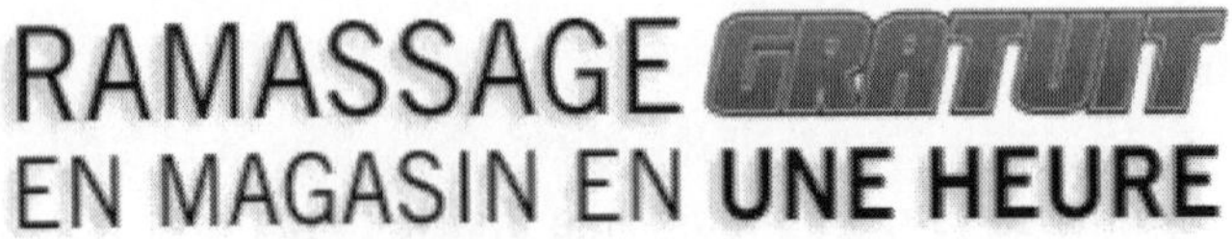

RAMASSAGE *GRATUIT* EN MAGASIN EN **UNE HEURE**

Figure 22 - Free pick-up in store in 1 hour[53]

9.1 The Future of Shopping?

Back in the happy days of the tech bubble, the internet was going to change the way we shopped forever. Of course it has, but not quite in the way that most of the bubble hype envisaged. Stores are not obsolete (although many retailers now have too many – see **Chapter 20**). Customers do not merely want to sit at their PCs buying and then hang around waiting for a delivery. Convenience is still a crucial motivator for customers, and a convenience advantage is still a key differentiator, but the key learning since the hyped-up days of 2000-1 is that convenience is defined not by the retailer but by the customer. It's a standard lesson in another form: multichannel has shifted power from the retailer to the consumer. The customer chooses what is convenient for *himself/herself*, the retailer needs to offer them options. And convenience is very difficult to "force" on customers, and extremely difficult to get them to pay a premium for: time-is-money may apply to airline travel, but it doesn't necessarily apply to shopping.

As online retailing starts up in a particular market, it is often able to offer a genuine step-change in convenience for customers. More transparent and (often) faster delivery than traditional mail-order, for example; stores which are indeed effectively open 7 x 24; grocery shopping without the toddler in tow. If you are in a country where online/multichannel is still relatively new, it is more than likely that a convenience advantage will help drive sales. See for example this delivery promise picked at random from my recent experience (**Figure 23**).

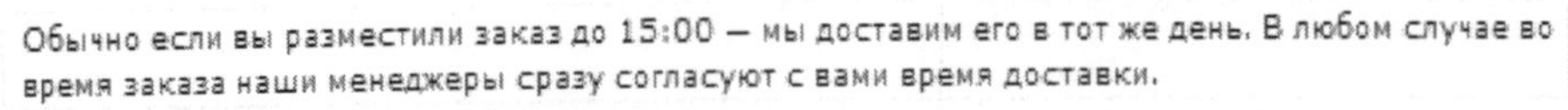

Обычно если вы разместили заказ до 15:00 — мы доставим его в тот же день. В любом случае во время заказа наши менеджеры сразу согласуют с вами время доставки.

Figure 23 - Order by 15:00 and we'll deliver the same day[54]

---

[53] www.lasource.ca, October 2012

What is certain in every country is that a convenience *disadvantage* will prevent sales. Perhaps the clearest illustration of this idea can be seen the adoption by Amazon of collection lockers (**Figure 24**) and its much hyped researches into delivery drones.

Figure 24 - Amazon Locker: collection point, London Tube station

It is NOT convenient for many customers to wait at home for deliveries during working-hours, or to go to a distant courier-company's offices; they want their good at a place they can reach, at a time they can reach it. In this space, pure-play retailers are at a clear differentiation disadvantage compared to the true multichannel retailer.

9.2 The Empire Strikes Back

"Our product mix lends itself to a multi-channel offer as customers often want further advice, a demonstration or fitting. Online purchasing patterns reflect this, with <u>86% of sales on Halfords.com</u> reserved and then collected from a store."[55] *[my underlining].*

Clearly collect-in-store is not the only way in which truly multichannel retailers can have an advantage over their pure-play opponents, but it is

---

[54] http://rozetka.com.ua/payments-and-deliveries/
[55] Annual Report & Accounts 2012, Halfords plc. More recently this has risen to >90%.

probably one of the most obvious. It also represents a true step-change to multichannel thinking, and is discussed in depth in **Chapter 21**. Nowhere is this more evident than in the grocery space (see **Chapter 25** for a much more detailed discussion of the very challenging online grocery model). France now has over 3000 grocery pick-up points, more than the number of grocery hypermarkets, and 80% of the population can reach a pick-up point within 10 minutes of their home or office.[56]

The first response of existing brick-and-mortar retailers to the challenge of internet pure-plays is often to simply open an internet channel themselves. This offers them all the disadvantages of their store estate – most basically a higher cost-base – without any of its corresponding advantages: their online offer is no better than the pure-plays and probably (due to lack of competence or focus) worse. It is multiple-channel where multichannel is required.

The "post-checkout" phases of customer purchase self-evidently offer many opportunities for true multichannel retailers to differentiate themselves, especially against pure-plays. In case this sounds dull, it's worth noting that this is an essential part of customer retention:

"74% of purchase decisions, before buying, are influenced by what your returns policy will be after buying."[57]

Interestingly, and at this stage speculatively, the steady development of mobile/smartphone as a channel, may well offer opportunities "pre-checkout". So far, mobile take-up of retail in countries with both the infrastructure and the smartphone wielding customer base is huge, but conversion remains a challenge. Conversion rates on smartphones (as distinct from tablets, which offer a completely different customer experience – much nearer to a traditional PC - and should not be blended in statistically under the umbrella term "mobile") are relatively poor (with the exception of China).[58] Where are these customers converting then?

---

[56] The State of Online Grocery Retail in Europe, Syndy, July 2015

[57] UPS/Comscore Pulse of the Online Shopper, 2012

[58] There are lots of conflicting data points. A reasonable example study (www.monetate.com) has PC conversion at 3.34%, tablet at 3.17%, but smart-phone at only 1.09% - importantly this study does not bundle tablets in as "mobile". 2015 update: increasingly this seems to be a consistent benchmark, with

Well, online via other devices or in-store, obviously. Capturing those missing conversions should be a key target for any retailer operating in a smartphone intensive country. For example online, one excellent way to achieve this is a shopping cart which the customer can add-to via mobile but then retrieve later on their PC to complete the keystroke intensive/security conscious checkout process. In-store, sophisticated multichannel retailers are realising they can't fight customers with smart-phones, much better to offer them free Wi-Fi, and use it as a differentiator and marketing channel. See the chapter on mobile for more discussion (**Chapter 23**).

Such concepts begin to overlap ever more with the final differentiation heading, Experience.

Figure 25 - Making the customer feel in control[59]

9.3 Top Takeaways

Convenience is defined by the customer, not the retailer.

Brick-and-mortar stores can offer a major convenience advantage over online pure-plays. For example, UK retailer Halfords sees 86% of its online orders collected in store, because customers value the follow-up services they can get there.

Online pure-play retailers need to counter this. For example, Amazon has introduced Amazon Locker as part of its response.

---

the exception of China where mobile conversion is much higher, partly due the availability of acceptable payment methods.
[59] Marks & Spencer, October 2012

Smartphones are convenient for customers but conversion rates are currently poor. Retailers need to ensure that a seamless multichannel customer experience drives non-converting smartphone customers to conveniently convert via other channels.

(Mobile is covered in depth in *Chapter 23*. Click-and-collect is covered in depth in *Chapter 21*.)

Chapter 10.   Experience

"If you got to ask, you ain't got it"[60]

10.1   Basics

If you are in a country with low online retail penetration, if you are an online pure-play anywhere, if you are not a premium trusted brand, or actually if you are just about anybody trying to sell through a non-store format, remember to reassure the customer. Many customers, even in very online literate markets, are still slightly dubious about it all. Lots of logos from organisations that specialise in trustworthiness are always worth the space (**Figure 26**):

Figure 26 - Reassuring German customers[61]

Clearly state policies, and make sure customers can find them. (I recently did a survey of top European sites, and it was surprising how often basic information like delivery prices and schedules were difficult to find). **Figure 27:**

Помощь	Help
Как сделать заказ	How to order
Доставка	Delivery
Оплата	Payment
Помощь	Help
Обратная связь	Feedback

Figure 27 - Basic Information Clearly Visible[62]

---

[60] Fats Waller explains rhythm
[61] From lidl.de
[62] From ozon.ru

Finally, make sure there is always a human available (***Figure 28*** is from Apple China):

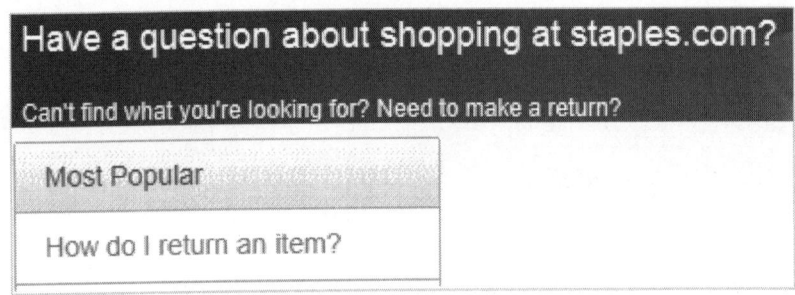

致电 400-666-8800
有疑问？尽管提问。周一至周五早八点至晚十点，
或周六至周日早八点至晚八点，您可以打电话，向
Apple 专家咨询专业意见。

Figure 28 - US brand, Chinese helpline[63]

OK, these are all nice for any non-store channel, but what about multichannel? Refunds and Returns are a great place to start. The prospect of returning by post, and being confident of a refund, is intimidating for customers in any country. Only customer familiarity and a reputation for trustworthiness has made online fashion retailing, with its inevitably high returns rates, viable. It is noticeable in all countries that consumers have to become educated to purchasing online first, via simpler categories such as electronics, before they will take the risk of purchasing clothing online. For the brick-and-mortar retailer, reassuring customers that they can always return-to-store is an important differentiator against the pure-plays. Don't miss the chance to reinforce it (***Figure 29***):

Have a question about shopping at staples.com?

Can't find what you're looking for? Need to make a return?

Most Popular

How do I return an item?

Figure 29 - Returns, the top confidence issue[64]

10.2   Everything Else

For the true multichannel retailer, the way forward is not merely imagination plus technology. The critical concept is that the customer experience must be coherent and joined up. The customer must perceive

---

[63] Apple's Chinese website
[64] Staples.com, US site, collage

that he/she is dealing with a single retailer, manifesting itself in different channels and formats, but still a single retailer. There must not be disconnects in the experience: to use a very simple example, store staff must know what to do when a customer who has ordered online wants to know why their order is late. It is this thinking which is behind two currently popular (and ugly) buzzwords – cross-channel and omni-channel. As usual in this field, there are many different definitions of the terms. The simplest way to think of them is that cross-channel retailing refers to joining up channels *after* checkout, omni-channel retailing to connecting channels *before* checkout.

Click-and-collect in store, is by this definition a cross-channel experience: the customer concludes checking out online, but then reverts to the store channel for delivery. Similarly endless aisles, where the customer orders in store but takes delivery at home are cross-channel.

Omni-channel, using the same definition, describes a customer purchasing experience which might include searching from a PC, reading reviews on a smartphone, getting recommendations from friends via Facebook on a tablet, adding to cart on smartphone, and placing an order at a kiosk in a store, tracking its progress on a tablet, and then writing a review on a PC again. See *Figure 7* for another example.

The terms are not as important as the underlying concept. In both cases, the key to a successful customer journey is that it must be <u>seamless</u>. If possible, each channel should know what the customer did on the previous channel. If this is technically impossible, then there should at least be no barriers. The future, which is only really starting to be developed in a fully multichannel way (as distinct from merely online), lies in personalising this experience – making it individually relevant to that customer. Personalisation is a topic of the later specific *Chapter 22*. However brick-and-mortar retailers should always remember that personal service, provided by a well-informed, service-focussed, human-being, is quite likely to be superior to most technology for the foreseeable future! This in turn leads to another important trend we discuss later: the potential need for more highly skilled sales staff in store (see *Chapter 20*).

10.3   Top Takeaways

Cross-channel retail is the joining up of retail channels from checkout and afterwards.

Omni-channel retail is the joining up of the customer's experience up to and including checkout.

Customer experience across all phases and channels should be seamless and consistent.

Basic reassurance regarding security, payment options, and what to do when things go wrong is essential on non-store channels.

Refunds and returns are the number one reason why online customers seek help and reassurance.

An online pure-play should never be able to offer an overall experience superior to a fully multichannel retailer!

Chapter 11.   The Customer Experience

11.1   Connecting Personas and Differentiation

It has been my aim in the preceding chapters to suggest how a fully multichannel retailer can create a customer offer superior to either pure-play online or pure brick-and-mortar competitors. Each channel is deployed to advantage, and the customer is offered beneficial options for the completion of his/her shopping journey. The price to pay for these advantages is of course in complexity. Every channel is both specialism in itself and a part of a joined-up overall whole, and to be successful it is necessary to execute both specialisms and overall experience well.

There is some risk that continuously striving to develop new channels, new ways of shopping, new cross- and omni-channel customer journeys can become an end in itself, and not just a means to encouraging customers to choose to spend with you instead of a competitor. One of the many benefits of a well-founded personas/missions based approach to defining the customer experience is that it clearly prioritises what is important for your customers and therefore for your implementation, in a way that facilitates shared definition and understanding. To demonstrate the approach, the next sections work through an artificially constructed example in some detail. I am conscious that hypothetical and simplified examples are just that – simple and hypothetical, and lacking in the complex context that always exists in the real world. However, although a real case-study might have merits in terms of more sophisticated illustration of the ideas, an artificial example has the advantage of clarity.

11.2   Simplified Example

Back in section 4.3, we created a simplified customer persona and mission – in this case, me trying to buy chocolates for my wife's birthday from an overseas hotel room. I will briefly illustrate how to use them to help define the multichannel differentiation and requirements for a hypothetical speciality retailer of chocolates. In the interests of simpler grammar, I will call this hypothetical confectionary retailer ChoxBox. Let us assume that ChoxBox is a reasonably well-known name, with a brick-and-mortar outlet of some kind (either small store or some kind of franchise) on many high streets. Gift-giving is clearly a core customer mission for such a retailer, and let us further assume that ChoxBox has carried out basic research indicating that I (or rather my persona) is representative of a significant addressable customer segment i.e. my persona and mission are relevant and applicable to ChoxBox.

I will break down my customer experience step-by-step, illustrating how ChoxBox might set about winning my custom, drawing on the P.R.I.C.E framework.

11.2.1 Experience: Seamlessly omni-channel

In the first place, notice that I will almost certainly NOT start from a search engine, looking for search terms like "chocolate gifts" or something similar. I might use a search engine to find the address of ChoxBox's website, but I will then proceed directly there. ChoxBox is already a high street name I am familiar with. Therefore it has a big advantage over any online-only chocolate retailers. To a significant extent, my custom is there for ChoxBox to lose. Provided they meet my needs at every step, I should be given no reasons to step aside and look elsewhere. This is a cornerstone of omni-channel retail thinking.

11.2.2 Experience: Reassurance

When I arrive at ChoxBox's website, I want to be sure it *is* the same people as I am familiar with on the high street. I also want to be clear, since I intend giving not only my details but also my wife's details to them, that they will take an appropriate approach to her (our) data. I am NOT, at this step, so interested in products or offers. Although it sometimes feels like a waste of screen space to describe these experience basics, in the case of this defined mission it assuredly is not.

If ChoxBox cannot provide this reassurance, this could be a point where I start to look at a competitor – my omni-channel journey already has a potential break-point in it. Remember the One Second Rule!

11.2.3 Convenience

I am still not so interested in the products or offers. The next thing I need to know is whether I can get a gift to my wife specifically ON her birthday, which happens to fall on a Saturday. Therefore, still in experience basics, I need to be able to find this out quickly. If I have to start hunting through the website, or worse still, I can only find out *after* I have added a product to my cart and started to check-out, then I will quickly get diverted to checking out the competition.

There are at least a couple of ways for ChoxBox to meet this need. Firstly they could offer a nominated day premium delivery service (notice that this is NOT an Express service, where the product just comes as fast as possible; it is a designated day that I want to achieve). If this is the proposed, I want to know who the delivery service is... and if it is the British postal service, then I probably want some alternative options!

Alternatively, I could arrange for my wife to collect a parcel from a ChoxBox store near our house. Quite possibly the same postal service will still be delivering the parcel but: a) I don't know this, and in fact I have the perception that the order is picked in the store (even though this is probably not true); b) I have time to place the order in advance, and rely on the store to hold the parcel for a day or two waiting for my wife instead of only relying on the postal service to be timely. I also need some information at this point: the location of the nearest store.

Offering both options gives the choice to the customer; in a multichannel world, the customer is in charge, not the retailer. For the purposes of my illustrative example, we will assume that I'm going to choose the collect-in-store option.

11.2.4 Information: Inspiration

Note that according to my defined persona and mission, I am currently working abroad. On which channel have I been checking out these basics? Probably on my smartphone (which my persona says I will have) whilst sitting in a taxi stuck in traffic. Having validated the essentials, I'm going to wait until I can use a PC to look at possible products.

The website now needs to give me some ideas for gifts. I need options to browse thematically: "gifts for her", "gifts for occasions", "birthday ideas" etc. Note again that I'm not at home in the UK, where it is almost certain that I would have high speed broadband access. It's important that the website design takes a view on typical bandwidth available to customers. Even the term "broadband" means quite different things in different countries: from 128K in India, typically 2Mb+ in the UK for example.

11.2.5 Range + Information

My wife does not like honey or Turkish delight, but she is fond of coffee flavours. Our son is allergic to nuts. Notice that I have still not been tempted to break my customer journey and go to a competitor site. Missing nut allergy information is one reason why I might do so. My memory of the very small local franchise store is that the selection was extremely limited, and in fact when I last wanted to buy my wife a gift, I could not find a coffee flavours selection. I am here on the website on the assumption that a complete range will be offered, possibly with some options to exclude nuts and honey.

11.2.6 Price

At this point I *might* be tempted to check out a competitor price. But notice how committed I already am to this purchase. I have already researched delivery options, store locations, gift ideas, specific range information, allergy facts; I might even have used some sort of online tool to let me put individual chocolates into a box, write a personal message etc. A birthday gift for my wife is anyway not a price-sensitive purchase.

Assuming I am not tempted to start price-comparison shopping, I will now checkout. This is not the place to discuss website design in general, and checkout design in particular (I recently read an article entitled "87 ways to improve your website checkout"…); there's more information in **Chapter 16**.

11.2.7 Experience

I need to know the progress of this order. ChoxBox could send me emails, but emails are not my preferred option when am I overseas and with clients: I would much rather get an SMS, which I can pick-up immediately and act on instantly if there is an issue.

If there *is* indeed an issue, the SMS needs to tell me what to do – at the very least whom to call. Assuming all is well, it needs to tell me how to collect the gift at the store. In fact I am going to forward this SMS to my teenage daughter, and get her to take my wife to the store on her birthday morning as a surprise.

11.2.8 Convenience again

Therefore, the SMS needs to restate the store address and its opening times – I may remember this as the original purchaser, but I am not going to be the one making the collection.

11.2.9 Experience: Multichannel

The ChoxBox store staff must know what to do when my daughter shows them the SMS. There must be a sensible and simple way to verify the purchase and prove my wife's ID, despite the original purchaser (me) not being present. The staff must be immediately able to locate the right box, and there must be control processes to ensure that my wife does not receive someone else's gift by mistake.

ChoxBox now has new customers in its store, because their collect-in-store offer has caused me (existing customer) to bring my wife and daughter (potential new customers) there. Apart from hopefully delighting my wife with her gift, ChoxBox needs to do something to exploit this visit. Looking again at my persona, we remember that my wife is unenthusiastic about technology, but my daughter is fully wired. Coupons are an obvious repeat visit driver, but remember that they may well need to work online *and* in-store. A coupon to my daughter's smartphone could be an option.

11.3   Example Evaluation

We have now designed ChoxBox's preferred multichannel shopping experience for a particular relevant core mission – absentee-professional last-minute gift-giving. I just want to state again that the above example is necessarily both artificial and simplified. The next step should be to evaluate the resulting proposition, and understand whether or not we actually have created something sufficiently differentiated from the competition. In creating the persona and mission(s), we should already have established that this is a sufficiently large target to be worth addressing, preferably supported by data or at least by good experience-based knowledge. Will ChoxBox have a competitive advantage in this space if it implements the proposed customer journey, or is more needed?

P.R.I.C.E. provides one possible simplified framework, particularly adapted to multichannel retail, to evaluate this. To take this a step further, obviously we need to evaluate the competition, and as it seems just too artificial to create ChoxBox-2 to illustrate this. I will confine myself to outlining a possible extension to our framework, based on a weighted scorecard.

Step 1: we score the relative importance of each element of P.R.I.C.E. differentiation for this Persona performing this mission.

Step 2: we score the implementations of ChoxBox and its competitors.

Step 3: we evaluate the resulting weighted scores.

To work an example, I will use weightings on a 1=bad/unimportant to 5=good/important scale. Firstly we consider the relative importance of each element of P.R.I.C.E. for me and my mission:

Factor	Price	Range	Information	Convenience	Experience
Importance	2	3	4	5	4

Secondly, we score ChoxBox's implementation of this Mission by comparison with its competitors:

Factor	Price	Range	Information	Convenience	Experience
ChoxBox	1	2	3	5	4
Competitor A	3	4	2	3	2
Competitor B	4	4	3	3	3

As a way to illustrate the process, I have given ChoxBox a significant price and assortment disadvantage compared to its competitors.

Next, we multiply the importance by the scores, to derive weighted scores:

Weighted Scores	Price	Range	Information	Convenience	Experience
ChoxBox	2	6	12	25	16

Competitor A	6	12	8	15	8
Competitor B	8	12	12	15	12

Finally we total up for ChoxBox and its competitors. Usually the results are expressed as a percentage of the maximum possible total – in this case 5 * (importance of each factor) = 5 * (2 + 3 + 4 + 5 + 4) = 90:

Competitor	Total Score	% Score
ChoxBox	61	68%
Competitor A	49	54%
Competitor B	59	65%

I would have every sympathy with a client who expressed the view that this is a bit too much management consultancy and a bit too little reality! Nevertheless, it provides some underpinning to the intuitively reasonable idea that by excelling on factors important to the customer, in this case most especially convenience, it is possible to overcome a disadvantage in both range and price. In other real-world examples, this technique has helped drive the concept and decision-making; not usually because of the actual scores and percentages, but because the debate around the weightings and the scorings helps focus everybody on what is important and/or crystallises the debate around its key points. In general this is true of most "management consultant tools" of this type: the value is in structuring the process and debate, not in the actual outcome.

11.4   A real world example: Amazon versus Best Buy

Hypothetical examples don't come alive for everybody, so I'm going to briefly repeat the exercise for a currently high profile rivalry: consumer electronics at Amazon versus Best Buy. I don't intend providing long subjective assessments of their relative strengths and weaknesses in each aspect. Instead I'd suggest you score them yourself and draw your own conclusions. Of course you should use personas, but in this case I invite you to become the stereotypical representative customer, and score them yourself. Imagine you are planning to buy something, for example a good quality camera for your vacation.

First we need to weight the importance of the factors. Here are mine, what are yours?

Factor	Price	Range	Information	Convenience	Experience
Importance	5	4	5	3	2

Price is very important to me for an expensive product like a high-quality camera. I want a good selection to choose from. I don't know much about cameras so I need information and help. For once I haven't left it too late, so convenience is less important than it sometimes is.

Next we score each competitor on these factors. Here are my scores.

Factor	Price	Range	Information	Convenience	Experience
Amazon	5	5	2	3	3
Best Buy	3	3	4	4	3

I have the perception that Amazon is cheaper and carries a much wider range. However it's not the easiest place to starting looking if you don't understand the product in the first place and I'd probably rather be helped with my decision. There's a store up the road. (This last statement is not true, but for the purposes of this exercise, I'll assume it is true – there used to be one until they closed it!).

Now for the arithmetic bit, creating the weighted scores.

Weighted Scores	Price	Range	Information	Convenience	Experience
Amazon	25	20	10	9	6
Best Buy	15	12	20	12	6

And finally the results:

Competitor	Total Score	% Score
Amazon	70	74%
Best Buy	65	68%

On this extremely superficial analysis, Best Buy needs to change something. Improving my price perception would improve their score fastest. Closing my local store moves them from a close second to a distant second — not only will their convenience rating drop, but so will their experience score. The implications of this latter point will be considered in more depth in the chapter on stores (**Chapter 20**).

11.5   P.R.I.C.E. Summary

11.5.1 For the online pure-play

It is very difficult for an online pure-play retailer to be superior to multichannel competitors in convenience.

Experience can be equivalent, albeit in different ways. The disadvantage of not having personal service must be overcome.

Range (assortment) can be comparable.

Information can be comparable, but a parasitical approach to showrooming will be required (i.e. let your brick-and-mortar competitors be your showroom for customers who want to touch and feel the products). A strategy for mobile (see **Chapter 23**) may be required for this.

Online pure-plays probably have a lower cost-base, which should in turn enable a price advantage.

11.5.2 For the multichannel retailer

In many aspects of retailing a retailer with stores that embraces multichannel should have a superior customer offer compared to an online pure-play; in information, in convenience, in experience.

It should be possible to offer comparable range/assortment, which can be easier to sell to customers via Endless Aisles supported by face-to-face service.

Establish a strategy to address <u>price</u>.

If you are in a country where online pure-plays in your categories have not really succeeding yet in scaling up, but are simply scalping the lower end price points, then a sensible strategy is to stop them scaling up in the first place.

If this is not an option, use the advantages of having stores to join them and then beat them. Even in the most challenging markets in the world, 80-90% of all retail still takes place in store.

> We have shops, call centres and a website giving you flexibility in how and when you buy from us. The level of service we offer can't therefore be equalled by online or mail-order only retailers - and it's for this reason we don't match their prices. Examples include Dixons, Amazon or Play.com.

Figure 30 - A line in the sand[65]

11.6 Top Takeaways

The P.R.I.C.E. framework can be combined with the personas/missions approach to give structure to the process of defining differentiated multichannel customer journeys.

The same framework can be used to evaluate comparison with competitors.

Online pure-plays typically have a cost-base advantage over multichannel competitors, which can be translated into a price advantage.

Online pure-plays need to plan a showrooming strategy.

Multichannel retailers hold most of the cards other than price when it comes to differentiation, and need to ensure they exploit these. If it is still possible, they should take steps to ensure pure-play competitors are stillborn. A strategy for addressing price is essential.

---

[65] John Lewis, price matching statement, 2012

Part B – Implementation

At its core, Part B is a "how to go online" guide for the retailer who is not yet online. There are three target audiences, but the first is probably the primary one:

i)   Existing brick-and-mortar retailers who are considering adding a serious eCommerce channel to their existing store channel. This is a multichannel retail handbook. Brick-and-mortar retailers planning to add new transactional channels are therefore one of its primary target audiences. This section generally approaches issues from the perspective of a retailer wishing to make this step from mono-channel to multichannel.

ii)   Executives in existing brick-and-mortar retailers where an online channel has been created in a very independent way, perhaps by a small team going it alone, who now need to understand better how this channel operates, so that they can consider how to re-integrate it into the main business. If you fall into this category, you are definitely not alone! See **Chapter 18** for more information.

iii)   A potential start-up online pure-play. However this book cannot be a guide to "how to become a retailer". Topics such as "How to Buy" are definitely out of scope. I assume you have all such basic retail competencies in place or available, and look only at the variations and additions that are implied by taking them online

Part B is structured to reflect the business case you will need to build, considering firstly estimating the sales opportunity, and then looking at the key cost areas in turn, to develop a new online store. Each implementation or operation area is considered in turn in the succeeding chapters.

Chapter 12.   Product Data

12.1   Introduction

Logically the place to start a business case is by considering the potential size of the prize. The next chapter is indeed devoted to that topic. Why, then, begin Part B with a lengthy chapter on an apparently obscure technical subject?

The first part of the answer is that you can only estimate the size of the prize when you know what you are going to sell. And the critical difference between selling online and selling offline is this:

> Brick-and-mortar stores sell products.
>
> Online stores don't sell products. They sell descriptions and promises.

Offline, customers swap their money for a product they can touch, feel, and takeaway now. Online customers swap their money for your description of what they are going to get, and your promise about when/how you will bring it to them. This simple insight is fundamental to all aspects of online retailing, including the business case.

(The apparent exception is cash-on-delivery, which is covered in more depth in the payment section in **Chapter 15**. However in this case this whole topic is actually even more critical, because customers initially swap *your* money – in the form of shipping costs – for a description and promise. If you don't match up to this description or promise, that shipping cost just becomes a straightforward operating loss on the order; you never get to see the customer's money).

The promise element of this key insight is discussed in more detail in **Chapter 15**. Briefly using here it to illustrate a simple example of how far this impacts your business-case: provided you can meet the promise you make to the customer, for example to deliver their order within the specified timeframe, there is no mandatory need to hold any stock of a given product, until after the customer has paid for it. How would your existing cash-flow and balance-sheet (and profitability!) look if you could do that in a brick-and-mortar situation?

The description element is the focus of the rest of this chapter.

12.2   Importance

The second part of the answer to the question 'why start part B with this?' is that the topic is absolutely critical. If you are already online, you will already be aware of how fundamental it is. If you are still planning to go online, then be warned: in every online implementation project I have ever seen or been involved with, product data management always ends up being *the* critical path task for launch.

It isn't just for implementation either. Even the smallest step-change to the multichannel proposition you offer to your customers tends to involve yet another product data management challenge. Adding click-and-collect? You need to flag all the eligible products. Adding cross-sells or recommendations? You need to manage all the connections or exclusions between products.   Adding an endless aisle in a category? Probably hundreds or thousands more products requiring their data managing. New season range change? More product data. Special festival period offer? Still more product data. You get the picture. The description and associated things like pictures IS the product as far as the customer is concerned. It needs to be accurate, enticing, and... descriptive.

Not only does product data describe what you are selling, it also describes *how* your online offer will behave, and how the product will appear. A very simple example to cheer up this page full of otherwise rather tough news: where does a nice bottle of red wine sit in the browsing hierarchy? Is it a 'red -> wine', or a 'wine -> red'? Somewhere, this decision and information has to be entered as an item of data. Strictly, this "how" data is not *master* data, it is *merchandising* data. For many practical purposes, the distinction is irrelevant because in all except the very largest and most complex organisations with the most sophisticated IT systems, the same people using the same systems end up doing the work. (We'll return to this topic in the IT section later *Chapter 16*. As with all things IT and multichannel, inevitably it somehow isn't quite as simple as I've painted it in this introduction).

Just to summarise:

- product master data defines *what* you are selling

- the closely related concept of merchandising data defines *how* you are selling it

Both concepts are of course fundamental to any retail business. Too see just how fundamental, we'll take a look in the next sections at how they impact the two main customer journeys on any retailer's website: searching and browsing. We'll start by searching.

12.3 Search

Search is almost entirely driven by product data. What is important to understand here is that the product search and navigation functions on a website do *not* work in the way that say Google, or any other search engine, does. Search engines like Google work by looking "from the outside in", scanning each page that you choose to display. They do not, in general[66], rely on any structure in what they find – every word, or data point, is equal. Retail website product search, by contrast, works "from the inside out". What does this mean?

Take a look again at **Figure 16**, that loaf of bread. The data about it includes a list of ingredients, one of which is unsurprisingly "flour". What happens on a grocery website if a customer enters the word "flour" in a search box? What you want to see is a list of packets of flour. What you don't want to see is a very long list of products which have flour as an ingredient, which will probably not be topped by packets of flour but by various breads and cakes. Simplifying (a lot), an "outside in" search-engine style search will see a lot of text, and with no other guidance, will treat all text as equal, so bread is just as much flour as flour itself is. The "inside out" search used by retail sites is given some more guidance by, or about, the product data. In this particular example, it would be told that text listed as "ingredients" is not as important as text listed as "product name". So when "flour" is entered by the customer, the more relevant products called "flour" are top of the list.

---

[66] This is gradually changing with the introduction of structured data and rich snippets. See schema.org for more information. It doesn't replace site search though, and in reality just adds yet another reason why product data is so important... and another task to manage.

As we head from search towards navigation, consider the same grocery website being contemplated by a customer who has gluten-allergy. The full ingredient listed for that loaf of bread is "wheat flour", which contains gluten. How do you tell this to a search engine? Again the "inside out" engines are given that advantage via either hidden data which is not text (such as a Yes/No flag for gluten-content) and/or extra rules information. So when a customer asks for "gluten free" in a search box, or ticks a "gluten-free" checkbox somewhere in the navigation structure, the engine is aware of the relationship between the ingredient "wheat flour" and the property "gluten free". This is pretty much impossible for a Google-type engine to do reliably; artificial intelligence hasn't yet reached this level, so the implementation reality is invariably extra hidden product data or rules.

> The key point: poor quality product data means poor search results. And if your customers can't find your products, they can't buy them.

12.4 Navigation

Checkboxes for "gluten free" are not strictly search, and more properly lie in the realm of navigation. Once again, product data is the foundation of effective navigation. Take a look at *Figure 31*.

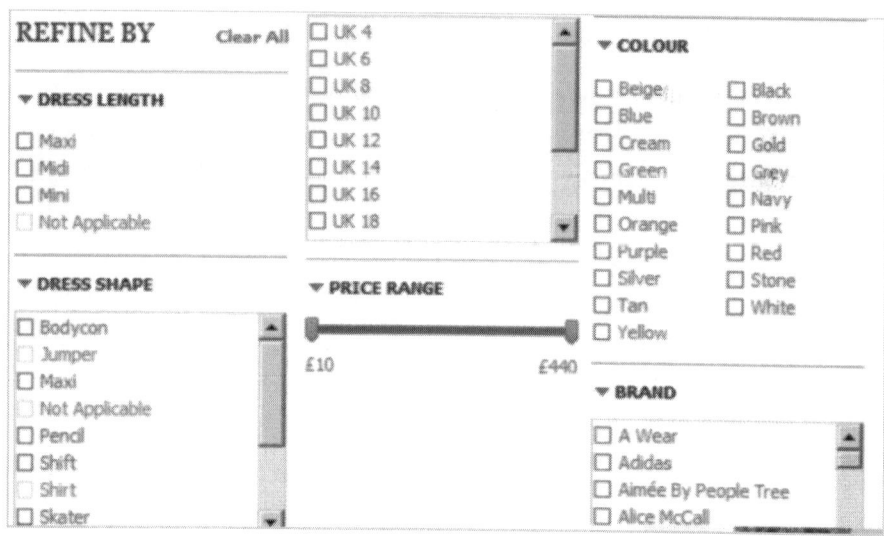

Figure 31 - Navigating to the right dress[67]

---

[67] Collage from asos.com, November 2012

This is a part (and only a part) of the navigational features to help you choose the right dress. The site in question sells over 2000 different dresses, so obviously the customer needs plenty of direction to finding the right one. To deliver that direction, every single dress has had its colour, size, shape, brand etc not only entered, but entered *consistently*. For example, there are 19 colours defined in this navigation. A child's box of crayons probably has more than 19 colours in it. To make this navigation work, some strict standards have been defined, for example the one that says that "red" is a valid colour but "scarlet" is not.

> The key point: such standards are necessary, and need business process, enforcement and quality control.

12.5   Browse and Taxonomy

An assortment's taxonomy is generally identified with the browsing hierarchy that you will be familiar with on any retail website, usually displayed at the top of the screen looking something like *Figure 32* (a display area known technically as a Breadcrumb Trail).

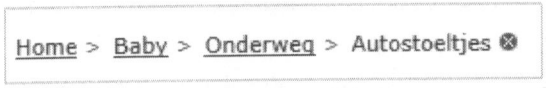

Figure 32 - Taxonomy / browsing hierarchy[68]

The most important part of any taxonomy is the Top- or 1st-Level of the hierarchy. In this example breadcrumb, the top-level is "Baby". Conventionally - and these conventions increasingly exist because they are proven to work - this top level will be visible on most/all of the key pages on your website.   *Figure 33* is a screenshot from the same website, showing the complete top menu section (incidentally notice the prominent "free delivery from 20 Euros" message):

Figure 33 - Website top menu, showing top level hierarchy[69]

---

[68] From bol.com, November 2012

Getting the correct top menu is a key task for any retail website. The reasons for this become particularly clear when we take a look at the same retailer's mobile site (*Figure 34*).

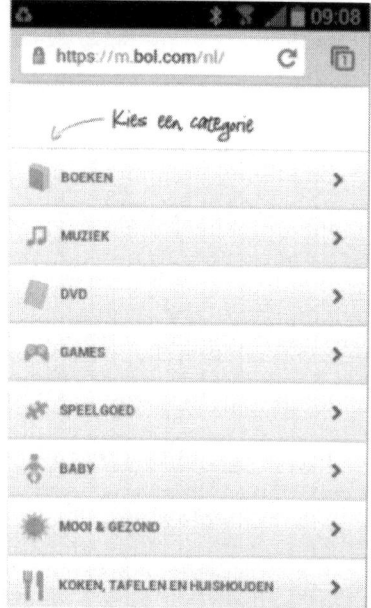

Figure 34 - Same taxonomy, mobile channel[70]

Excluding Search, the *only* route into this retailer's assortment is via this very short list of words. It follows that organising these categories in the right way is one of the most important tasks for any online retail proposition, and one that tends to get neglected in amongst more exciting possibilities. By the way, the moment you decide to launch a mobile site as an extension to an existing desktop website (or vice versa) is a very good moment to take another look at the efficiency of your taxonomy.

An assortment's taxonomy is NOT product master data. It is a property of *how* you sell, not *what* you sell, and is therefore merchandising. There are some sophisticated logical-data-structure arguments behind this which are important, but it is not so easy to demonstrate these convincingly to anyone outside a rather specialist IT-architecture audience. Fortunately there are some much simpler practical reasons. The most obvious is that a product may sit in multiple places in a hierarchy. Consider a fashion

---

[69] ibid
[70] ibid

website, which invites customers to browse both by garment-type (e.g. coats, dresses, trousers) and by brand. Such a site will have *at least* a double hierarchy. If you add in further navigation routes for the customer, such as perhaps a special offers section, it is easy to see that a single product can end up occupying multiple slots in the hierarchy structure. Another reason is that you might have different sales channels with different hierarchies; a specialist clearance site for example, or a branded micro-site.

The implication of such multiple hierarchies lies primarily in the process you should use to manage the taxonomy:

WRONG WAY: make a big table of your products, and then next to each product list its position in the hierarchy;

RIGHT WAY: make a big map - which will look rather like a diagram of a tree - of your hierarchy, and then drop your products onto its "leaves". You can quite easily drop the same product onto several different leaves if that is what is required.

This is not just true when first creating a taxonomy, it's true for managing it ongoing as well. The process should always be 1) define/refine the taxonomy; 2) the taxonomy "pulls" the products onto itself. Do not accept being given processes in which your products "push" themselves into places on the taxonomy by apparently knowing about it by themselves. (Incidentally for smaller retailers using entry-level software solutions, this distinction in process approach is strongly recommended as one of the various ways to tell a good solution + supplier from a bad one). *Figure 35* illustrates the idea.

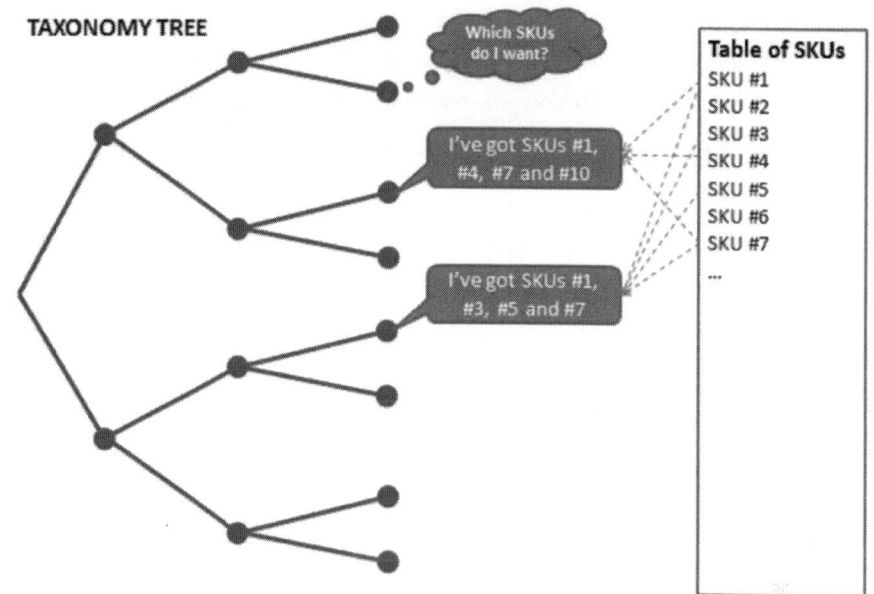

Figure 35 - Taxonomy creation "pull" process

Note that there is (or should be) no requirement that every leaf on the taxonomy has the same depth so products themselves could sit at the 2nd level (Home -> Special Offers) and the 4th level (Home -> Baby -> On the move -> Car Seats) within the same taxonomy. Good practice is to try to ensure that all the leaves have a reasonably consistent number of products in them, typically between 10 and 50. Having one leaf with 1000 products and another with only 3 not only looks silly, but can cause issues with inconsistent site behaviour.

Note also that a retailer's pre-existing <u>buying</u> hierarchy is almost never a hierarchy which should simply be shown to customers. As a simple example, I worked with a client whose buying hierarchy included the term "dry drinks". In actual fact it meant things like teabags and coffee powder (despite my mental pictures of alcohol-free beer and wine, or in madder moments of powdered water), but it certainly wasn't a term to display to customers. Even simply using a more customer-friendly name is not usually adequate. For example, you might have your buying for a particular category split into domestic and overseas, but you probably don't want to display this distinction to your customers.

There is no simple labour-saving way to avoid creating the taxonomy from scratch and then placing your products one by one, although there will probably be shortcuts at least at sub-sub-category level. Many retailers maintain their taxonomy using index cards on the wall (or floor if they have a lot of products!), which sounds oddly un-technical but seems to be the best way in practice; if you want to use software, you need an extremely large screen.

> The key point: taxonomy is probably the most important area where product data and merchandising data meet. Both are necessary for a fully operational retail website.
>
> Like all aspects of managing such data, it is a labour intensive task. Just re-using the buying hierarchy isn't sufficient.

12.6 Business Process

Figure 36 shows a possible outline business process flow for the capture of data. In practice it can only be illustrative, because the landscape, especially in existing supply chain or purchasing functions, will vary. In some way or other every step described here will need to be addressed somewhere in your own flow.

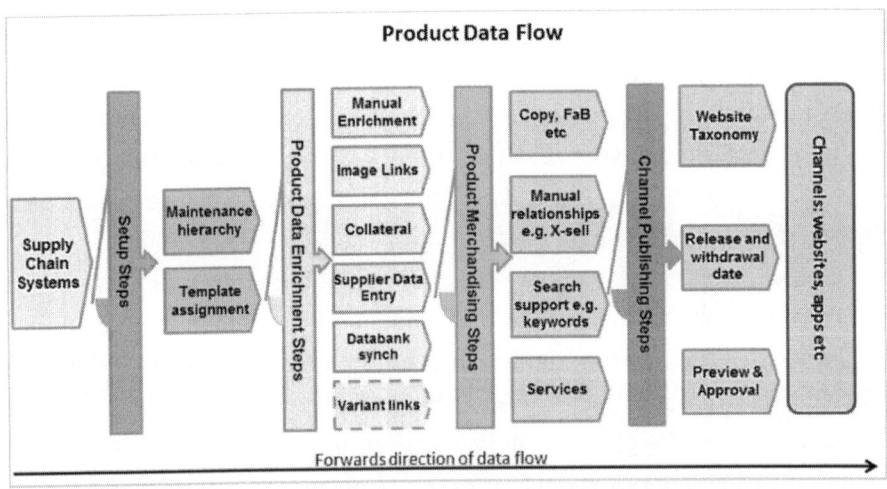

Figure 36 - Product Data Capture Schematic Flow

We will very briefly run through each of these steps and explain their purpose.

Supply Chain Systems: most retailers of any size having buying or supply chain systems in which at least some basic data is captured, not least the allocation of the SKU number. Even what data there exists here is frequently of limited use online: compressed titles instead of full descriptive ones, dimensions of inbound shipping units instead of the unwrapped product etc. But given this is where the key field – SKU number – gets allocated, it's almost always the starting point.

Template assignment: a cabbage and a camera need rather different data capturing. You need to decide how many different templates you need (try to have as few as reasonably possible, because it scales cost elsewhere too). Every product needs to belong to one.

Maintenance hierarchy: often the buying or supply chain hierarchy will do this job. Rather simply – you need to be able to find products in your product data flow in some sort of hierarchy too and/or allocate the tasks of enriching their product data to different teams.

Manual enrichment: speaks for itself. Someone has to key in data about the product.

Image links: similarly products need pictures (or videos etc). It's usual to store them somewhere else for performance reasons, but you still have to associate pictures to their corresponding products.

Collateral: very similar to pictures. Sometimes you might want other material such as instruction-manuals associated with products.

Supplier data entry: sometimes, if you are very big and therefore have the muscle, or alternatively if your supplier is very enlightened and volunteers this, you will be able to get data directly from the supplier. Typically they will provide files to upload plus possible some sort of QA service. For most retailers in most categories, the best advice is: don't count on it!

Databank synch: as noted below, in a few specific categories (and even more specific languages), you might be fortunate and be able to subscribe to a databank, free or otherwise. You then need to keep your data in synch with this databank.

Variant links: this is very product, category and system specific. You may need to capture that product are closely related and should be presented "as one" to the customer, for example because they are colour variations on the same style. This will need to be considered in detail depending on your specific circumstances; it is impossible to generalise, almost every retailer has different challenges here.

Copy & FaB (features and benefits): it is extremely unlikely that your existing buying systems will contain selling copy or FaB. Even if they do, they are often inappropriate for presenting directly to consumers. Someone has to create this, and give it a tone of voice. This is a very time consuming part of the job, but usually essential to online selling.

Relationships: Does the product have a natural partner product, for example a stand that goes with a TV, or trousers to match the jacket? This task might be manual, or might use software to automate it inside the selling channel itself: see also *Chapter 22* on personalisation.

Search support: as we saw in the example above about gluten-allergy, it is often necessary to provide extra data to support search or navigation. Additional hidden keywords is another potential requirement - I might, for example, put the hidden keyword "omnichannel" into the data about this book.

Services: do you offer installation, removal of previous product, set-up at home etc?

Taxonomy: as discussed above.

Release and withdrawal date: you may be able to handle this manually. Often products should be published to the site altogether, for example for a new season or range. Some semi-automatic control may be needed, depending on the size of your assortment.

Preview and approval: you should QA as much as possible throughout the process. A final "what does it look like to customers?" step is strongly recommended.

12.7   Simplified Example

I'm keen to stress that word 'simplified' before presenting this example; this is an especially relevant word if some of this data is interfaced from other IT systems. The practical task of managing the data and the proper definition of IT logical data structures to support it can seem quite far apart, and a discussion of IT enterprise architecture considerations is definitely not in scope for this book; some of what follows might therefore make the purist wince. Be that as it may, I already started using dresses as an example, so let's continue on the same theme: a new hypothetical retailer, MegaClothes, selling a party frock from its exciting MegaFrocks range.

Product data is generally specified in attribute-value pairs. For example the attribute might be "weight" and the value might be "400 grammes". Of course nothing is ever quite so simple, and in this case the specification in a real system might be in an attribute-value-unit triple, so the value would be "400" and the unit would be "grammes". I'm keen to keep this example simplified though, so I'm going to avoid (or should that be evade?) these kinds of additional complications.

Attributes are divided into those which are common across all your products – for example "brand" – and those which are specific to a category or sub-category. *Figure 31* showed "dress shape" as one of the attributes of a dress. Clearly this is no use when describing bras, when a cup-size attribute would be relevant instead. For every category, or sub-category, it is necessary to define what category-specific attributes you require: this is the Template as described in the data flow above. (Applying this to the taxonomy topic, position in taxonomy should *never* be managed as though it were an attribute of the product.)

Some attributes are visible to customers. Others are used internally in various ways: they might be hidden in support of navigation like the "gluten free" example above; they might involve parts of the operation that you don't want to directly display to customers, such as the packaged-weight of the product which you might use to calculate the shipping charge; they might be part of controlling the work-flow of creating and completing the product data itself, such as a QA-sign off without which the product will not be listed on your website. For simplicity I'm going to stick with referring to all of these as attributes, even though in a more complex IT system they might well be managed in quite different ways, especially the work-flow aspects and/or data interfaced from other systems such as price.

We'll look at organisational issues in *Chapter 18* below, but responsibility for collating this information is often spread across your organisation, with a coordinating function adding the specifically "website" parts and performing quality assurance.

NB: *Figure 37* is NOT intended to be a definitive list of all the likely attributes for a dress, just those selected to make illustrative points.

Attribute	Value	Visible/ Internal	Step in the process	Comment
Common Attributes				
SKU#	12345678	Internal	Buying or supply chain	
Catalogue number	12-34-56	Visible	Manual enrichment	Don't use the SKU number for this; you'll find that causes problems later on. You need a number to display on invoices and catalogues
Brand	Megafrocks	Visible	Buying or supply chain	
Size	12	Visible	Buying or supply chain	This type of attribute is known as a "variant"; a website will not list ten dresses identical except for size, rather it will list one dress with ten size options
Name	MegaFrocks Little Black Party Frock	Visible	Manual enrichment	Typical buying/supply chain systems provide only abbreviated product names: you will need a full-length, SEO-friendly one for an online channel.
Description	Ideal for Xmas parties	Visible	Copy/FaB	There is often a big process difference between attributes which are "facts" and attributes which are "opinions". For example "opinions"

				are not usually very high priority for Search.
Shipping weight	400g	Internal	Manual enrichment	You might hope this would be in supply chain, but typical legacy supply chains don't capture the outbound shipping weight of the product as a single item in a customer order.
Stock Locations	Warehouses #1 and #3	Internal	Supply chain.	This type of attribute might be explicitly stated, or it might be "deduced" from the interface with your other logistics systems. This tends to depend on the complexity of your existing brick-and-mortar operation if you have one.
Overseas shipping?	No	Internal	Services	
First day on sale	15th November	Internal	Release (and withdrawal) date.	
QA sign-off	Yes	Internal	Preview and approval.	Processes are required to make sure you don't "publish" a product to your website until it is completely prepared in all its aspects.
Price	£100	Visible	Buying (note to those who design II	Attributes such as price are often sourced

			architecture: price is always merchandising data)	"automatically" from the central merchandising systems. It is necessary to put in place processes to ensure the systems stay in synch, and also that the price can be overridden on the web in emergencies.
You may also like	SKU #9876	Visible	Manual relationships	Most retailers have to maintain this data manually.
Get the look	SKU #7777 + SKU #6666	Visible	Manual relationships	There is no way to avoid maintaining this data manually!
Search priority	2	Internal	Search support	Instructions to your internal search, in this case that it should be high up a list of results but not at the top
New until	15th February	Internal	Usually part of Copy/FaB etc	Instructions to your website itself, in this case that a "New!" splash logo should be displayed next to the image
Images	url-name X	Internal	Image links	Where to look for the main picture of this item
Attributes Specific to Dresses Categories				
Colour	Black	Visible	Buying/supply chain	This type of attribute has a strictly controlled set of valid values, so entering "dark grey" will be rejected – it's either

				black or grey. This may require a step in Manual Enrichment to apply the standardised set of customer-facing colours in place of the supplier-provided colours.
Dress shape	Shift	Visible	Usually buying/supply chain.	Might be in manual enrichment if a "standards" mapping is needed.
Dress length	Mini	Visible	Usually buying/supply chain.	Might be in manual enrichment if a "standards" mapping is needed.

Figure 37 - Simplified product data example

As you can see, I have already identified 18 attributes for this simple black party frock just when constructing an artificial illustrative example. Real world situations are usually more complex.

There are some possible external sources of such data. A few companies specialise in providing it for specific categories (BrandBank for branded groceries, for example – as always, no recommendation or otherwise implied. The consumer electronics industry has a free-to-use collaboration called icecat[71], which offers ways to source and manage this data in 35 languages.) You need to carefully evaluate the quality of such sources before enthusiastically subscribing as a way of avoiding all this internal labour. Even if you use an external source, there is still a big organisational task to do; when they work well, they are still not a silver bullet, and you should never omit quality control steps.

12.8 Costs

The standard baseline planning benchmark is that it takes 25 FTE minutes per SKU to set-up or maintain the necessary data. Or put another way, 1 FTE can manage 4000 SKUs per year. One of my clients had 800,000

---

[71] See www.icecat.biz

SKUs... As with all benchmark data points, this is only valid until you have your own direct experience of course.

The resultant cost benefit case can be quite challenging. One take on this, as discussed in more depth already in **Chapter 8**, is to take a hard look at exactly how much data you need to capture – do you really need to become *the* reference source for this information online – and use that approach to reduce the costs. The alternative, of course, is to increase the benefits, and adapt a truly multichannel approach to the exploitation of master data. This is discussed further in **Chapter 20**.

Unfortunately many retailers adopt a third alternative: economising on the quality of such data. Given how fundamental it is, cutting corners on quality is unadvisable; if you are looking for savings, reduce the quantity of information and/or streamline the process. One way to tackle the latter is to consider *who* is doing the task; this is discussed further in **Chapter 18**.

Of course you also need some sort of IT system to organise it in, which can vary from spreadsheets to multimillion dollar/pound/euro solutions, which is a topic we will cover in the later chapter on IT (**Chapter 16**). Be warned, however: no system, however good – or expensive! – will prevent the task of product data management being a labour intensive, mission-critical, highly manual, slog.

12.9   Top Takeaways

Product master data is the foundation of multichannel retailing.

If it is a new discipline for your retailer, put it on the project critical path and start now!

An online retail channel is not selling products, it is selling descriptions of products (plus a fulfilment promise). These descriptions are therefore critical.

Master data describes the products (the *what*) you are selling. Merchandising data describes *how* you sell them. For smaller retailers, or with less complex IT systems, the distinction may be theoretical rather than practical.

The planning benchmark assumption is that good quality master data requires 25 minutes per SKU to source and capture. 4000 SKUs therefore require approximately 1 man-year to set up.

If the costs look like being a problem, look for savings in data quantity or in streamlining capture/maintenance processes: do *not* compromise on data quality.

Browse and Search are the two main methods customers use to find products on a website.

Taxonomy, usually identified with the assortment browsing hierarchy on a website, is the browsing gateway to your products. Taxonomy is part of merchandising.

A taxonomy should have a root-branch-leaf structure; leaves should be of approximately equal size. It is critical to get the root-level right for customers, especially on mobile sites.

A taxonomy should *never* be defined via product master data attributes. Products should always be "pulled" into a taxonomy; they should never push their own way in.

Existing buying hierarchies are typically inappropriate to map one-for-one into customer-facing taxonomies.

Internal website search differs from Google-style search; an internal search will receive more data/rules guidance for prioritising its results, be more focussed on merchandising, and be able to access invisible data attributes.

Search and navigation are enabled by product master data and merchandising data. Such data is typically structured in attribute/value pairs such as colour/red. It may be visible or invisible to customers.

The management of this data requires formally defined and documented business processes for all common use-cases, as well as standards for data entry into each attribute.

Getting suppliers to participate is often challenging, especially if either you are small or they are small.

Databanks exists to help in a few specialised categories and languages.

Never omit quality control checks on product data, no matter how/where you are sourcing it.

Good product data is the biggest difference between a good website and a bad one. It does not come cheap. Managing it is very labour intensive.

Chapter 13.   Forecasting Sales

13.1   Introduction

The previous chapter presented a lengthy description of a wholly incremental, and rather expensive, addition to your cost-base. Obviously it would be nice to counterbalance this with wholly incremental sales. Unfortunately, unless you are reading this as a start-up pure-play, this is unlikely to be the case, which is why the first sub-section in this chapter is about cannibalisation of existing store sales.

The remainder of the chapter presents some very simple models to use as a starting point for forecasting sales. As always with these kinds of "consultant" models, the point is in the process and rationalisation of your thought processes, not in the actual direct outcome of the model itself, without further business thinking, experience and judgment applied to it.

13.2   Cannibalisation

Any new channel will cannibalise an existing one. A new eCommerce channel will, therefore, cannibalise sales from your stores. It is extremely difficult to measure this effect, and so the usual rule of thumb applied is that around 50% of any "new" sales will in fact not be incremental overall. The few data points available tend to suggest that this might be rather pessimistic, but to a significant extent it depends heavily on whether your competitors are already online as well.

Before you halve the benefits line in your business case, and then disgustedly decide it isn't actually worth it at all, it is worth returning to some basics.

Figure 38 - Non-Food Retail Growth Trend in UK[72]

Figure 38 illustrates a critical point: eCommerce does NOT create new money in customers' wallets. In the UK, with its very well developed online retail sector within an already mature retail environment, overall non-food retail sales have effectively remained flat over the last dozen years once inflation effects are removed. Sales have simply switched channel.

(The exception may be in categories which store-only customers simply found impossible to access until they could buy online. To some extent this is the case in places such as China, where offline retail was also relatively undeveloped away from the bigger cities, and therefore where eCommerce is enabling customers to access a range of products and categories that were previously unavailable to them locally.)

New channels are competing for wallet-share with existing channels. You may recall from *Chapter 2* that your best customers will be expecting you to be on multiple channels, a proportion which will grow as adoption of new channels grows in your market. If you aren't on these new channels, they may well switch to a competitor who is. This leads to a key point:

---

[72] Data from UK Office of National Statistics & British Retail Consortium. CPI used as the inflation measure.

> If you don't cannibalise your brick-and-mortar stores yourself, then somebody else will cannibalise them instead!

It is very important to separate this statement into its two different consequences.

> Firstly, your eCommerce business case should claim <u>all</u> its forecast sales, not just the truly incremental part.
>
> Secondly a completely different business case should consider the consequences to your stores of potentially reduced sales (see **Chapter 20**).

The overall picture is depicted in **Figure 39.** In a fast-developing market, where both you and your competitors are rapidly headed online simultaneously, the "incremental" element may well be very small, of course. The self-cannibalisation part will certainly exist: you may find you end up with the same total sales from a more complex business. Most retailers find this preferably to the alternative of fewer sales from a simpler business.

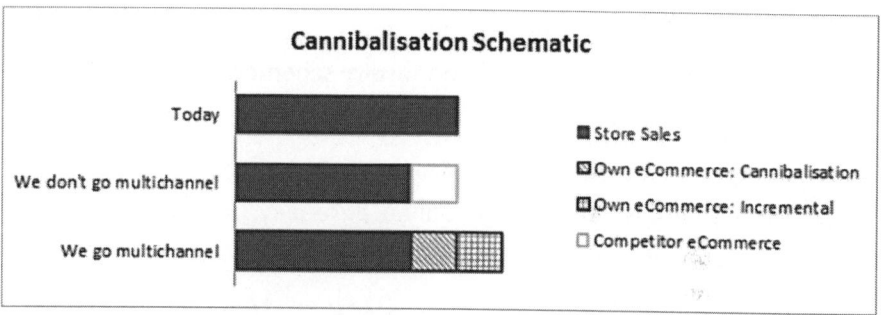

Figure 39 - Cannibalisation Schematic

Failing to accept the idea that, in a mature retail market, brick-and-mortar store sales will almost certainly fall as eCommerce takes off in your categories is a recipe for disaster. You might not want it to happen, but it will, driven by your customers... or worse by your competitors. Plan for it.

13.3 Competitive Landscape Structure

In order to effectively model the sales opportunity, it is helpful to consider the key states in which an online market might be, in your countries/categories. The three basic situations are: 1) Highly developed online; 2) undeveloped online; 3) fragmented. A simple template is provided for each in turn. I have created example high level assessments for illustration. *Please be aware that I have made up the data and examples for illustration only.*

13.3.1 Highly developed online market

...but not including you!

The size of the potential eCommerce market can usually be determined from publicly available data, and competitors are usually well known. The general growth of eCommerce is also usually well tracked and projected out in various publicly available studies. Suggested assessment template with example:

Market: UK B2C Wine

Market Size: around GBP 500M

Growth: approximately 11% per year

General landscape: a very developed market, dominated by three large players. There are also numerous specialist and non-specialist "wine-clubs", especially those run by the Sunday newspapers or offered as rewards by the major points-based loyalty schemes. Many of these are in fact fulfilled by the big three.

Key competitor #1: AAAA.com, 40% share. Differentiated by Range and Experience. *Range*: deep-range online pure-play. Subscription models drive a significant proportion of revenues. *Experience*: celebrity wine-writers add cachet to the site.

Key competitor #2: BBBB.com operated by a leading supermarket, 15% share. Narrow core range with approximately 2000 SKUs. Differentiated by Convenience, Experience and Information. *Convenience*: leverages online grocery delivery vans to offer precisely timed delivery slots. *Experience*: exclusive club feel. Multichannel strongly leveraged, with store-based events branded as club-exclusives, and promotional calendars synchronised offline and online. *Information*: magazine and associated secondary club brand.

The focus when considering how to model sales in such a market (see below) will be on how your differentiation will allow you to capture some market share from these established competitors. Your differentiation approach will need to be very strong.

13.3.2 Undeveloped Online Market

The reality is that such markets are increasingly rare as eCommerce develops rapidly worldwide. In such a market the focus will be on understanding the category offline market, and then extrapolate by understanding general online trends. It is also necessary in such a market to examine whether basic hygiene factors for online retailing such as broadband, banks offering secure online payment connections, or last-mile delivery exist. In some markets (Indonesia is a good example) these are "just happening" and a first mover opportunity may well exist. Secondary evidence is often available from information on non B2C online commerce, such as eBay for example.

Suggested assessment template with example:

Market: India, Jewellery

Total market size: Approximately 65000 crore Rs

Online market size: 80 crore Rs, approximately 0.1% of all sales

General landscape: Highly fragmented market. Approx 6% of market taken by large players such as YYYY (4%). Some single-state chains. Otherwise all local players. However an item of jewellery sells on Amazon, eBay, Snapdeal or Flipkart in India every few seconds.

General online retail landscape: Retail eCommerce as a whole is forecast to grow by at least 30% year on year, over and above underlying retail growth of 15% year on year.

Constraints: Delivery. Last mile delivery, especially of high value items, is available only in large cities. Cross state-border taxation issues remain a concern.

Constraints: Payment. Payment infrastructure is established, with large banks such as HDFC, ICICI and SBI all offering appropriate gateways.

Constraints: Consumer acceptance. Consumer acceptance of "non-face-to-face" purchase is relatively low but growing rapidly.

Constraints: Broadband penetration. Penetration of broadband (256K) into large Metros is now significant, and at least in Metros is no longer a constraint. Outside of the big cities, it remains an obstacle to effective eCommerce.

Why is there an opportunity? We have a large range of mid-price jewellery which can be sold as a commodity without "touch and feel" selling. The progress of marketplaces in India is a strong indicator of the opportunity. Many constraints have now been removed, and it is therefore believed that a real first-mover opportunity exists in this space. With the exception of YYYY, there is no other player with the nationwide reach or resources to quickly dominate this space.

13.3.3 Fragmented Market

In some ways this is the ideal situation. The "perfect" market for an online proposition is one with a strong mail-order (or telesales) heritage, but where the mail-order players have not generally become multichannel yet. Consumers are used to distance buying, infrastructure such as delivery capability generally exists, but possibly for single-issue reasons such as access to broadband, or just consumer acceptance in the category, internet has not become a preferred channel. Alternatively the market can be fragmented, or dominated by niche players, usually small online pure-play start-ups. This is frequently the situation in "simple to start" categories, such as consumer electronics, in emerging online countries. Suggested assessment template with example:

Market: UK professional catering equipment

***Addressable* market size**: approximately GBP 650M

Growth: approximately 11% per year

General landscape: a very fragmented market. The only scale player is XXXX.

Key competitor #1: XXXX. Differentiated by Experience, Range and Convenience. *Experience*: A bricks'n'clicks'n'flicks offer including telephone ordering, with a strong mail order heritage. *Range*: A big book catalogue is published twice a year with 50,000 listed SKUs.

Convenience: Very aggressive convenience promise based around next day delivery.

Other competitors: fragmented players operating in very narrow specialist niches.

In reality there is not so much data which can be captured for assessment in this situation. The key difference from previous templates is the focus on addressable market. Niche players may well operate in extreme niches, such as very local geographies or extraordinarily specialised categories, which will therefore be exceptionally difficult for you to address even with an endless aisle. Excluding such extreme cases, an ideal market, will consist of mail-order, telesales and similar, where it is possible to compete through superior multichannel behaviour, plus basic online pure-plays who may struggle to compete with a more sophisticated player. Some approximation is inevitable. The potential sales opportunity is in any case more likely to be identified by looking at specific existing players and "taking" a share of their sales from them (see the Predator model below).

13.4   Assessing the Sales Opportunity

Three very simple models are provided here to use as a starting point.

Comparative fair-share: intended primarily for highly developed markets – essentially it looks for justification as to why you should end up with more/less than the same share online as you currently have offline;

Predator: Intended either for undeveloped markets or for start-ups seeking to take share off existing players;

Bottom-up: intended primarily for fragmented markets or where other reasonable top-down models are not appropriate

13.4.1 Comparative fair-share

This is a two stage model. In the first stage, we simply calculate what a fair share of the new channel (online/eCommerce) market would look like for your target market or categories, starting from the assumption that you capture the same market share online as you currently do offline.

Our share of the offline market / total size of the offline market = our fair share %.

Forecast (or current) online market size * our fair share % = our expected online fair share.

For example, if the offline market is worth 500M and you have sales of 25M, then you have a 5% share. If the online market is estimated to be worth 40M, then your 5% fair share of it will be worth 2M.

In the second stage, we simply look to justify why you might be entitled to more or less of your fair share. The basis proposed is the P.R.I.C.E. differentiation model described in **Chapter 5** and onwards (**Figure 40**).

Our fair share online	Price versus competitors	Range versus competitors	Information versus competitors	Convenience versus competitors	Experience versus competitors	PRICE Summary	Fair Share multiplier	Our sales opportunity
5M	Green	Amber	Amber	Green	Amber	GREEN	2.5	12.5 M
5M	Amber	Red	Red	Green	Red	RED	0.5	2.5M
5M	Green	Amber	Red	Green	Amber	AMBER	1	5M

Figure 40 - Fair Share Assessment Template Stage 2

Step 1: Grade (RAG) the proposed eCommerce proposition against the 5 key differentiators: Price, Range, Information, Convenience, Experience. RAG is not complex: **Green**: better than most competitors (for our target customers); **Amber**: about the same as most competitors; **Red**: not as good as most competitors.

Step 2: summarise the 5 RAG-grades into a single summary RAG.

Step 3: Uplift or reduce the fair-share opportunity according to the summary RAG: **Green**: you will be able to take significantly more than your fair share; **Amber**: you will only take your fair share (at best); **Red**: you will not take your fair share, and 50% is a very(!) optimistic default multiplier.

Step 4: Identify the resulting sales opportunity

There is no especially numerical basis proposed for summarising the differentiation, and although one could be built I suspect it would be rather arbitrary even by the standards of these tools. Similarly the proposed multipliers, suggesting that a better (green) differentiation should entitle you to two-and-a-half times your fair share while a worse (red) differentiation should entitle you to only half are also completely arbitrary although not unreasonable.

13.4.2 Predator

A similar but rather simpler process is proposed for the predator model. The same differentiation assessment is applied, but to the specific competitor's business, as illustrated in *Figure 41.* Again the assumption of capturing 25%/5%/1% of a competitor target's sales when differentiation is rated green/amber/red is arbitrary.

Target	Target sales	Price versus competitor	Range versus competitor	Information versus competitor	Convenience versus competitor	Experience versus competitor	PRICE Summary	Expected share of target's sales	Our sales opportunity
Brand X	50	Green	Amber	Amber	Green	Amber	GREEN	25%	12.5M
Brand Y	100	Amber	Green	Green	Green	Red	AMBER	5%	5M
Brand Z	200	Red	Red	Red	Green	Amber	RED	1%	2M

Figure 41 - Predator Assessment Template

An obvious, but sometimes easy to forget, point is that the competition is allowed to fight back! You will not instantly capture the share you identify: typically it might take 5 years or more. During this time, your competitors will also be developing their offering and business model.

13.4.3 Bottom up

In this situation there are no obvious large-scale benchmark figures such as existing brick-and-mortar or predator-target businesses to use as a baseline. It is therefore necessary to proceed customer-segment by customer-segment. Some care is needed in modelling new channel behaviour based on existing behaviour: customers may not purchase in the same way online as they do offline. For example online may be for distress purchases or specialised items while brick-and-mortar remains for regular large purchases.

Five different customer behaviour changes are suggested here, but of course in reality the number of possibilities is endless:

Increased frequency: increased frequency of shop by existing customers; brick-and-mortar customers use a new channel for additional purchases. Estimate the number of additional checkouts per year per customer, and the expected online cart-size. Note that online carts may be different from offline carts, depending on the mission statements you have associated with your personas (see *Chapter 11*).

Increased cart-size: increased size of shop; brick-and-mortar customers transfer a portion of their spending to a new channel (cannibalisation) but at the same time spend more when doing so. For example this might be a consequence of offering a larger assortment online.

New customers locally: new customers in current segments from the existing catchment areas of your brick-and-mortar stores.

New customers in new geographies: new customers in current segments but from outside your current store catchment areas (obviously a particularly good target for an online offer).

New customers in new segments: totally new customer segments not covered by the previous classifications.

13.5   Ramp-up / Phasing

Obviously no new business reaches its sales targets overnight. Nevertheless, new channel propositions can grow remarkably quickly, and behaviour changes by customers in response can be surprisingly fast. Amazon isn't exactly an old established company, but its sales are almost USD 90 Bn worldwide, with some startling year-on-year growth figures; overall up 85% in the 3 years since the first edition of this Handbook.

I'm conscious that it's rather meaningless to propose numbers, but for completeness I suggest a default ratio of 1:2:4:7:10 over the first 5 years, just as a starting assumption, based on a few business cases I've worked on with clients. Having put this into your spread-sheets, overwrite it with something better founded on your own evaluation as soon as possible.

13.6   Top Takeaways

Multichannel does *not* create new money in customers' wallets. A new channel will inevitably cannibalise existing ones. When considering going online, if you don't cannibalise yourself, someone else will do it for you.

It is legitimate to treat *all* forecast online sales as incremental. However a separate, but parallel, model should consider the consequences to existing channels of reduced sales due to cannibalisation from online.

In a market where both you and competitors are simultaneously going online, there may be no incrementality, only cannibalisation. Most retailers prefer eating their own sales to finding them being eaten by competitors instead!

Three standard situations are suggested for assessing the competitive landscape: highly developed online, undeveloped online, fragmented.

Three models are proposed for assessing the sales opportunity, using the P.R.I.C.E. framework: comparative fair-share, predator, bottom-up. The bottom-up model is further subdivided into increased frequency, increased cart-size, new customers locally, new customers new geography, new customer segments.

Growth may be fast but won't be instantaneous; a ramp-up phasing model is required.

Chapter 14.   Online Marketing

14.1   Top Down Benchmarks

Unsurprisingly this is an area where public domain data is fairly difficult to source, especially for a "starting out" operation: online pure-play start-ups are not big enough to be required to publish this data, multichannel players don't separate it out in their accounts. However the larger pure-plays do sometimes publish useful benchmarks, and so it is possible to use these as a starting point. Amazon for instance, in its most recent 10-K, shows that marketing spending was 4.9% of turnover, incidentally quite a big step up on recent years where the average typically just under 4%.[73] Asos, investing heavily in overseas expansion, has seen spend of approximately 4% grow to 5.7%.[74] These figures are not wildly out of line with what a "typical" (if there is such a thing) brick-and-mortar retailer might spend; maybe a little higher driven by new market growth.

A multichannel player might budget 7% of first year turnover in the new channel, with the premium being spent on creating awareness of the new channel (i.e. *not* on general marketing, but specifically within the new channel). I'm not entirely sure why, but this figure seems to be fairly consistently applied in this context.

A benchmark planning assumption for an online start-up, which of course also needs to therefore build awareness and brand, might be a *minimum* 17% of first year turnover; in a conversation with one CEO with a track-record of building new online brands, a figure nearer 100% of first year turnover was mentioned.

Traditionally, if it is possible to use such a word in connection with disciplines less than 20 years old, this budget would be spent on a mixture of any/all of the following: search engine optimisation (SEO); search engine marketing (SEM); other pay-per-click / pay-per-impression (PPC, PPM) activities; affiliate marketing; price comparison engine enrolment; social network marketing; eMail or SMS marketing; others. It would be possible to write several complete books on each of these disciplines. Consistent

---

[73] Amazon.com inc, form 10-K, for fiscal year ending 31st December 2014.

[74] Asos plc, annual report for year 2014

with my aim of producing a more comprehensive, but inevitably therefore less deep, guide, each is introduced briefly in turn in a section below.

However, tradition is fine, but unfortunately it ain't so simple.

14.2   Logistics is the new Marketing

A steadily developing trend in online retailing is subsidised, or even free, delivery. Particularly noticeable is a trend to offer free shipping even on larger (and therefore expensive to ship) articles. Worldwide, Amazon Prime is both well established and increasingly copied. Obviously this comes at a cost. So who should pay for this? Returning to both Amazon and Asos again as leading examples of pure-plays who also conveniently publish accessible accounts, they both tell us the answer:

"While costs associated with Amazon Prime memberships and other shipping offers are not included in marketing expense, we view these offers as effective worldwide marketing tools, and intend to continue offering them indefinitely."[75]

OK, they don't actually include it in the quoted marketing spend as such, but quite clearly it is considered to be marketing. How much marketing? Excluding services such as marketplace or hosting which clearly don't require shipping, Amazon spends approximately 4.7% of turnover on these "worldwide marketing tools" (shipping revenue of 5.1%, shipping costs of 9.8% of sales). So suddenly instead of 4.9% of sales, Amazon appears to be spending 9.6% of sales on marketing once the cost of subsidising shipping is included.

Asos is even more explicit:

*"...the Group has reclassified delivery costs from cost of sales to operating expenses to reflect their increasing deployment as a marketing expenditure. Prior year comparatives have been reclassified accordingly."*76

How much is this costing them? A quite staggering 13.4%[77] of net sales!

And of course it isn't just pure-plays that are doing this. Moreover it is extremely unusual (and I would suggest, also counterproductive) for

---

[75] Amazon.com inc, form 10-K, for fiscal year ending 31st December 2011
[76] Asos plc, annual accounts 2011-12
[77] Asos plc annual accounts 2014

retailers offering click-and-collect to charge for it, even when the associated parcels are still shipped to store and therefore incur shipping charges (see click-and-collect in **Chapter 21**).

Finally, Amazon has recently taken the whole idea that shipping costs are a marketing expense to its logical conclusion: a marketing event for which the shipping offer is the central concept – Prime Day, the first of which took place on July 15th 2015. They've seen that shipping offers already work for retention and conversion, and simply extended the idea to be an acquisition tool too!

14.3   SEO

As a child I was frequently given copies of the annual Guinness Book of Records as a Christmas present. Its style and language have subsequently modernised, but the 1977 edition[78] still lurking on my bookshelves remains memorable for the following choice of phraseology:

"No single subject is more obscured by vanity, deceit, falsehood and deliberate fraud than…"

And this was written twenty years before SEO was invented! (Actually the quotation then ends *"…the extremes of human longevity.")* Search Engine Optimisation is the gentle art of getting your site to appear at the top of the results of a search-engine query. At least it should be a gentle art, with maybe a small dollop of science. Unfortunately it has been through a protracted iteration of pseudo-science, with a whole sub-industry concentrated on "gaming" the search-engines by second-guessing the rules used to prioritise query results and then modifying sites in artificial ways aligned with these rules. The search-engines, most especially Google, are now fighting back and steadily making these gaming approaches ineffective, and a back-to-basics approach is increasingly likely to be more useful.

What does back-to-basics look like? Essentially it consists of getting some key hygiene factors in place, things that make it easy for the search engines to scan your site; this is the small dollop of science. And then it consists of a lot of hard work, creating and maintaining original and relevant content, product descriptions etc; the gentle art. Search engines

---

[78] Twenty third edition, ISBN 0 900424 37 0

are increasingly rewarding this hard work by moving you up the results rankings, which is anyway what they were always aiming to do in the first place – relevant results from relevant content.

Why is it so important? Although the percentage of shopping missions that start from a search page is slowly eroding, a lot still do. If you are my hypothetical example retailer ChoxBox from *Chapter 11*, and a customer starts by typing "chocolate gifts" into Google, then being top of the results list is a huge advantage. There are slightly varying data on how big an advantage, but roughly the curve looks like *Figure 42.* Some key takeaways are that the number #1 rank gets more click-throughs than ranks #2, #3, #4 combined, and that it is fairly useless being on the second page or below (although actually being top of page 2 is marginally better than being bottom of page 1).

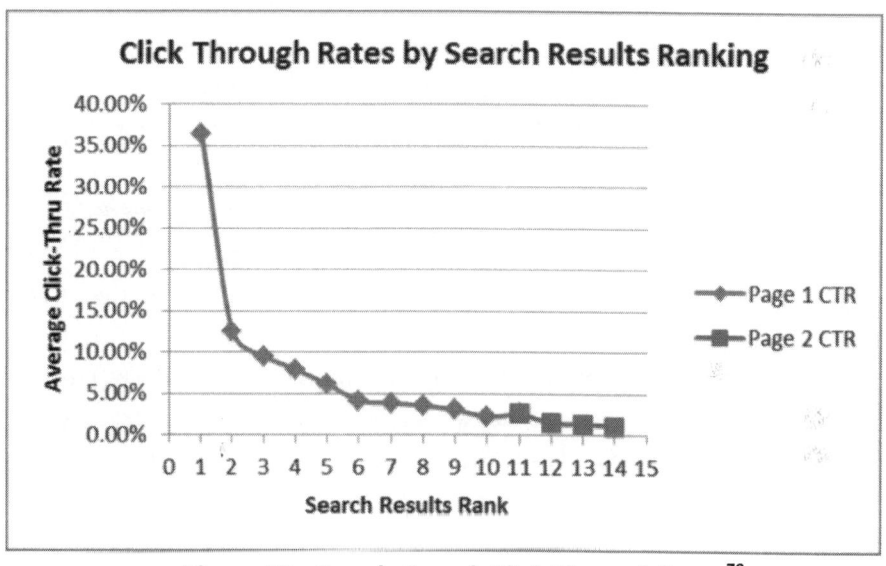

Figure 42 - Google Search Click-Through Rates[79]

Having I hope demonstrated the importance of SEO, I will very briefly touch on its core techniques – despite asserting that it will continue to become a less technique-based discipline. A practical recommendation is that you should consult an SEO specialist... having first listened to whether he/she focusses on artificial gaming-style approaches or more natural, and more intelligible(!), methods, and made your selection of specialist

---

[79] See for example data from http://searchenginewatch.com/article/2049695

accordingly. A reasonable investment in SEO can have a far stronger business case than any other marketing technique available, especially if you are small niche player without an existing strong brand, but beware of it becoming an end in itself. It is very much a discipline where 80/20 thinking should apply.

14.3.1 SEO Basic Hygiene

Bluntly, if whoever builds your website doesn't get the technical basics in place, then find someone else. These include ensuring that every page has header tags, titles and meta-descriptions which are linked to content, with relevant and short-as-possible urls. Since any retail site will consist of a lot of product pages, as far as possible these should be generated automatically and consistently. Similarly if your site is too slow for the crawlers/spiders which the search engines use to read your content (which will kill any customer usage of it anyway), or it is not architected with links that they can easily follow from page to page, then find another supplier. And if you find your site stuffed with hidden keywords, then not only find another supplier but sue the previous one.

Content basics are also straightforward: the content needs to be consistently relevant to its topic, and contain key phrases and words that customers are likely to search for. It must not be artificial, as the search engines will penalise this. So it is no good having your brand as every second word in a large amount of hidden content, nor is it (usually!) helpful to write pages including hot keywords like sex when you actually sell furniture or vegetables. If an SEO "expert" recommends buying links, having search-engine-only pages (i.e. not intended for humans), spamming blogs and other content with back-links to your site, or other dubious techniques, find another expert. Search engines now routinely penalise such methods.

14.3.2 Natural SEO

SEO techniques are focussed on what is known as "natural" search i.e. the standard searching process and consequent results that a normal customer would follow, without any bias due to paid sponsorship. Search engines increasingly reward natural content with natural search priority. Content needs to be new, fresh, original, in depth, frequently updated, contain content relevant to both the rest of the site and the specific page. In other words, it requires continuous hard work.

As is well known, since it was what originally made Google's algorithms stand out in a crowded field in the early days, a major contribution to the ranking of your site and pages is driven by the links to it from other respected sites: respected, quality sites, not link farms. Links from other respected sites are driven primarily by having content which is worth linking to.

If you operate in multiple countries, or even, as search gets ever more sophisticated, in multiple regions, then localised or locality-specific content also helps. For a discussion of which search engines matter most in which countries, see *Chapter 26*.

14.3.3 Advanced SEO

Google, most especially, but other search engines too, are constantly bringing out new features. Keeping track of all these is another area where an SEO-specialist might prove worthwhile. An example of such a feature which is particularly relevant to retailers is the use of structured data to create rich snippets[80] that appear in search results. Amazon is an enthusiastic user of this feature for example (*Figure 43*):

Lava Lamp Classic Lava Lamp, 14.5-inch, Purple/ Yellow ...
www.amazon.co.uk › ... › Specialty & Decorative Lighting › Lava Lamps ▾
★★★★☆ Rating: 3.8 - 595 reviews
The Original Classic Lava Lamp; Melted wax flows for a calming effect; Provides relaxing soft light; Brushed aluminium base and cap; 25 watt light bulb included.

Figure 43 - Rich product snippet example

14.4   SEM

SEO and natural search is nice because it is "free" – well apart from all the effort you need to put in creating suitable content, specialist consultancy you need to pay for, and IT work to present your sites in the right format. By contrast Search Engine Marketing is explicitly not free –

---

[80] As already noted previously, see schema.org for more information about structured data. For information on how Google supports them, try https://developers.google.com/structured-data/rich-snippets/?hl=en

you are paying the appearance money to the search engines. Take a look at this desktop screenshot (*Figure 44*).

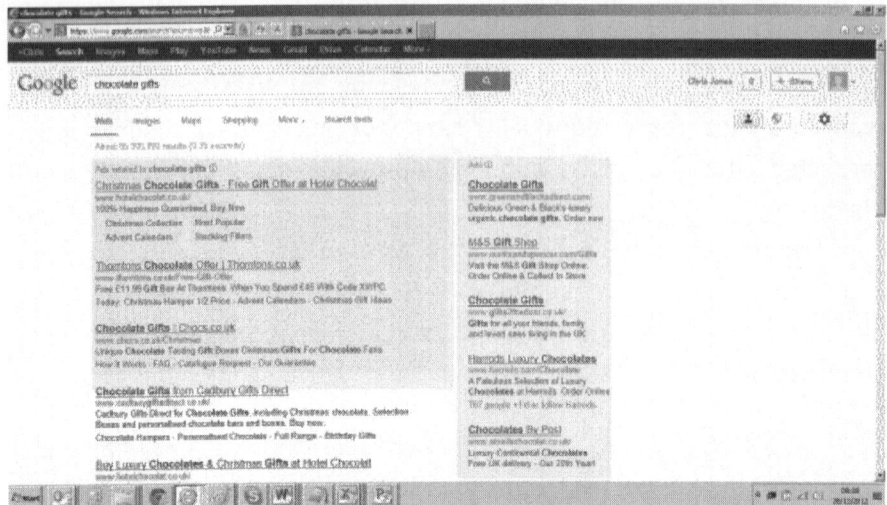

Figure 44 - Google Search Results – shaded areas are paid adverts[81]

The shaded areas are the SEM paid-for areas. Not a lot of space is left for the natural results, an observation which possibly explains the statistics in the SEO section above. There are in fact only two natural results visible on the page, and people are notoriously reluctant to scroll "below the fold" (I've seen data points as high as 87% of people never scroll below the fold, depending on the type of page in question). The rest of it is entirely SEM results, although to be fair there is some additional bias due to choosing a Christmas gift search term ("Chocolate Gifts") during the Christmas gift-buying season. The effect is even more obvious when I try the same search on my mobile (*Figure 45*):

---

[81] Screenshot, November 2012. For clarity I have retained this screenshot, and its smartphone partner in the next figure, instead of using a more recent one containing other types of listing such as snippets, google shopping etc. See Figure 47 for a newer example

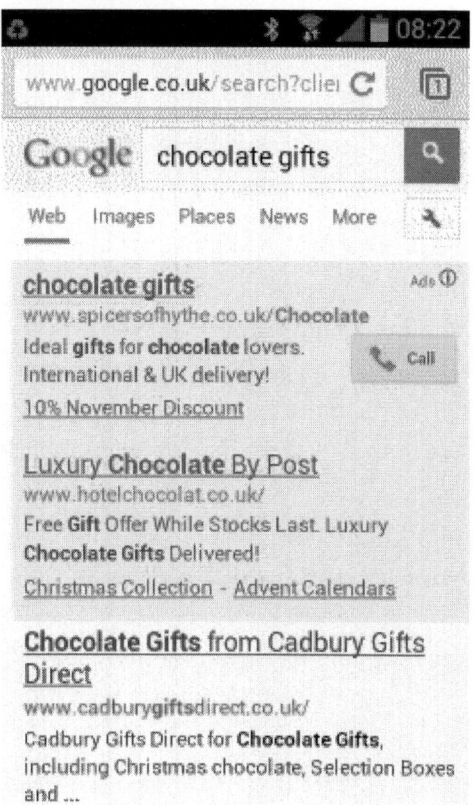

Figure 45 - Same search results on smart phone

We'll discuss mobile in its own chapter later (**Chapter 23**), but just to observe briefly here that increasingly the "research" phase of purchasing is headed towards mobile devices, even if the eventual completion of the purchase still takes place on another channel. When two thirds of the results are SEM results and only one third SEO, then it gives some idea of Google's revenue strategy, and therefore the potential cost implications for the retailer pursuing search-based marketing in general. Just for interest, the estimated cost per click (CPC) of buying a top 2 ranking in the UK results for "chocolate gifts" was around GBP 2.50 on the day I did this test, which is a large bite out of the gross margins even for products like gift chocolates, especially when you remember that most clicks don't lead to a conversion. Other search-engines, such as China's Baidu, can be even more paid-biased.

Note the preferred CPC measure. Conventionally online advertising is measured (and charged) in units of:

CPM: cost per thousand impressions

CPC: cost per click-through

CPA: cost per action (usually the "action" is a checkout, although of course this is technically quite complex to actually capture and measure)

For retailers online CPM advertising is generally considered almost irrelevant; it might have some purpose if you simply need to build the brand, but with the much better CPC also available, most retailers focus on CPC-based targets. The technical challenges in tracking CPA, theoretically the "best" measure of effectiveness, tend to confine it to affiliate marketing (see below).

Unlike other forms of marketing CPC also has the benefit of being directly measurable. You can see which keywords work and which don't, and this feedback is often statistically significant after quite short periods of time. A plan-do-review-refine/re-plan methodology should therefore be adopted, aiming to continuously improve the effectiveness of SEM spending (*Figure 46*).

Figure 46 - Classic plan-do-review cycle

Although this may not look like much of an insight, it is important to stress the difference with offline activities. Online, it is possibly to quickly, accurately and directly measure the success of any change with genuine confidence that the results are statistically valid (see also website A/B testing in the section on Analytics below - section **16.5**). This is particularly true of SEM; typically clients I have worked with run the complete plan-plan cycle every 2-4 weeks.

14.4.1 Google shopping

Just in case the revenues it makes from its usual SEM activities aren't quite enough, Google also maintains a specifically retail targeted version of SEM: Google Shopping. The principle isn't very different at all: they include your products prominently in search results, you pay for the privilege of being clicked.

A look at the results for a search for "lava lamps" shows many of the techniques described above on a single screenshot (*Figure 47*):

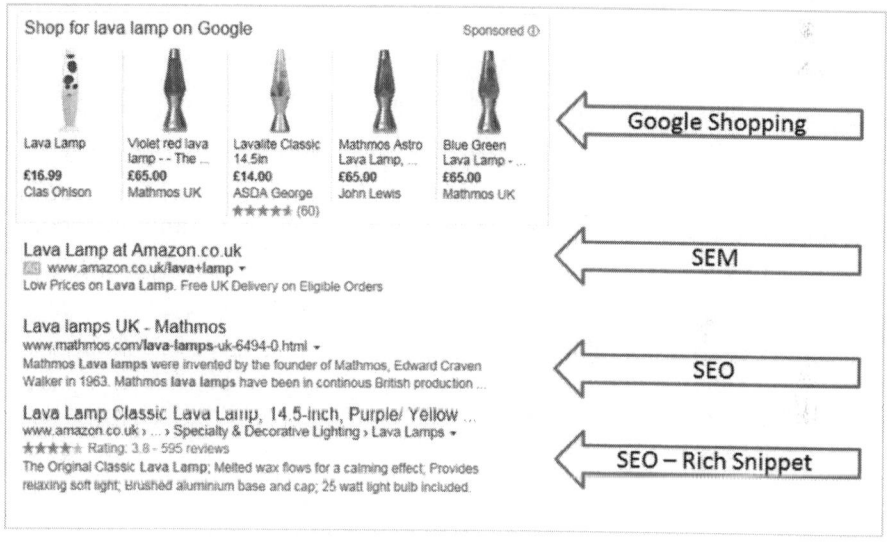

Figure 47 - SEO, SEM, Snippets and Shopping

14.5   Other pay-per-click activities

Not all customer journeys start from a search engine. Of course best of all, you have such a strong brand that they will start directly on your website. Most retailers are less lucky (or even if they are so fortunate, half the visits will be price-comparison visits anyway), and their customers start on another site. It may therefore make sense to have links from that site. If you sell cameras, and there is a leading online camera magazine, then it's probably a fairly good place to advertise.

Traditionally, that alarming word again when it comes to such young disciplines, an affiliate marketing scheme (see next section) may be the best way to tackle this. There are a number of reasons why you might not prefer this approach. Firstly, affiliate marketing is relatively expensive. Secondly it has a slightly questionable reputation on which you will need to form your own view. Thirdly, and perhaps most interestingly, the rise of mobile – with its great place to research, poor place to checkout status at present – makes it worthwhile driving traffic to your site even if it does not immediately lead to conversion/checkout: there is increasing value in capturing the customer at the research stage.

There are also various alternative networks, in addition to search engines and affiliate-marketing themselves, whose business is to place adverts on a network third-party sites (from which the third-party earns revenue) and then derive revenue when customers click-through to your site. As with the search-engines, their revenue improves as they optimise the placement of such adverts across their partner network, so they have a strong incentive to be effective.

The recent rise of ad-blocking software, especially on Apple's products, is not yet significant enough 'at the time of writing' to really impact on these techniques – but in a technical world that moves quickly, it might have become so 'at the time of reading'.

14.6   Affiliate Marketing

As discussed in the SEM section above, CPA – cost per action – is the most attractive way to measure marketing. For a retailer, the desired customer action is a checkout, or even better a series of checkouts. Marketing spending that leads directly from spend to checkout, via a proven and verifiable chain of customer events, is self-evidently well-targeted. Online retail gives you the technical means to make this direct link. Firstly let's look quickly at how it works. It's easiest to start by looking at from the perspective of the affiliate, not the retailer. Theoretically it couldn't be easier (*Figure 48*):

Figure 48 - Affiliate marketing, from the affiliate's perspective

Amazon Associates is by far the best known such programme, and (summarising a rather complicated structure) pays the affiliate different commissions by category, varying from 4% to 10% of the transaction value. The Amazon scheme works particularly well for them because they are able to leverage a huge number of niche microsites proposing correspondingly niche-interest books and media; there is a strong correspondence between the customer interests and their likely propensity to purchase items connected to that interest. Other similar and fairly visible schemes outside of retail include those operated by online gambling sites of various kinds, which typically pay a percentage of the turnover of any new victim you persuade to sign-up to them by linking from your "predicting horse racing results using biorhythms and star signs" niche microsite. So far so simple.

Where it all gets a bit messy is when the checkout does not immediately follow the action (click-through from the link). What happens if an affiliate draws a customer to your site, who browses, adds to cart, but then doesn't checkout until the next visit? And then in the meantime a different affiliate also attracts that same customer, who adds another item to their cart, but still doesn't checkout? You will almost certainly have to use an affiliate management partner, who should have various solutions in place to manage this. Nevertheless not all retailers think it worthwhile to give away commission for a customer who might well have arrived there anyway by cheaper means. Asos.com rather famously closed its generally open affiliate programme, and restarted it as a more controlled, invitation only affair, accompanying this change with a memorably rude quote from its CEO:

"I'm not saying we couldn't do more in the online marketing space. Next year we'll reintroduce affiliate marketing, but as it should be. No silly

commissions being paid to grubby little people in grubby studios growing income at our expense, getting in the way of genuine sales."[82]

Affiliate marketing can be very effective indeed, but you have to make a decision whether or not it is a) appropriate; b) controllable and manageable; c) available as a technical solution in your locale; d) affordable in your market and categories (I still have a vivid memory of explaining the concept to an Indian client who had not previously encountered it, and watching jaws hit the table when I mentioned the usual levels of commission and consequent implied lost gross margin). Unlike SEO and SEM, it should not be an automatic choice.

14.7   Price Comparison Engines

The top price comparison sites draw a huge amount of traffic. A top of listing spot for a hot ticket item will attract a large percentage of that traffic to you. But… you have to pay for it twice. Firstly, although the commercial models of course vary, price comparison is essentially a variation on affiliate marketing. The engine has to earn its money from somewhere, and this is either from retailer or brand advertising, retailer subscriptions, or direct commissions. You are probably paying either affiliate-style or SEM-style for the privilege of your share of all this traffic. Secondly, you then have to be amongst the cheapest anyway. Unless you already have a price advantage, there is a double cost.

In extreme cases, the cost is so great that the opposing business model applies: retailers make an effort to block price comparison sites from harvesting their online prices. In general this is a futile battle that you are almost certain to lose, by technical means anyway. Nevertheless, active engagement with price comparison sites generally has a net positive cost-benefit case only to those retailers with a stable price advantage in the first place. Otherwise, you may have no choice but to be a passive victim, but don't deliberately solicit (and pay for!) victimisation.

---

[82] http://econsultancy.com/uk/blog/918-affiliates-close-rank-after-asos-ceo-calls-them-grubby

14.8 Social Network Marketing

Writing this section made me nervous in the first edition of this book, and still makes me nervous for the 2016 edition. Which is a sign of the power of social networks. They seem to have the ability to start revolutions, lose elections, and create celebrities overnight. As a way to promote your brand, and as a traffic driver to your website, they can be tremendously effective.

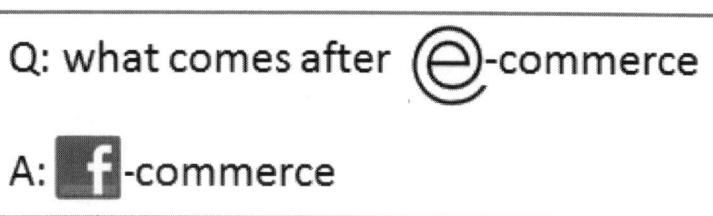

Figure 49 - Already an old joke?

What hasn't happened, *yet,* or should that be *still,* is the transfer of the actual purchasing from the retailer's website to a store hosted within Facebook or some other social platform. In the West, there's little sign that it's going to happen in the immediate future. (China, with its ubiquitous social app WeChat, and high mobile propensity, is a rather different story).

Traffic driven to your website from social channels typically may converts reasonably well, and such advertising is a reasonable addition to your online marketing mix, but pay close attention to which social traffic is actually working for you; conversion rates vary enormously (***Figure 50***).

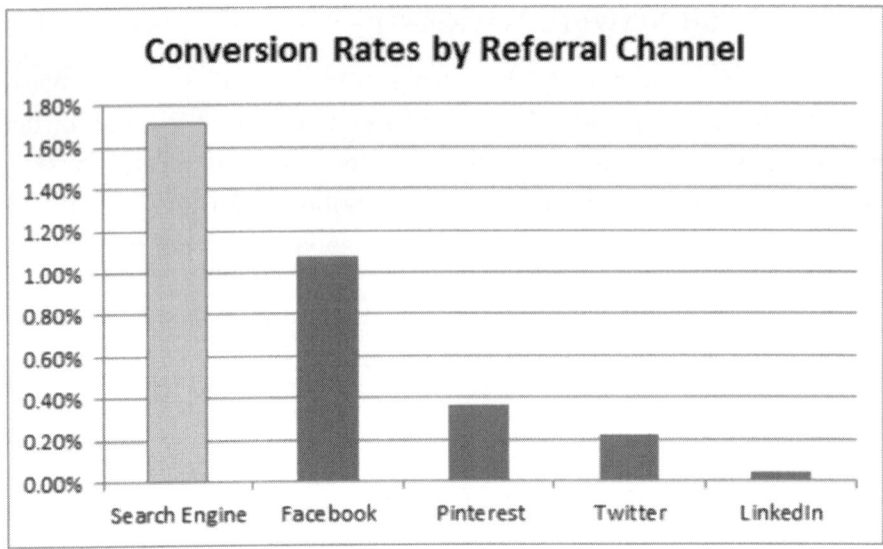

Figure 50 - Conversion Rates by Social Referral Channel[83]

14.9   eMail marketing

It would be possible to write a complete book on email marketing, and a glance at Amazon shows that plenty of people have done so. So, to address the challenge of summarising several books into a concise sub-chapter, how about a memorable acronym? Email marketing should be TART: Timely; Actionable; Relevant; Triangular. I'll take a brief look at each of these points in turn, with a particular focus on their specific application to retail.

14.9.1 Timely

Firstly, customers have often actually asked you for emails. For example, customers like to be updated about the status of their orders, and will agree to these emails even if they opt out of others. It is important to deliver this information to reduce the number of expensive calls to your contact-centre anyway, but it is also a perfectly legitimate marketing opportunity. Don't let the marketing obstructing the information the customer wanted - such an email should be roughly "here is your information, by the way what about..." in structure – and don't expect

---

[83] SmartInsights: http://www.smartinsights.com/ecommerce/ecommerce-analytics/ecommerce-conversion-rates/

fantastic take-up, but nevertheless don't miss the opportunity. The customer wants to be communicated with, you know exactly who the customer is (see *relevant* below), you can propose something they might have a high propensity to want, even if it's only the cross-sell products for their ordered items that they maybe didn't take up when you first suggested them on the website.

Secondly, there are moments when it is both very effective and also reasonably legitimate to jump down a customer's throat with an email. The best-known is probably cart-abandonment. If you observe a cart built, but then not checked-out in a reasonably timely manner, send that customer an encouraging email. When this is both well-timed and appropriate, conversion rates can be spectacular. I'd like to quote a data point with a reference, but they are either client confidential or dubiously biased because they are quoted by suppliers of email marketing solutions; so as an unreferenced data-point assumption for planning, well-executed cart-abandonment emails have approximately 6-times higher conversion rates than a default "blast" email. Note how important timing is here. The average first-site-visit-to-purchase journey time is around 18-19 hours. The cart-to-checkout part of that is less than half. If you jump on the customer in the middle, especially when they are just using the cart as a holding area for products in their consideration-set, you'll probably put them off. Leave it too long, and you won't get the benefit. As with all things online, the fact that you can directly measure means that constant experimentation and tuning is the key to success.

Anecdotally illustrating the pitfalls of these techniques, Amazon have developed a flavour of this which could be described as "browse abandonment": they notice when I have looked at a category without purchasing, and then start emailing me about it. As this is invariably after I have been using them either as a price comparison site, or to take a screenshot to illustrate a point to a client, it is distinctly counter-productive to the extent that the only reason I don't relegate their emails to my spam-filter is that I have a professional interest in following their methods.

And with spam-filters firmly in mind, thirdly, there is a good ol' regular email blast. Most of the success factors for these lie in the other areas to be discussed shortly, but timing still plays its part. An empirical approach is still the best. For example, split your customers into random groups, and try twice-weekly, weekly, bi-weekly and measure the take-up. Similarly, try different times of day (a nice study suggested that the early hours of Sunday night works best in the UK, aiming for the Monday-morning inbox) and measure the response.

Fourthly, and better than the simple blast, if you have relevant news, such as a sale event, of course tell customers about it. The increasing number of successful private-sale sites are particularly dependent on this approach; the customer, by subscribing to such a private-sale club, has effectively requested such emails, and of course are much more likely to open a mail they have asked for than an unsolicited one. Even if your business model is more conventional, emails about a genuine sale event with real benefits for the customer will have far better take-up than just another deal.

14.9.2 Actionable

Firstly the Actionable you don't want: in many (most) countries, there is legislation requiring customers to opt-in to emails before you start sending them. Don't forget to capture this opt-in in any interaction where you ask customer's for an email address. A big database of contactable customers that you are not legally permitted to contact is extremely frustrating, although not as frustrating as a big pile of lawyers' letters complaining when you did contact them without permission. Of course you can choose to ignore this, but at your brand's peril. (And even if you are just trying to make a quick buck, it is exactly the kind of thing even basic due-diligence processes look at when you try to sell the business, precisely because it's such obvious territory for lawyers).

The Actionable you do want is your customers doing something positive in response to your emails – opening them, preferably clicking-through to a website, and then doing something good when they get there. The opening step is dealt with under *triangular* below. The next step is clicking through. It is genuinely astonishing how many emails don't get this simple step right: it needs to be obvious where to click to get what response. Remember our One Second Rule from the introductory chapters? For emails, you are very lucky if you even get one second. Don't make the customer actually have to read it like Sherlock Holmes, put things in it that scream "click here" at them. I won't give examples, because there are hundreds and hundreds online; check a few of them out.

The second part is that the click-through has to arrive at the intended landing-page. Make sure your landing page url is statically named (i.e. your IT system does not dynamically generate a new temporary url every time the page is accessed). And when the customer arrives, measure and record it, because you will need this data for the next email you send out.

14.9.3 Relevant

I'm talking to you.

Not just a generic you, but specifically you the individual. Personalisation is a critical topic for multichannel, and therefore discussed at length in its own *Chapter 22* below. I'll use a very simple example now to illustrate the point. Suppose your website sells wine. You know that I have occasionally bought red wine from it, but never white wine. Should you send me an email with a white wine offer?

14.9.4 Triangular

There are a bunch of best practice guidelines to follow when preparing emails. For example titles should be as short as possible, three-to-five words being optimal. The guideline which gives this section its title is that the body of an email should also be a tapering triangle like this (*Figure 51*) for maximum impact and response.

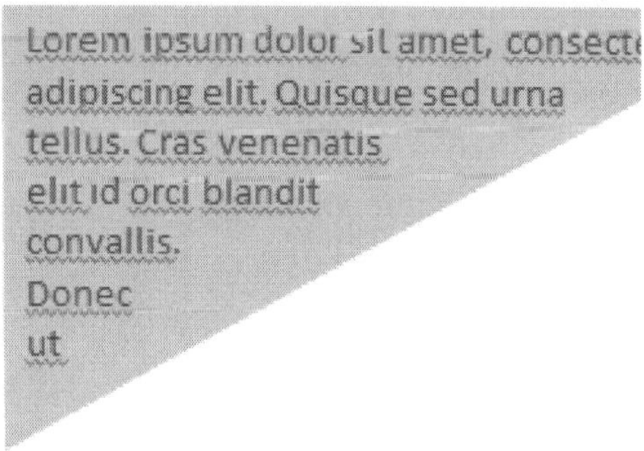

Figure 51 - The perfect shape for an email?

At least, several experts on the topic have assured me that this is so. I haven't yet met an Arabic (or other right-to-left language) expert who can confirm that this behaviour should be mirrored in these cultures.

I picked this particular guideline as an illustration of something that might well be unexpected. The point is that there is a tremendous pool of knowledge available, either online or via appropriate consultants, in this particular space. The "rules" are not necessarily intuitively obvious, since they rely on bizarre human psychological responses, and have generally been learned empirically by practitioners. I am not, in this book, going to be able to cover such a specialist topic in depth, and therefore in this particular space, rather like SEO, I recommend strongly that you <u>consult a domain expert</u>, of which there are many.

14.10 SMS marketing

Having found a memorable acronym (TART) to define the approach you should take to email marketing, I have spent some time trying to find one suitable for describing what should happen with SMS marketing. Alas, considerable cogitation has failed to inspire me with anything that the letters B.A.N.N.E.D. could stand for.

OK, this is not really fair. The problem with SMS is that it can be extremely effective. Why is this a problem? Because its effectiveness is achieved via intrusiveness and generates subsequent resentment. With a huge health-warning around the validity of these statistics, a quick comparison of SMS with email (***Figure 52***):

	eMail[84]	SMS
Open rate	Up to 38% (if you are very lucky)	Up to 98%
Click-thru rate	Averages between 10-22%	Approx 15-20%
Conversion rate	Averages between 1-3%	Up to 16%

Figure 52 - Dubious comparison of eMail and SMS marketing

Just to repeat, these statistics are extremely suspect, especially those for SMS. They depend entirely on circumstances, content, brand, purpose, target and a thousand-and-one other factors. The only practical way to determine the effectiveness of such campaigns for your business is to try

---

[84] Various sources, including US Direct Marketing Association

them, and establish some baselines. The basic message is that SMS is a more powerful tool for getting attention and also for causing irritation, and if your objective is click-throughs then SMS obviously has some challenges, not least the existence of a mobile site to land on.

Unsolicited SMS is not a recipe for commercial success – at least in retail - as anybody who followed the high profile Papa Johns story in the US will be aware. (If you have not seen this, Papa Johns pizza chain faced a USD 250M class action lawsuit as a consequence of an unsolicited SMS marketing campaign, and eventually settled for USD 16.5M).[85] However, there are legitimate *solicited* SMS situations: providing updates on order status for example, which of course can also become marketing opportunities. In countries with less developed online infrastructure and where an individual's email addresses can be fickle, SMS might well be a more reliable means of contacting the customer, and in these cultures semi-solicited SMS is generally more acceptable.

14.11 Offline

The general principle of online marketing – that almost everything can be measured directly, and therefore should be measured directly – should be very evident. By implication, there is usually an investment in software and/or services required to do it well. Those who provide such services should be experts themselves, and any negotiation with such a potential partner should include obtaining a few free days of consulting on these sometimes very specific specialist topics.

Despite all these wonderfully measurable online methods, and depending on the preferred customer journeys you have identified (see Part A of this book), then offline marketing may still be a very valid option. A particularly common combination – because it is an effective combination – is flicks'n'clicks: combining a paper catalogue with a website (or its multichannel extension flicks'n'clicks'n'bricks... Yeah OK.) Websites, and mobile sites, are good places to search but relatively bad places to browse. If your customer behaviour involves a significant level of browse behaviour, then paper catalogues may well still make a lot of sense. You do need to coordinate the product numbers in the catalogue with what is

---

[85] See for example http://www.law360.com/articles/442855/papa-john-s-will-deliver-16-5m-to-end-tcpa-claims

displayed (and searchable for) on your website, which adds yet another piece of data to capture in that, by now familiar challenge, product data management.

14.12 Top Takeaways

A first-year of operation marketing budget might be 7% of total sales for a multichannel proposition. For a new online pure-play, 17% is probably an absolute minimum.

Amazon currently spends 4.9% of turnover on marketing. However when shipping offers are included, which Amazon regards as marketing, then this rises to almost 10%. Comparable figures for Asos are 5.7% and 13.4(!)%.

Logistics is the New Marketing. Traditional online marketing might include any or all of: search engine optimisation (SEO); search engine marketing (SEM); other pay-per-click activities; affiliate marketing; price comparison engine enrolment; social network marketing; eMail or SMS marketing; others.

The impact of most online marketing spending is directly measurable. Implement a very frequent plan-do-measure-review cycle.

SEO is an essential discipline. Get the hygiene right, consult a specialist, but remember that engines are increasingly rewarding content in preference to technique.

SEO impact is strongly skewed towards the top few positions.

When planning SEM campaigns, take care to ensure that you get as much benefit as the search engine does.

Take advantage of specialised options on search engines, such as rich snippets and Google Shopping.

Cost-per-action is a more direct measure of effectiveness than cost-per-click is a more direct measure than cost-per-thousand-impressions. CPA > CPC > CPM.

Affiliate marketing can be measured by CPA (=good). However managing it effectively is more than usually challenging.

Social media marketing forms a legitimate element of an online marketing mix. Direct social commerce – purchasing within the social site itself – has not really taken off in the West. (WeChat in China may be a special case.)

Email marketing is a very specialist skill. An outline is that it should be TART: timely, actionable, relevant and triangular.

SMS marketing needs to be strongly validated for appropriateness. Unsolicited SMS can have negative consequences.

Data protection legislation is especially applicable online.

Don't omit offline techniques. Bricks'n'clicks'n'flicks can be a powerful mixture. Always relate back to your customer personas and missions.

Chapter 15.   Order Lifecycle

15.1   Definition

This rather bureaucratic-sounding term refers to everything that happens after the wonderful moment when the customer hits that "submit order" button on your checkout. In summary it covers payment, warehousing, pick-pack-ship, returns, (much of) customer-services, and often a lot of financial system tracking. In less officious language it's "getting the stuff to customers that they've paid for".

That there is reasonably close linkage between these elements should be self-evident. Just how closely coupled they are becomes especially plain when you start to consider what happens when something goes wrong. Linking back with the previous chapter for example, what happens when you arrive at the pick-face in your warehouse ready to pick your customer-order, only to find that the last MegaFrocks little black party dress remaining in stock actually has a large rip down the back? Probably you now have to contact the customer, re-price the order, re-price the shipping, re-label the parcel, re-print the invoice, change the shipping company collection manifest, write-off the stock, possibly refund some of the payment...

For mail-order companies, 80% of this stuff is business-as-usual when they go online, which is part of the reason taking mail-order online is usually a relatively simple business model development. For brick-and-mortar retailers, 80% of it is both new and often causes conflict with existing well-established business-processes.

15.2   Available-to-Promise

The first element of Order Lifecycle actually happens before the checkout. It's where the "front-end" (website and so forth) meets the "back-end" (order capture and fulfilment).

As stated in the introduction to **Chapter 12,** in any online retail proposition you are selling a description of a product, plus a promise to somehow get the described product to the customer. That chapter discussed the description, this chapter discusses the promise. The promise actually consists of two parts:

A shipping promise. This is straightforward, and might include various options for the customer such as express delivery, pick-up-in-store, nominated time etc.

A stock promise: when will the items be available to start shipping to the customer?

Available-to-Promise (ATP) is usually considered to refer to the second point – the Stock. ATP is actually a bit of IT jargon, but the concept is so fundamental to multichannel retail that it deserves better in life than relegation to an IT three letter acronym (TLA...).

15.2.1 Implementation

For many people ATP's most familiar manifestation is seen on Amazon's website (see *Figure 53*), with its statements such as "usually despatched within 5 to 10 days".

£14.50 Paperback
Usually dispatched within 4 to 6 weeks

£18.98 **£18.24** Hardcover
Only 2 left in stock - order soon.

£12.99 **£11.69** Paperback
In stock but may require up to 2 additional days to deliver

Figure 53 - Availability Promises[86]

Notice how this promise varies from the very specific "2 left in stock" to the rather vague "usually dispatched within 4 to 6 weeks", which really doesn't commit to anything except an expectation that it will turn up eventually but you might be waiting a long time. This spectrum from specific to vague reflects Amazon's control over the stock and the processes. One might reasonably infer that the two left in stock are in an Amazon warehouse, whereas the four to six week item has to be purchased from a secondary supplier (and in the case I used to make this collage, actually from overseas).

---

[86] Collage from Amazon.co.uk, November 2012

There are some important refinements of this that are particularly relevant to multichannel retailers. Specific promises can only be made when you have tight control over stock and processes. How many retailers really have firm control over their in-store stock? You may well have good processes at start and end of day, but what about intraday, when (hopefully) your stores are full of customers with items in their shopping baskets which are neither on your shelves – and therefore available – nor rung through your POS – and therefore unavailable. In-basket stock is in a kind of limbo for the purposes of availability promises. This is especially important if you are operating some sort of click-and-collect proposition where the items are pre-picked in store (see **Chapter 21**).

Similarly if you operate, as many multichannel retailers do, a supply chain where the Fulfilment Centre for eCommerce receives its stock from the same source(s) as your stores, can you realistically make any commitment to the level of stock deliveries into that Fulfilment Centre tomorrow? There are a number of reasons why this might not be the case. For example:

Uncertain supply: you can't guarantee the precise timing and volumes which will be delivered by your suppliers;

High efficiency: you currently have very efficient logistics, with strong "one touch" processes operating, but where breakages, non-conformance and similar issues which affect saleability are therefore only discovered at the last possible moment;

Channel conflict: you prefer not to prioritise allocations of stock to eCommerce over allocations to stores in the event of any shortage;

Unpredictable velocity: you have items whose rate of sale is hard to predict. Typically this applies especially to the long tail.

In a brick-and-mortar store environment, none of this precision matters quite as much. The item is either on the shelf when the customer tries to pick it up or it isn't. Availability is of course important, and you will disappoint customers if items are missing, but there is no complicated promise for the future. Shelf availability is an instantaneous fact. In an online environment, by contrast, the item is not picked immediately the customer puts it into their cart. It is probably not picked immediately the customer checks-out either. Availability on the shelf or pick-face is an accumulation of results of complex business processes spread over an extended time period.

ATP is also probably the most complex area of your IT, for the simple reason that it lies on the interface between multiple systems – maybe at least website, stores, logistics, shipping, order management, and probably others. In almost all IT ecosystems and projects, the "difficult" bit is interfacing *between* component systems, not the implementation of the self-contained components themselves. Having a critical business process spread across boundaries in this way intrinsically adds complexity.

So in ATP lies an inherent conflict. You want to make the best possible promise to your customers, maximising both availability itself and also optimising the promise as part of competing on convenience. Making best possible promises means diving headlong into some of the most complex business processes and IT systems in your business. Complex processes are risky processes. Disappointing customers who believe they have successfully checked-out and are just waiting for their goods to be delivered is extremely bad, much worse than not having an item available on a brick-and-mortar store shelf. Very likely such a customer will need a lot of convincing to return to you and try again.

For the retailer new to multichannel, the best advice is to *keep it simple*. Only promise what you are 100% certain you can deliver, even at the apparent risk of missing sales opportunities. Experience says that the cost of any sales lost in this way will be far lower than the cost of disappointing large numbers of your most loyal customers. The realisation of such a policy clearly depends on how you set up your fulfilment, but the simplest case is that of a dedicated stock location, and a policy that says you will only promise to customers stock which is definitely in that stock location in a fit condition for sale, and which has not already been sold to another customer.

For the multichannel retailer scaling up, these and related issues lie behind the justification for major investments in the implementation of sophisticated order-management engines, often running to into millions (in any currency!) of costs.

15.2.2 Not available to promise

This question invariably comes up in any discussion of the topic so I've included it here: what should an online channel (usually the website) display when a particular SKU is theoretically included in the range but is temporarily out of stock?

Back-orders are notoriously challenging to handle, especially if your IT back-office systems are not yet very sophisticated. Therefore the choice often boils down to either display it but tell the customer they cannot add it to their cart, or don't display it at all. Displaying it unavailable risks disappointment, not displaying it damages your marketing (especially SEO).

The recommended answer, assuming you don't feel confident to handle back-orders (and I strongly recommend that you don't unless you are *very* confident of the back-office system provision – don't improvise it), is to consider the issue at a category or sub-category level. A category with say 5% of its items out of stock actually looks fine, and anecdotally is actually a positive statement to customers: we are in control of our stock, our promises are real, there are sufficient sales on this website to cause out-of-stock situations to occur. A category with 50% of its items unavailable just looks pathetic and tells the customer to try a competitor instead: don't display the unavailable items in such a category.

15.3   Payment

15.3.1 Payment Policy

Depending on the market in which you are operating, you will offer various different payment options to your customers. These might range from credit card to bank transfer to cash on delivery. When planning order lifecycle the important thing to define is *when* the payment takes place.

Firstly note that payment card transactions are typically actually a two-stage process. Stage 1, known as "authorisation", is the process of reserving funds against the customer's card. A variety of validation checks will be performed by the various participants in this process, all aimed at ensuring that the card is valid and that the funds are available. The most familiar example of such transactions are when you are asked in hotels to present a credit card at the start of your stay, which will be blocked for a certain pre-reserved amount. Stage 2, known as "capture", actually moves the money from the card to the merchant i.e. pays! If you pay for something by card over the counter in a store, authorisation usually takes place on the spot, but capture quite often is an overnight process, and the time-lapse generally doesn't matter. Payment Policy is about deciding when authorisation and capture will take place, and applies to non-card transactions by implication as well.

Typically authorisation will take place either during, or immediately after, the website checkout. This is usually fine, but suppose you are selling made-to-order billiard tables, which take 15 weeks to build? It is not reasonable to block a large amount of the customer's card limit for 15 weeks, and in fact generally card companies automatically release authorisations after somewhere between 2 and 5 days anyway. In this situation you would probably prefer to authorise just before shipping. Many websites with this kind delayed payment will typically do a trial authorisation for a small minimum amount during the checkout, whose purpose is essentially just to validate that the card is genuine and has no silly issues such as an expiry date before the likely payment is required.

Payment capture usually takes place at one of three moments: pay-on-order; pay-on-despatch; pay-on-delivery.

Pay-on-order is what you would normally expect to do for an eBay transaction for example, while Amazon generally operates pay-on-despatch. Pay-on-delivery usually means payment on the door-step, but could also mean waiting for the shipping company to confirm the delivery and then executing the capture step.

If your preferred payment method is cash-on-delivery, then your payment policy in general is both obvious and mandatory. For other methods, it is essential to make the choice, stick with it, and accept the consequences throughout the order lifecycle. In the sub-section on returns policy just below, I'll define most of the archetypal situations that need to be considered. There is no "best" or "worse" choice of payment policy, it depends on your business, although in some countries this choice is partially or completely prescribed by the local regulatory system. In general, in all countries you should ensure that you are aware of distance-selling laws, which often give customers additional rights over-and-above what you might be used to in a brick-and-mortar environment. On a similar regulatory note, beware as well of different PCI/DSS-compliance requirements for online transactions[87].

15.3.2 Fraud

Payments on a website are defined as CNP transactions – Customer Not Present or Card Not Present. Most payment schemes charge higher merchant fees for CNP transactions, reflecting the higher risk of fraud and chargeback. The higher your track-record rate of chargebacks, the higher your merchant fees will become. The worst case I have ever seen was a retailer generally paying typical fees of 1.0-2.5% on most in-store transactions which found itself facing proposed fees of 10% online. Such charges will cripple most business models, so it is worth doing something about it proactively.

Firstly Verified-by-Visa[88] and Mastercard Securecode[89] should be implemented by default if you plan to accept credit card payments at all and there is any existing customer acceptance of these schemes in your region. Similarly any schemes specific to your country's preferred payment methods should always be implemented. Secondly, have a very hard think about whether or not you want to accept credit cards from overseas. Particularly if you don't ship overseas, the lost business from occasional frustrated expats may well be more than offset by the reduced fraud risk of blocking their cards. Many retailers maintain BIN range (the first 6 digits of the card number) tables defining ranges they find unacceptable, which can be managed at country level, so for example a Belgian site might decide to accept Dutch and French cards, but not Bulgarian ones. Brick-and-mortar retailers also often have private hot-card lists, still sometimes just pinned to the check-out, and these should be uploaded to website checkout if possible.

Finally, there are specialist fraud-prevention solutions available. Complete solutions are generally only worthwhile for larger players, but slightly less specialised solutions are often available from your chosen card

---

[87] See https://www.pcisecuritystandards.org, although I recommend speaking to a specialist, not wading through the material yourself

[88] See for example http://www.visaeurope.com/en/cardholders/verified_by_visa.aspx

[89] See for example http://www.mastercard.us/securecode.html

payment gateway provider (or payment service provider – PSP - the two terms are more-or-less interchangeable). A PSP is a specialised service that sits as an interface between a website and (normally) your usual acquiring bank. There are slightly different configurations possible, but the outline set-up is shown in *Figure 54.*

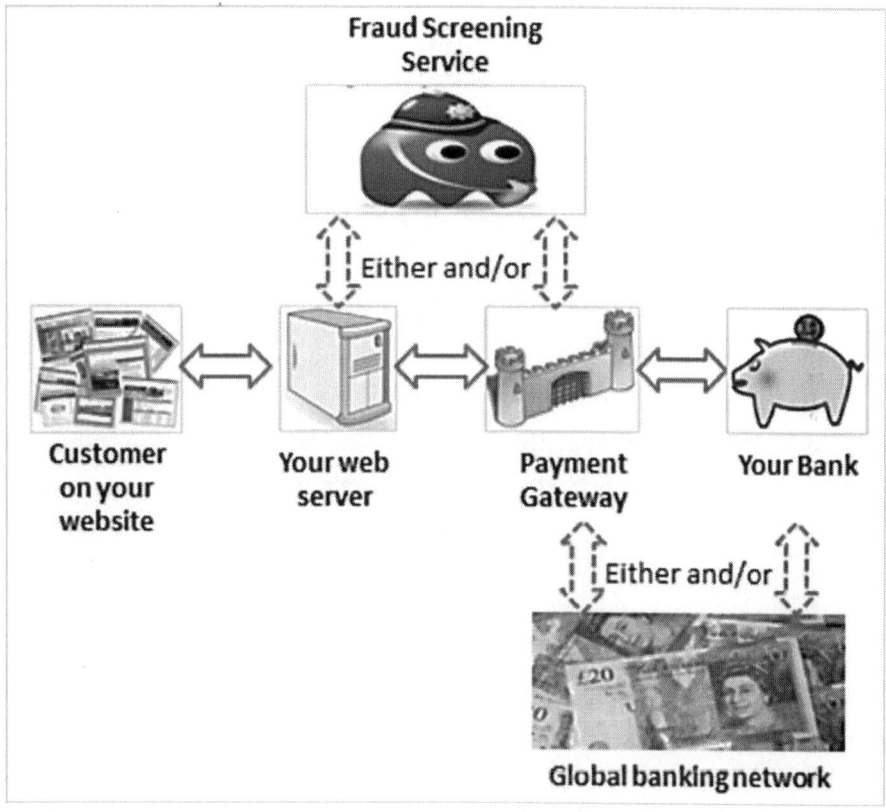

Figure 54 - Payment Gateway and Fraud Screening

Many banks, especially in "developing" online retail countries (I have found this to be particularly true in Eastern Europe and India), operate their own PSPs; in more developed markets they are usually specialised services. If you intend taking payments from global customers, you may find a specialist more able to access the bewildering variety of payment schemes prevailing in different regions, although accessing them is one thing, delivering them effectively on your site checkout is another.

From a business case perspective, a reasonable default planning assumption prior to engaging in detailed negotiations with your banks and/or PSP, is that some combination of either fraud, increased CNP merchant fees, or fraud prevention services is likely to add around 1% of gross sales to your costs, in addition to PSP service/transactional costs themselves.

15.3.3 Address-checking

Depending on the country in which you live, and the stringency of its post-code/zip-code/address-structures, it might make sense to validate shipping (and possibly billing) addresses using a service.

It has a place helping reduce fraud, and helps reduce unwanted customer service issues and returns. Just as important, it often helps reduce the amount of data a customer has to key at checkout; anything that makes checkout easier is always worthwhile.

There's usually a small cost associated with each check.

15.3.4 Accounting Policy

Some of the most thrilling days of my professional life have been spent with accountants, creating the T-diagrams for online retail operations. In brick-and-mortar retailing the stock movement out of the store, the payment by the customer, and the moment of recognising the sale are simultaneous at the point-of-sale. In online retailing, by contrast, there is almost always some sort of timing/phasing issue, which inevitably makes the standard double-entry book-keeping more intricate.

Some national accounting standards will prescribe the moment when an online sale can be recognised – typically the instant when the despatch of goods first takes place; otherwise a pure policy decision can be taken. Depending on your payment policy – on order, on despatch, on delivery (or collection) – then this is probably not simultaneous with the customer payment. Various messy accruals (especially across period boundaries) and reconciliation challenges need to be addressed. The messiness is increased if you are obliged to run two payment policies (**Figure 55**), for example card payments but also cash-payment on delivery, and/or if orders can be split across multiple deliveries.

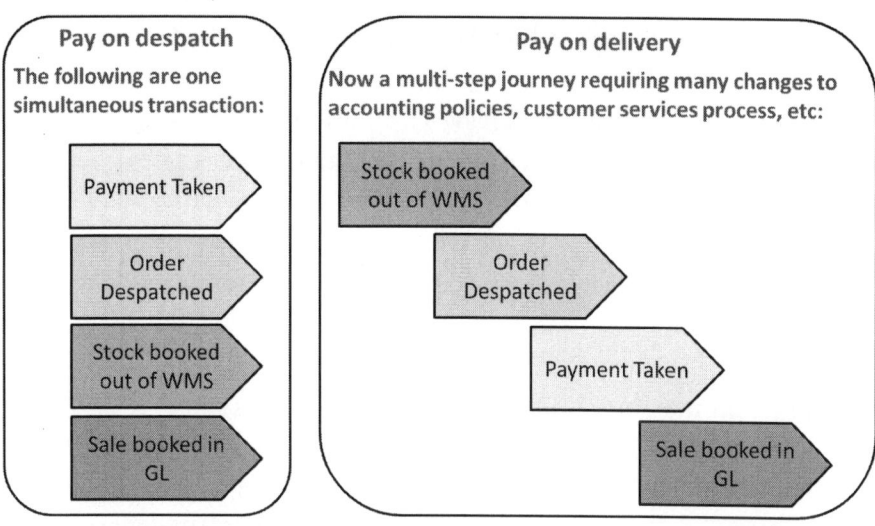

Figure 55 - Accounting flow for differing payment policies

It isn't so much that these are especially difficult as that they are frequently inconsistent with the existing processes used in brick-and-mortar stores, which generally mirror a pay-on-despatch process, and therefore require parallel accounting processes to be established.

15.4 Fulfilment

"Stocking, picking, packing, shipping,
All without our standards slipping,"

sang Mary Poppins to the children, as she waited for the sweeps to collect another batch of parcels ready to drop down the chimneys of London.[90]

You may struggle to find this particular song in the original movie, but nevertheless these are the fundamental business processes of fulfilment. **Figure 56** describes it rather more professionally. (Click-and-collect deserves a complete chapter to itself - Chapter 21 - so it is out-of-scope for the purposes of this chapter.)

Figure 56 - Fundamental fulfilment steps

---

[90] OK, I made this one up

I'll take a look at each in turn in the next sections, but first you should consider the option of outsourcing some or all of fulfilment. To start with, you are very likely to be outsourcing most of the shipping stage, although man-and-van delivery operations in metropolitan areas close to your stock location(s) are especially popular in Eastern Europe, with startling service levels (e.g. receive your order within 2 hours of placing it, for example). Many of the large shipping companies offer complete solutions, which may extend to customer service management, and which often also solve one of the nastier IT challenges too.

Aside from the pure economics of the business case for outsourcing, it has some other advantages. Despite the Mary Poppins ditty at the start of the section, the fulfilment cycle is much harder than it looks to perform consistently and reliably "without our standards slipping". Even a 2% failure rate in fulfilment can prove catastrophic to your overall business case, simply because errors are so costly to remedy. Take a look again at how many steps, and therefore potential staff time as well as direct costs, are involved in fixing the rather basic problem of the ripped party frock example I gave at the start of this chapter. Outsourcing can represent a significant de-risking of the whole project.

Where businesses re-introduce more risk instead of reducing it is when the fulfilment is partially outsourced, or outsourced to multiple third parties, without clearly defining the interfaces and boundaries. To the customer it looks like one process, which as far as they are concerned, you the retailer are performing. When a parcel arrives damaged, they are not interested in whether the goods were damaged in a warehouse or in a delivery van. Since you will have to remedy any failures, it is essential to tightly control the handover processes between each stage. For example the shipping company must agree that all the parcels it received from the packing stage for delivery were received in good condition, and that therefore any subsequent damage was their fault. This needs to be very tightly controlled in any contracts and standard operating procedures.

Perhaps the worst example I have seen is a retailer who outsourced warehousing (stocking and picking) to one third party, shipping to another, but then insisted on specifying, purchasing and designating the packing materials used themselves. They then economised by using substandard materials, and it cost them far more resolving endless disputes about liability for parcels arriving at customers with the goods in poor condition than they saved on materials (although to be honest I also think their shipping partner should have refused to accept such a contractual stipulation the first place).

15.5   Stock

The simplest and cheapest way to manage stock is to not have any.

Ensuring that the endless aisle does not require endless buying is often done by selling third party assortments through your website. When a customer places an order, you divert it to the third party. The difference from a marketplace-style offer, such as Amazon Marketplace, is that you are still deciding which products to list on your site and also that the customer is (usually) not aware that there is a third party involved. The extent to which you take ownership of the final shipping process to the customer varies. If you are working with a professional drop-ship vendor (DSV) who specialises in this business model – and these exist in many markets, including less mature markets (I've worked with one in Romania for example), especially in categories such as consumer electronics – then probably you will just hand-off this part of the order to the DSV, and expect order progress-status updates. On the other hand, if you are sourcing some specialist items from a cottage-industry supplier more focussed on quality-making-to-measure than on managing deliveries, you may prefer to handle the whole journey to the customer yourself. (There is also the question of branding the paperwork to consider – shipping notes, invoices etc – see below). Clearly the savings are not just less buying effort; it's also a way of avoiding stock risk on lower stock-turn items which are nevertheless necessary for a complete online range.

Otherwise you'll need some stock, and therefore a place to put it. At this point I suggest you re-read the available-to-promise section above. As a general rule, you will need a pool of stock which is isolated and dedicated to the online channel. That doesn't mean you aren't allowed to move stock in and out of this pool in a controlled way, but it does mean that it should not be "shared" in an uncontrolled way and subjected to competition from other channels. The products which are fast-moving online are probably the same products which are fast-moving in brick-and-mortar, and shared stock pools will just generate too many situations where you are out-of-stock but your website doesn't realise this and keeps on selling the product.

Stock holding locations in brick-and-mortar retailing are usually stores and distribution centres (DCs). Using store shelf-stock is a recipe for out-of-stock situations as just defined. Using back-of-store stock usually *only* works if you ring-fence the website stock separately; it is a rare retailer which otherwise has such tight controls on back-of-store stock that it requires it to be booked in and out before moving it to the showroom floor. On the other hand properly ring-fenced back-of-store areas can be an excellent use of the space in under-performing stores! As soon as you try to employ more than one such store, however, the whole available-to-promise story can get a little more complicated – what if a customer orders two items, each of which is only in stock in different stores? It isn't unmanageable, but each small step in increased complexity needs to be taken carefully.

Using an existing DC presents a different challenge for most retailers. The first is that IT systems usually don't like it much. The second, much more important, is that DC operations for many retailers are simply not designed for the single-item picking processes required for customer order fulfilment; they are designed to optimise the bulk replenishment to stores, not fiddly picking and packing to customers. Breaking open supply chain shipping cases, for example, is not something you would do in bulk replenishment – it usually takes place when the goods are moved onto the store shelves – but is clearly mandatory for customer orders.

Therefore, the standard solution is another specialist warehousing operation, typically named a Fulfilment Centre (FC) to distinguish its operating model from a DC. That doesn't, of course, oblige it to be in a different physical location, but probably does oblige it to be treated almost as though it is (clients I have worked with who share the location refer to the separation of the DC from the FC as the "red line", regardless of whether one is really painted down the middle). Incidentally this specialisation of the FC operation away from the DC operation is another argument in favour of outsourcing until you have sufficient scale.

For business case planning assumption purposes, British Imperial measurements provide a particularly memorable rule-of-thumb: you can handle orders worth 1000 GBP per year per square foot of FC space[91]. In a more broadly useful metric measurement, this same rule-of-thumb translates roughly to the rather less memorable 13,450 EUR per year per square metre. Since sales density in practice is going to vary enormously depending on your assortment, then like all rules-of-thumb this one is only useful until you have the practical experience to ignore it (although it has actually proven surprisingly generally robust).

15.6   Picking

There are a couple of issues which might cause picking online orders to have somewhat different operating procedures and priorities compared to your existing processes. The first of these is specific, order level, service level agreement commitments to customers, which are probably the main step-change from traditional mail-order. *Figure 57* shows some of the options currently offered by Amazon in the UK for example:

	Free Super Saver Delivery	One-Day Delivery	First Class (Standard Delivery)	Express Delivery	Evening Delivery	Expedited Delivery
Delivery Time	3 to 5 business days after despatch	One business day (including Saturdays) after dispatch	1 to 2 business days after dispatch	Orders before the Express deadline guaranteed to arrive by 1pm the next day	Orders before the Evening deadline guaranteed to arrive on the same day	Delivery times can vary from 1 to 3 days. Estimate shown in the order form

Figure 57 - Six delivery options offered by Amazon UK[92]

This section of the book is targeted at retailers starting out in online, to whom the best advice is... don't try this at home, especially options like "evening delivery". While six different classes of delivery service might be

---

[91] See for example data published by Asos.com, planning £1.2Bn of sales from 1M sq ft of warehouse. Amazon's 2011 10-K filing quotes $42Bn of product sales from 44M sq ft of warehouse, equating to around 600 GP per year per square foot, or roughly 8000 Euros per year per square metre; this probably reflects the relatively low price points of books and media, and may be slightly understated anyway as this space is referred to as "fulfilment and other" without giving any clues about the "and other".

[92] From amazon.co.uk, October 2015

great customer differentiation, a single extra express option is more reasonable. An obvious, but related point, is not to over-promise, especially about order cut-off deadlines. "Order by 6pm for next day delivery" is a common type of promise, especially in the geographically compact countries of Europe. Remember all the steps that this involves, and especially the scheduled time when the courier will come and pick up your parcels which is an absolute cut-off (**Figure 58**). It's not going to be practical to make this particular promise if the courier arrives at 18:15 (unless you know a multi-drop van driver who is happy to hang around? I thought not).

Figure 58 - The long road to express delivery

The second issue is that generally it is worth prioritising accuracy at the expense of efficiency, especially if you are setting up this sort of operation for the first time, and this is often in contrast to how the rest of your logistics is set up. A 98% KPI might be very good for store replenishment logistics, but it's dreadful for customer order fulfilment because of the high cost of each error. Typically this is addressed by picking-by-order even if the resulting picking-tours are not optimal, and by additional use of 4-eyes quality control processes. One retailer I worked with deliberately laid out its FC counter-intuitively, with the aim of ensuring that no two adjacent pick-faces had similar products in them, and thereby reducing the risk of accidentally picking a similar-looking but incorrect item.

15.7   Packing

The usual caveats about using planning rules-of-thumb are even more appropriate when budgeting for packing materials. Following the business-case theme of this section I feel obliged to quote a benchmark, so I suggest you start out targeting USD 1.50 per customer order. The quickest way to attack this figure is to purchase in bulk, but the quickest way to throw away some cash is to purchase in bulk before you have concrete experience of the way in which your customers order.

A typical, standard, non-food, B2C online operation, will have order sizes of somewhere between 1.5 and 2.5 items per order (although this often looks like 1,1,1,1,1,10 rather than 2,3,2,3,2,3 items). As far as possible you want to ship orders in as few deliveries as possible to keep costs down, but predicting in advance the "shape" of the packaging you might need is almost impossible. Start by buying a small number of various sizes of packets, and then see which ones you use the most of. I'd like to suggest a more scientific predictive approach, but practical experience is by far the best guide.

Whatever you do, don't economise excessively on materials quality. Similarly, don't economise on double checking the contents of those boxes before you seal them up for the shipper. Just keep remembering how much it's going to cost to remedy errors, never mind the reputational and brand damage. Just as an example, wine typically comes from the supplier in 6-bottle or 12-bottle cardboard cases. These are perfectly adequate when piled up into pallets, but are not really robust enough to just send as a parcel. *Figure 59* shows an example of protective repackaging (it's pretty heavy-duty cardboard too).

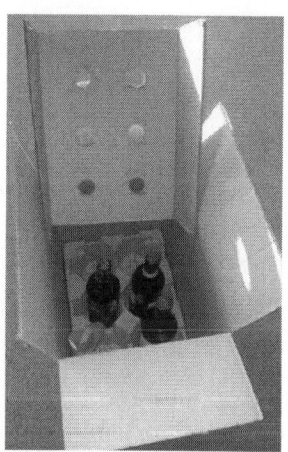

Figure 59 - Re-packaging an online wine order

15.7.1 Printing

Every package will need to be accompanied by some form of documentation. There are six possible documents that most retailers need to consider: shipping note; invoice; returns form; shipping label; non-physical product documentation (especially extended warranties); marketing flyers and leaflets.

The shipping note is obvious – it says who from, who to, and what the package contains. What it usually does not do is mention prices and costs. The most practical reasons not to do so are twofold: a) it might be a gift; b) it is not ideal to tell anybody who might inspect the external documentation how much they would gain by stealing the contents. The second reason is nice, but doesn't take into account customs officials or pay-on-delivery processes. If cross-border shipping or payment on the doorstep are going to apply, then a paper invoice is mandatory (otherwise this is usually exclusively an email document in countries where fiscal printing is not anyway mandatory for tax reasons).

Clothing retailers include the documentation making returns easy, because this is a fundamental part of the proposition of selling clothing remotely. Other retailers, while not exactly obstructing returns, should consider at least making the customer put some effort into it. Provide the form on your website to be printed and completed by the customer, or possibly demand a call to your contact-centre first, especially if this gives you a chance to proactively intervene to prevent a return happening at all; anything to discourage gratuitous returns without preventing genuine ones.

All except the smallest man-and-van couriers will expect you to print the shipping label, usually machine readable, using software which they will typically provide, or at least to their specification. For any retailer big enough to have the courier collect, rather than themselves going to the post-office, some basic IT customisation to link shipping label numbers with your internal order numbers is usually worthwhile to make subsequent customer service simpler.

Warranty documentation is often sent separately by post, but of course you have to put the separate processes in place to do this. Occasionally this might also involve notifying the third-party providing the warranty at the same time.

Marketing material such as paper flyers are an obvious thing to do, and in fact can serve as a secondary revenue source if you can find partners who are interested in contacting your customers and don't represent any competition.

15.8   Shipping

Shipping is a two stage process: moving the goods from point A to point B; possibly then doing something at point B. Taking the "moving" part first, this is generally pretty straight forwards, until you start dealing with large items. Depending on exact health and safety regime you have to operate within, somewhere between 20Kg and 30Kg there will be a limit that says this is no longer a parcel that can be shipped by parcel-post. Equally even a lighter item, such as a very good racing bike or an aluminium ladder, will fall outside limits on awkwardly shaped packages. There are various ways these limits are defined by different carriers, but in general any single dimension larger than about one metre is going to prove challenging.

If you sell furniture, large electrical items, or very large quantities of commodity products (e.g. printer paper), you may find you need either a large item specialist service (the jargon is usually "2-man" service) or a pallet-shipper. The downside of such services is the cost of delivery, typically in the 30-40 Euro range in a compact European country, and potentially an awful lot more if you want to ship from say Sydney to Perth, or Moscow to Vladivostok. Even in a world of subsidising delivery out of marketing costs, some items may become completely uneconomic; typically these are bulky products with low margins – you won't find many online retailers who sell coffee tables for example, because these exactly fall between small=reasonable shipping costs and large=profitable enough to share shipping costs with the customer.

The upside of these carriers, especially a "2 man" specialist, is that they often offer a wide portfolio of possible premium services, which customers will be willing to pay extra for: delivery to room of choice, morning/afternoon/evening options, WEEE (old product) disposal, gas-fitting, plumbing-in, TV-set up. Their business model – in which a failed delivery because the customer was not available is an extremely expensive issue – tends to naturally promote premium service. Calling ahead, multiple SMS messages reminding the customer about delivery all feel like excellent service even though their primary objective is actually to keep costs down.

This leads naturally to the "possibly doing something at point B" side of shipping. Payment-on-delivery is the most obvious such something, either by cash or credit-card depending on the local prevailing consumer preference. But proof-of-delivery, delivery to room of choice, morning/afternoon options and so on, all offer possibilities for premium service (and fees) without significant additional cost. Furthermore there may possibly be local legal issues to contend with, such as ensuring that an adult signs for the receipt of products containing alcohol (restricted products vary bizarrely from country to country).

In summary, don't overlook the opportunities to make shipping into more than just delivering parcels. It can become an inherent part of your proposition and differentiation, without this necessarily driving excessive cost. However do plan ahead for the consequences, especially if you are proposing to sell "2 man" products. A customer who creates a perfectly reasonable seeming order such as a photocopier with an extended warranty and installation, some paper, and an ink cartridge for it, all in the same shopping cart, may well find themselves receiving four separate shipments, each handled by a different specialist shipping company (photocopier + installation = 2-man, paper= pallet-shipment, ink=standard parcel delivery, warranty=postal service). This has implications not just about cost, but about the whole order lifecycle – what happens if the ink gets spilled but the rest of the order arrives OK? Do you need four separate sets of paperwork, four partial invoices, four different payments collected on the door-step? Is the installation service a "product" as far as your IT and finance systems are concerned? How will you explain all this during the website checkout?

15.9   Issues and Returns

One aspect of retailing where you will be truly multichannel right from day one is handling returns and refunds. Even if your intention is to keep your brick-and-mortar and online channels as mostly separate propositions and operations to start with, customers will bring returns to your stores. It is impossible to prevent this (without major brand damage) by creating determined policies requiring online orders to be returned via online process – customers will still bring online issue to stores, where they can be sure of dealing with a person they can pin down and not an evasive email.

A lot can go wrong between an order being checked out and the customer receiving it satisfactorily. While returns may seem like a tedious side issue, returns rates even when your service is good can be quite high.

As usual, I offer some benchmark planning figures with the warning that reality might be very different (**Figure 60**).

Category	Business Case Planning rule-of-thumb Returns Rate
B2C Food	<1%
B2C Wine	Approx 1.5%
B2C General Merchandise	Budget for 8%, probably a bit less if you are small
Consumer Electronics	Budget for 9-10%
Clothing	Budget for 30%

Figure 60 - Benchmark planning returns rates[93]

In almost all categories the returns rate will increase as the price-point of the items increases. The highest reported figure I have heard was for a website selling very expensive shoes. Being both (broadly) in the clothing category and having a high price point, the returns rate reached a spectacular 85% without this actually being indicative of any real issues. Clearly such a business is only sustainable if you have gross margins to match! By contrast, cheap plain white T-shirts have negligible returns rates.

(In general note that to sell clothing online, you probably want to *encourage* returns; better still if you are multichannel and customers can return to store. Online clothing is partially predicated on the mantra that the customer "wants one, tries three, keeps two".)

Customer expectations of returns policies vary widely by country, and especially by the strength of consumer protection legislation, and so it is impossible to define best-practice. Worst-practice is easier to define: defining your returns policy *after* selecting your third-party fulfilment partners, *after* briefing your IT teams, or *before* talking to your brick-and-mortar store managers.

---

[93] Reliable public domain data is very difficult to source, but see for example http://www.e-commercefacts.com/background/2011/08/10-tipps-to-reduce-return/

15.9.1 Standard Issues List

What follows is a starting-point list of typical issues, for which I suggest that you should have a pre-defined documented process in place. There is no country I am aware of where it is acceptable to take the money and then not deliver the goods, so this is an obvious starting point. Inevitably there will be a thousand-and-one edge-cases, strange exceptions, and obstreperous customers which you cannot possibly pre-define, but it's always easier to improvise from solidly built foundations. Remember that many issues will involve a problem with a single product in a multi-product order. Incidentally, the key to writing basic procedures for these kinds of "infinite possibilities" situations is always to <u>write them assuming that only one thing goes wrong at once</u>.

Pick Fail: Failure to pick the complete order, due to stock issues

Missing Goods: Goods which the customer claims are missing a) when there is no proof they received them; b) when it would appear that someone else received them (this is particular important if you are operating pay-on-order or pay-on-despatch policies)

Damaged property: Customer's property damaged during the delivery, even though the goods themselves are fine

Unacceptably damaged goods: Goods delivered damaged. NB, many retailers have a "secret" threshold, typically around the $30 level, below which they judge it is cheaper to just send the same goods again for free without requiring a corresponding return, rather than manage a whole returns process

Acceptably damaged goods: Goods delivered damaged, but in a condition which the customer will accept if given a discount (for example a scratch on the side of an oven, which will be hidden from view when fitted in the kitchen)

Serial Offenders: Spotting serial offenders (customers whose orders apparently always have some sort of issue...)

Notified Returns: Returns notified by the customer; what process should they follow to get the goods back to you, where should they send them, what documentation is required?

Returned to store: Ordered online returned to store processes, especially for products not normally included in that store's assortment

Returns QA: QA process on receiving a return (ensuring that the box contains a faulty laptop, not a faulty brick)

Refund: Refund process. In many situations/countries there is a requirement that the return is issued to the same tender as the payment was made on because of a) credit card scheme rules; b) money laundering legislation

Unexpected returns: Un-notified returns (a box with some documentation just arrives spontaneously in the post)

Discretionary returns: Discretionary returns allowed ("I just didn't like it")? This is probably mandatory for clothing.

DSV returns: Returns to drop-ship vendors

Overseas returns: Returns from orders shipped overseas

15.10 Customer contacts and customer service

It is usual to measure customer contacts as a ratio of contacts-per-order. A contact is any message from the customer, including emails, phone calls, click-to-chat, web-forms and certain kinds of social network interactions (those which imply an action is required) especially twitter used as a more public version of email. There is of course a decision to take about what contact channels you will make available to customers. There is a tradition for online pureplays to avoid publishing telephone numbers to keep costs down – not so long ago it was almost impossible to call Amazon for example. The business case for this has to be set against the long-term reputational issues caused by very disgruntled customers and more directly the short-term issue of lost sales because the customer is just not confident to order from such a site. "No phone number" sites are decreasing, which suggests that this business case is tipping in favour of better customer service preferred to lower costs.

An excessive contacts-per-order ratio is a key reason for an online store to become unprofitable, as they are often disproportionately expensive to address. Customer contacts occur for one of three basic reasons:

Pre-sales, for information. Some are unavoidable, but a high rate (> 0.1 / order for a typical business) can be a sign of insufficient information on your sites or, dare I say it, poor quality product data;

Pre-sales, for ordering. In markets where customers typically may not have access to online payment methods such as credit cards, and therefore pay by offline processes such as funds transfer from a bank, a website can become a sort of online catalogue in support of what is really a telesales operation. This model is particularly common in countries such as Russia where internet literacy is quite high but payment infrastructure is still developing. If you are in such a market, or if you decide that telesales are part of your business model anyway (there is only a small difference, so if you are building the infrastructure for eCommerce you may well want to consider adding telesales to it), then clearly such calls are probably a "good thing", and certainly should not be "counted" towards the contacts-per-order ratio ("bad thing");

Post-sales, due to some sort of order lifecycle issue. Universally these are a "bad thing".

The key to a successful customer-contact process is to ensure that the *agent handling the issue has at least the same information available as the customer does*. For example, if handling a pre-sales issue, the agent should be able to see the same website as the customer. If handling a post-sales issue, the agent should have timely information regarding the progress of all the items in the order, the financial/payment status etc.

For business-case planning purpose a benchmark is needed. Such data is extremely difficult to source in the public domain, so for this benchmark I am obliged to quote numbers from experience without really backing them up with representative quoted data. Counting only pre-sales for information plus post-sales for issues reasons (i.e. excluding "good" contacts for placing orders) combined, then *Figure 61* shows some reasonable numbers:

Contacts per Order	Applicable situations
0.2	About as good as it gets
1.0	What you can expect directly after launching
0.5 to 0.6	Where you should aim for 6-12 months after launch
Over 2.0	A major problem, stop focussing on driving sales and focus on fixing the process issues before your brand is ruined!

Figure 61 - Contacts per Order Benchmarks

If you are operating in a market where "good" pre-sales calls are the norm, then it is interesting to compare with eBay, who anecdotally have contacts-per-order ratios heading towards a grim-sounding 5.0 / order, the vast majority of which are pre-sales contacts, but allegedly have lower post-sales contacts rates, and more importantly much lower returns rates as a result. A variation on the same theme – providing information up-front reduces post-sales dissatisfaction - is that items with large numbers of customer reviews tend to have lower contact rates overall, another argument in favour of including ratings and reviews.

15.11 Top Takeaways

Order lifecycle includes the closely coupled topics of payment, warehousing, pick-pack-ship, returns, customer-services, some financial system tracking.

15.11.1 Available to Promise

An online retail channel is not selling products, it is selling descriptions of products plus a delivery promise. The promise is made up of a shipping promise and a stock promise. Available to Promise (ATP) usually refers to the latter.

Stock promises made about in-store stock are especially challenging.

Channel conflict can impact multichannel retail ATP.

ATP is relatively more critical for online channels than general stock availability is for brick-and-mortar channels.

ATP can become very complex: it typically lies at the nexus of many of your systems and processes. Keeping it simple is important to start with; once you want to go beyond simple, expect to need to make a significant investment in systems.

Low frequency out-of-stocks may add credibility to a category online; high frequency out-of-stocks reduce it.

15.11.2 Payment, PSPs, Fraud, Accounting

Payment policies can be: pay-on-order, pay-on-despatch, pay-on-delivery. The choice of payment policy can have a major impact on order lifecycle. Payment is a two stage process: authorisation followed by capture.

Ensure you are familiar with local payment method processes, distance selling regulations, PCI/DSS compliance implications before selecting a payment policy.

Card/Customer Not Present (CNP) transactions are more expensive than face-to-face transactions. The costs rise when fraud prevention measures are inadequate. A budget of 1% of sales value should be allowed for either fraud costs or fraud prevention.

Payment Service Providers (PSP)/Payment Gateways process non-cash payment methods. PSPs may also include fraud prevention services. In many countries PSPs are operated by banks, but independent gateways exist in more developed online markets.

Accounting for online sales is different from store sales, because of the non-simultaneity of movement of cash and goods.

Address/post-code/zip-code checking services are usually worthwhile, for assisting fraud prevention, reducing shipping and returns issues, and facilitating checkout.

15.11.3 Stocking, picking, packing, shipping

Drop ship vendors (DSVs) exist in many markets, and can be used to operate stock-less models, especially in support of endless aisles.

Stocked models should usually ensure that stock is ring-fenced, consistent with the intended available-to-promise.

The operating model of a Fulfilment Centre (FC) is different from a traditionally store replenishment Distribution Centre (DC). Even if the two are co-located a "red-line" approach is recommended, to ring-fence stock and permit alternative operating procedures.

A benchmark rule-of-thumb for sizing a Fulfilment Centre is £1000 of orders per square foot per annum (=13450 Euro per square metre).

Fulfilment is very sensitive to error; errors are relatively very expensive to correct. Fulfilment Centre processes therefore emphasise accuracy at the expense of efficiency.

Multiple delivery options, especially express delivery to SLA cut-offs, require special processes. The cycle - place order, send to FC, print pick note, pick order , 4-eyes check, pack, label for courier, collected by courier – requires sufficient time to complete after the cut-off.

A rule-of-thumb benchmark planning figure for packing materials is $1.50 per order. Packaging needs to be robust enough to survive the stresses of the journey.

There are six possible documents that most online retailers need to consider: shipping note; invoice; returns form; shipping label; non-physical product documentation (especially extended warranties); marketing flyers and leaflets.

Oversized or heavy goods will require specialist shippers: pallet delivery or 2-man delivery. The cost of such services is much higher than parcel shipment. However they frequently offer the opportunity for additional differentiating services such as room-of-choice, installation/setup, old-item disposal.

Plan for orders which might require split shipment - such as the example of a photocopier plus pallet of paper plus ink cartridge plus warranty - and consider the impact on website checkout.

15.11.4 Returns and refunds

Returns will be multichannel from day one. Returns to store should not be resisted or refused. They could include items not normally ranged at that store.

Benchmark planning rates include 8% on general merchandise and 30% on clothing. Returns-rates increase with price-point.

Pre-plan returns policy for one level of issue per order (only): pick fail, missing goods, damaged property, unacceptably damaged goods, acceptably damaged goods, serial offenders, notified returns, returns to store, unexpected returns, QA, refunds, discretionary returns, DSV returns, overseas returns.

Returns and refunds issues may affect only a single item in a multi-item order.

Refund policy must take into account payment scheme rules and money laundering regulations.

Customer contacts occur for three main reasons: pre-sales for information, pre-sales for order, post-sales due to order lifecycle issues.

Customer contacts-per-order is a key measure of inefficiency. A distinction should be made between good contacts (offering sales opportunities) and bad contacts (due to bad product information or order lifecycle issues). Steady state rates should be between 0.2 and 0.6.

Chapter 16. I.T.

16.1 Introduction

Condensing complex topics like SEO or eMail marketing for retail, about which there are already shelves of books, into brief chapters is challenging. Condensing the entire libraries of material about I.T. for online retail is trebly so. (Full disclosure: I.T. was my first career before I decided that multichannel retail is more fun, and I still derive a proportion of my consulting income from I.T. related work in the multichannel field, such as project design, business analysis, enterprise architecture, or platform/vendor selection processes.)

Firstly a reminder of the scope of this part of the book: going online. Broader multichannel integration issues are therefore excluded from this chapter. Also deliberately excluded is any attempt to compare particular I.T. products or their suppliers. The eCommerce forums on the internet are full of questions of the "is software product X better than software product Y" type; this is the wrong question anyway. So what is the right question?

16.1.1 All the same

I'll start with a deliberately provocative assertion: all online retail stores are exactly the same. This is almost true of mobile retail, where the conventions and best-practice standards are steadily settling down, and is very much true of websites aimed at PCs and tablets. They all do the same few things:

Help: Help and information, and information functions (such as store locators);

My Account: Some sort of "my account" functionality, from the very basic where-is-my-order (known as WISMO) up to the quite sophisticated online wallets, personal preferences etc;

Home: A home page;

Category pages: A series of intermediate taxonomy pages i.e. the home pages for categories and sub-categories, special or seasonal offers etc;

Search: a search box, and search results pages;

Navigation: Various navigational filters which apply to the taxonomy pages or search results to help the customer drill down to the product he/she actually wants;

Product pages: Product pages themselves, including all the merchandising extras that go with them such as cross-sells, ratings, recommendations etc;

Basket: Shopping cart;

Checkout: Checkout, which normally has sub-steps asking who you are, how you want the goods delivered, where you want them sent to, and how you want to pay.

Behind the scenes are a number of key components supporting the online business, which again are almost the same at all retailers. The main differences in these parts of the ecosystem usually occur deep into the "back end integration" of the systems, and depend on the way in which the management of Order Lifecycle is coupled into existing systems, especially if you operate some sort of ERP.

16.1.2 All different

Where solutions do differ is firstly in their scalability. Amazon took 37 million orders during their peak 24 hour period in 2013[94]. A spread-sheet solution for order management probably wouldn't hack it for them. Secondly, in the depth of the functionality they offer. For example search or navigation can be very sophisticated, including features such as personalising the results to the customer, or dynamically tuning the search results to prioritise products which are proven to lead to better conversion. However, these sophisticated features need sophisticated teams to manage them; they always require complex set-up and continuous ongoing tuning and monitoring. It is impossible to become Amazon on the day that you launch, and retailers who try to leapfrog over five years learning in five weeks tend to come a cropper. Of course there is no need to work it all out from scratch as the pioneering online retailers did, but a first class fully

---

[94] See for example http://www.theverge.com/2013/12/26/5245008/amazon-sees-prime-spike-in-2013-holiday-season

functioning I.T. ecosystem with all the processes and skills in place to support it is not something you can magic into being.

The third factor where there are some genuine differences between solutions are if your basic building blocks of retail – customers, products or prices – are unusually complex in some way and don't fit a standard B2C model. If any of the following considerations apply to your retail business model, then get these on the table up-front in any discussions with software solutions or suppliers:

Complex customers: If there are any relationships or restrictions between two separate customers (this is usually only applicable to B2B, where one logon might be allowed to build a cart, but only the supervisor logon can checkout);

Complex pricing: If your pricing is not a one-price-fits-all model at SKU level i.e. there is not always a single "current price" for a given SKU which does not vary with the purchase volume or (especially) the identity of the customer;

Complex promotions: If you absolutely *must* have promotional structures where the existence of one product in a cart can affect the price of another (e.g. buy two shirts and get a free neck-tie). If you study most leading online sites you will find that they tend to avoid promotional pricing structures like link-saves, multi-saves, multi-buys and so on – these structures are awkward to handle in an online environment. Many retailers who operate these offers in store do not replicate them online, and in fact a trend partly driven by multichannel is to reduce the complexity of promotional structures in general, to keep promotions consistent across channels;

Complex products: If you have any of the following "complex" types of product:

1. Items with variants (e.g. colours or sizes). Most solutions will handle these OK, but check there are no limits like only one dimension (e.g. colour but not size simultaneously)

2. Loose-weight (e.g. screws or nails) or catch-weight (e.g. chickens) products where the item is priced per Kg not per unit

3. Any items where the calculation of ATP will be difficult (e.g. two three-metre ropes do not make a six-metre rope)

4. Any items which are not added to cart in whole numbers (e.g. 1.2 metres of rope)

5. Non-physical products (e.g. warranties). Most solutions will be OK, but double check

6. Configurable items like PCs (or BMWs!), where the customer could add different features

7. Any products where a single item in a cart could generate multiple lines on an invoice (e.g. a dining table + chairs)

8. Listings i.e. where the same SKU from two different suppliers are two different products

9. Almost anything else where a simple model 'one item added to cart = one item to pick in the warehouse = one item to ship = one line on an invoice' is not appropriate

10. Products which require specialist shipping (i.e. anything that won't fit in a small parcel).

16.1.3 Archetypal architecture

Without further ado, here is a (very!) high level overview diagram of an archetypal online retail I.T. ecosystem (*Figure 62*):

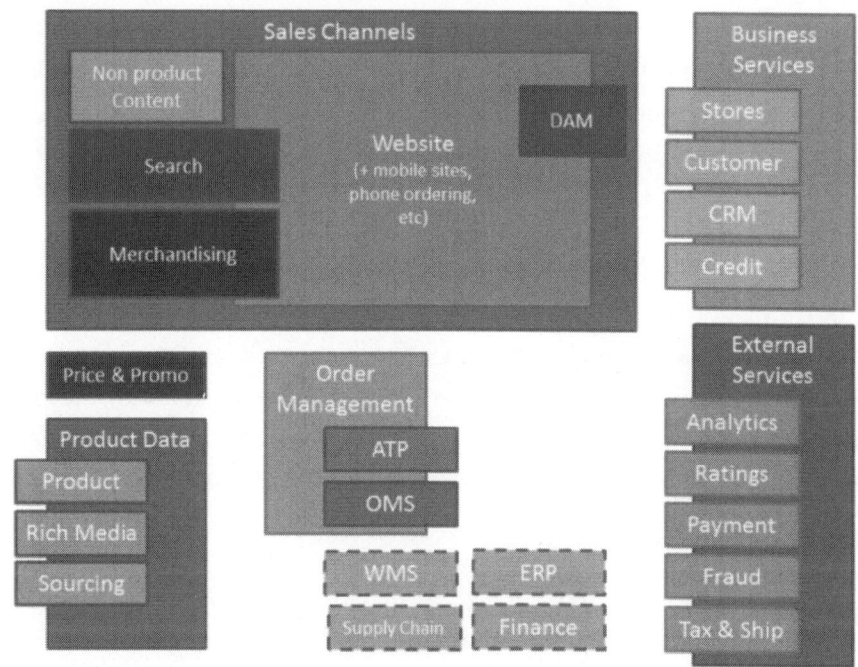

Figure 62 - I.T. ecosystem archetype

Quickly getting the acronyms and abbreviations out of the way:

CRM: customer relationship management;

OMS: order management system;

ATP: available to promise;

WMS: warehouse management system;

ERP: enterprise resource planning (system);

Rich Media: digital asset management – managing pictures and videos, often a separate system for high volume sites primarily for performance reasons;

Analytics: will be described below;

Tax & Ship: only necessary in certain countries (such as the US), external services for the calculation of sales taxes and shipping rates;

Credit: or any other special payment arrangements such as accounts, subscriptions etc;

Ratings: shorthand for Ratings & Reviews.

At its most simplistic, if you can firstly tick all these boxes, and then secondly tick integrating the boxes together, then you have all systems go,

The fundamental difference between a billion dollar website and a kitchen-table web-store is that the big player will tend to have high-performance, high-availability, full-featured, specialist products doing each of these jobs while the small player might well have a single generic package supplemented by a few spreadsheets; even the smallest players might still use some specialist components (for analytics for example).

Standard components are cheap. Specialist components are expensive (I'm sure any IT managers reading this will identify with the experience of shuddering when a vendor announces that theirs is an "enterprise class solution" – a euphemism for adding a couple of extra zeros to the price tag). Getting components to work by themselves is straightforward=cheap. Integrating different components together is difficult=expensive.

16.2   Choosing solutions

I asserted in the introduction to this chapter that forum questions like "is software product X better than software product Y?" are the wrong question. This class of questions are typically posted on online forums by small-medium retailers trying to wade through a jargon ridden and technology-biased swamp, and it is to them that this section is particularly aimed.

Online retail I.T. differs in two extremely helpful ways from other I.T. Firstly, all retail websites genuinely do perform broadly the same functions. Secondly they are all on view in public, unlike say a back-office finance system or warehouse management system, where you are unlikely to be able to view the functionality details of large numbers on a daily basis. You can quickly gain insight even into the less visible parts on an online retail solution by ordering something from the site and then returning what you ordered. (Professionally I have to look at large numbers of websites, and I always start by reading the delivery options and returns pages, and then experimenting with the checkout, which together tell me far more about how the business works than browsing the assortment might.)

A "classic" I.T. selection process will consists of making a very detailed list of all the things you need the solution to do, and then inviting suppliers to tick the items in the list. The trouble with this approach for something as standard as online retail is that you will end up with everybody ticking 97 out of 100 boxes. This is just as true for the very top-end systems as it is for the most basic ones – as soon as you are comparing solutions in the same "class", it's like comparing Coke with Pepsi. However this idea of "class" does give a good starting point. I.T. solutions can be divided into the following (extremely broad) clusters (*Figure 63*):

Target Solution Tier	High Level Delivery Approach	
	Software packages which need to be "installed" by someone	Cloud / SaaS (software as a service) / Hosted
Only for the biggest players	Large scale frameworks, intended to be integrated with lots of specialist components	
For 2nd or 3rd generation larger websites	Fairly complete packages, with a good number of well-defined integration points	"Complete" solutions with globally applicable functionality
Small-medium retailer or 1st generation websites	As above, but usually without the scalability or integration flexibility	Fairly complete solutions but usually only applicable in single countries and for the more standard types of products
Very Small	"OK, now install the CD-ROM" packages	In many countries 1001 "online cart" options, often provided by generic web players (such as the search engines)
Kitchen-table	Freeware	C2C Marketplaces

Figure 63 - IT solution classes

So what? Now is a good moment to go back to the "all different" subsection just above. It isn't an accident that Amazon started with books, or that if you look at all but the most developed multichannel markets many or most of the top online stores are all in media or consumer electronics.[95] These are very "standard" online categories i.e. <u>simple</u>. The

---

[95] See for example internet retailer top 300 Europe guide

right place to start when selecting solutions is to ask "how is my business model, differentiation, proposition or operating model different from just being a vanilla online book-store?" (Don't picture Amazon, picture a plain basic store!). If the answer to this question is "not much if at all", then head towards the right-hand column at a scale that fits your budget and ambitions. If the answer is "a lot" then aim left and higher. If you are larger retailer reading this section anyway despite its introduction, then at this point the Forrester Waves, Gartner Quadrants et al are a good idea.

The next step is to always *simultaneously* choose software and implementation partner (even if this partner is your own I.T. department, or just yourself if you are a very small start-up). Never pick one and then the other ("I want someone who can implement package X", "Z are good, let's get them to implement package X"). Package X is not better than package Y, live business solution X is better than live business solution Y. If you force a good implementation partner to use unfamiliar technology, or give a good package to a bad partner, you will most likely end up with business solution which is poor, expensive or late; a few minor extra features will be no compensation.

Then focus again on those *differences* from the standard book-store; they are where 80% of the challenge in the project will be. If at all possible (i.e. unless you have created something quite unique), do not be the first to do this specific functionality with this partner with this software. Insist on talking to someone else who has already been there, and don't focus on the standard/easy 80% of the functionality - every retail website has product pages. And insist that your partner demonstrates how it proposes to tackle these specific differences.

Define any expected integrations with existing systems you may already have. Focussing again on the differences from the book-store, are there any places where you will need to integrate some specialised, or best-in-class, bits of software? Integration is the most difficult part of I.T.

Finally, never sign a contract until you have done a workshop to design how the checkout is going to work. Don't get excited (yet!) by things like beautiful artwork depicting your home-page design (in fact, do NOT talk about the home page at all until as late as possible). Sitting down and working through the checkout process will tell you whether your partner and software is going to be able to do the job, because a) it will force you to consider almost all the difficult details of your proposition and b) it will tell you if you and your partner can communicate. All I.T. projects discover small surprises along the way; the trick is to try and avoid large surprises which completely invalidate half the work already built.

16.3   Key components

In the next few sub-sections, we'll take a brief look at a few of the key components listed in *Figure 62*. Many of them have in effect already been covered elsewhere, so for example I'm not intending to talk *again* about product data from a peculiarly I.T. perspective. Some are indicative of integrations back into existing areas of your I.T. (for example a CRM system or Finance system), and so again won't be covered. Some, like WMS or Payment Gateway, are generic solutions anyway, and their requirements have already been covered previously; a WMS solution for online retail is not, apart from what has been discussed in *Chapter 15*, so different from any other WMS.

16.4   Site Design

Once again, I'm going to take you back to Moscow 1960, only this time with a slight change from the previously presented *Figure 9*.

Figure 64 - Moscow 1960 bishops on offer

Figure 64 is the same chess position, but with a bit of promotional hype. And I can now guarantee that those same experienced chess-players who could digest and recognise this whole position in less than one second will be completely unable to perform that feat now the layout has been mucked around slightly, despite exactly the same data being on display. The same logic extends to website design. All good online retail websites look pretty much the same and do pretty much the same things. This is not lack of imagination on the part of retailers, nor is it imposed by limitations of their I.T. systems. It is because customers *need* to be able to rapidly digest the information presented. If they can't, they don't spend time being intrigued by the fascinating new design paradigm, instead they quickly switch to someone offering a more familiar pattern.

A whole set of conventions has emerged through trial and error, best-practice is quite easy (if lengthy) to describe, and customers are turned off not just by poor design but by unfamiliar design. This is increasingly true for mobile sites too (of which more later in **Chapter 23**). Compare for example these three top-level navigation screens from three different European countries (*Figure 65*):

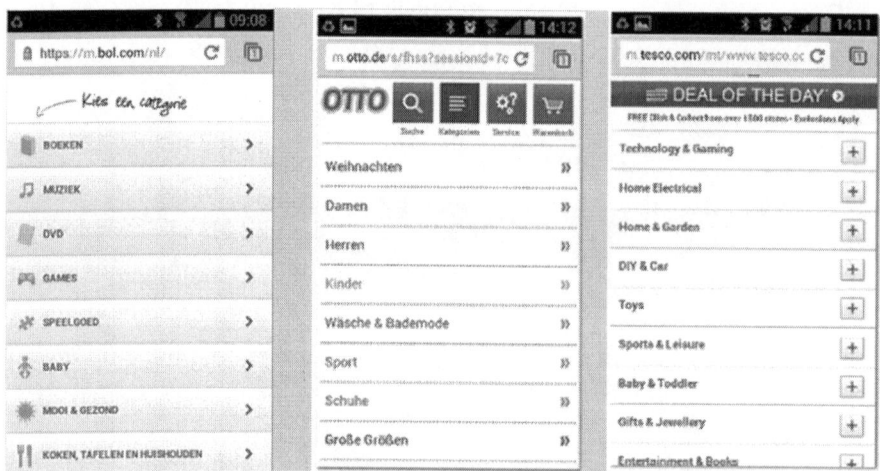

Figure 65 - 3 countries, 3 mobile navigation screens[96]

These are top general-merchandise retail sites in their respective different countries and yet are remarkably similar when you think how many different ways there could be to lay out navigation. In this area, at

---

[96] Collage from bol.com Netherlands, otto.de Germany, Tesco direct UK

least, mobile is headed the way of the good old PC – to standardisation of the user interface experience. In fact if you have a read of the technical documentation for developing Android applications, theoretically an open platform where imagination could rule, in fact a great deal of it is focussed on standardisation of the user interface.

That isn't to say that there are not cultural differences, but they tend to be common across the entire culture, and to exist for a well-proven and founded reason. Take a quick look at a Chinese eCommerce site, for example, and you will typically be confronted by a wall of text; a designer familiar only with western design patterns will be able to explain at length to you why this is not best practice and how it will put consumers off. But Chinese is a relatively slow language to type in, and so the home-page typically has to perform the duties that a search box would perform on an alphabetic language site. Chinese consumers want to click a mouse on a link, not painfully type into a box, and so navigational links tend to predominate in the use of space. They also like a very high-energy experience in general. Best practice is different, but best practice and consumer familiarity are still fundamental.

Much as I might enjoy writing such a text, this book cannot possibly be a comprehensive guide to retail website design (maybe the next book if this one sells well); the screenshots required alone would double its size, let alone the commentary. I will therefore confine myself to the following top ten tips:

16.4.1 Fast response times

Find out what is the slowest connection bandwidth that covers 90-95% of your target customers. If the majority will connect via GSM-mobile links, or via 56K dial-up modem – and this is still true in many regions – then design your website for them; lots of high quality images or video might look beautiful over the fast link in your offices, but will take a few hours to load over GSM. "Broadband" is a variable concept too, so state a precisely-defined benchmark connection speed and make sure all your pages load on that connection in less than 2 seconds.

There are some well-publicised statistics about page-loading times and their impact on sales/conversion rates. One of those "source of the Amazon" quotes which is widely touted but the original seems to be lost in myth is that each 0.1s (100 milliseconds) extra delay in loading pages costs 1% of sales.[97] A better founded, and more recent, data-point suggests that a one second extension in page-load times results in 7% lower conversion[98]. It's that old favourite One Second Rule again in a slightly different form.

16.4.2 No roadblocks or locked doors

Never *require* your customers to log in or register in order to checkout (or worse still, browse). Always have a guest checkout option. In general, never make any "extra" data *mandatory* over-and-above the minimum needed to successfully complete the transaction. The temptation to capture extra for re-marketing purposes later may be strong but making it compulsory should be resisted; there's no harm in optional requirements so long as it is very clear they are optional and the incentives for doing so are plain (e.g. loyalty points). There is a famous and oft quoted example: "the 300 million dollar button", in which simply removing the requirement to register during checkout generated $300M of extra sales for the website in question (OK, it was already a big site).[99]

16.4.3 Make sure checkout is about checking out

Online checkout is a complicated process. Getting a customer to the end of it requires focussing them on the job at hand. Enclose the customer in it. Do not distract them with new offers half-way through (save them until after the customer has confirmed the order!), and do give them a progress overview (*Figure 66*) to encourage them on the journey when they start to ask "are we nearly there yet?"

Figure 66 - Checkout Progress Bar

---

[97] Amusingly this statistic is even quoted in academic papers, for example this one –
http://wwwdb.inf.tu-dresden.de/misc/team/boehm/pubs/diss_final.pdf - but the very formally quoted source then turns out to be someone's blog with (yet another) anecdotal reference in it!
[98]   http://www.aberdeen.com/Aberdeen-Library/5136/RA-performance-web-application.aspx
[99] http://www.uie.com/articles/three_hund_million_button/

16.4.4 No nasty surprises

The top reason for customers to abandon their shopping carts is "sticker shock" – finding out that their order is going to cost a whole lot more than they thought by the time they arrive at the order summary page. Give them the bad news up front. Sucking the customer into the transaction only to play them for a sucker at the end is for budget airlines. It says you are a "cheap" (in every sense of that word) brand.

16.4.5 It's the products stupid

Every page on a retail website (except checkout!) is a product page. It should always be possible to add something directly to the shopping cart from every non-checkout page on a retail site.

True product pages should focus first on ensuring that the customer knows what they are buying if they choose *this* product, and only second on trying to sell them alternative or extra products.

16.4.6 It's the stupid customer

Every page should have a Call to Action: it must be possible to decide what to do next within one second, and the Call to Action should stand out on the page; remember the One Second Rule. It should not be necessary to read the page as though it is a mortgage contract before knowing what to do or where to click.

16.4.7 Below the fold is another county

80% of customers won't read any part of a web-page that requires them to scroll down. One of the more esoteric, although perfectly valid, disciplines that has developed significantly as a consequence of the web is eyeball-tracking; monitoring where on a page users are focussed, and then creating a heat-map indicating where user attention is most concentrated on average. I've drawn an artificial one in *Figure 67*.

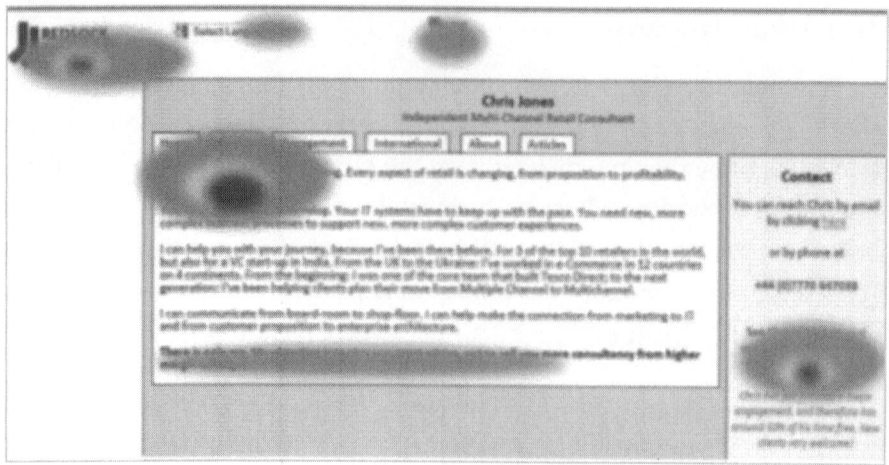

Figure 67 - Web page heat map

One thing such maps show fairly clearly is that below the fold is foreign territory for the majority of customers. This does NOT mean you should cram the top part of every web-page full of as much information as possible; you will end up without clear Calls To Action, which is far more fatal. But it does mean that whenever your design agency brings you yet another "portrait layout" screen design, you should be ready with a ruler and a blank piece of card to place across it and see what it would look like if you only view the un-scrolled area.

16.4.8 Be conventional

As already discussed, there is a standard layout that customers expect for each language layout family (left-to-right alphabetic like English, right-to-left alphabetic like Arabic, Chinese, etc). An English language page should flow from top-left to bottom-right, have top navigation, left-filtering navigation, top-to-bottom forms flow etc. Don't break these conventions, they are the result of years of trial and error, and are now so familiar to customers that they are self-fulfilling.

16.4.9 Tell customers where to find or get help

FAQ and help pages are not an optional afterthought to be written in the 25 minutes before you finally go live. If you don't reassure your customers that it's all going to be OK if they risk giving their money to a screen instead of a human, then they won't.

16.4.10 Don't believe any of the previous nine tips

Online, there is no need to *believe* anything. You can *always* measure it. Guidelines like these top ten tips are nice, but only useful until you have some empirical data to replace them. In order to capture such data you will need an Analytics tool…

16.5   Analytics

On any single channel, every click or interaction by every customer can be recorded. Analytics is both the process of recording, and much more importantly, the process of analysing the resulting mass of data to draw useful insights.

Failing to do all this is flying blind, like running a corner-store without ever watching your customers shopping in it. Since there are even freeware tools available (such as Google Analytics – as always no endorsement or otherwise implied), there is no excuse not to implement a site analytics solution. It's one of the absolute basic disciplines.

Much more information on this topic is in **Chapter 19** covering measurement and reporting.

16.6   Order Management

Order Lifecycles, as discussed in **Chapter 15**, can be complex. The need for some sort of I.T. system to manage them depends largely on scale. If you are retailing from your kitchen table, and your order lifecycle process consists of picking and packing a dozen orders each morning and then taking them down to the local post-office, you can just keep track on a spreadsheet. If you are Amazon doing 37 million orders in a peak 24 hour period, then something a bit grander is going to be required. The difference between the most basic and the grandest includes (but is by no means limited to!) the following key factors. The first, scale, is obvious.

The second is the complexity of your orders. As soon as a single customer order can consist of more than one shipment, then complexity increases exponentially, especially if your order lifecycle might accompany split shipments with split payments. The underlying structure (of which this is only the tip of the iceberg) might start to look like **Figure 68**.

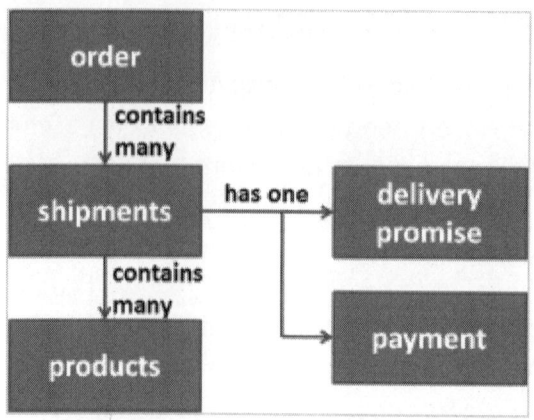

Figure 68 - Order complexity, 2nd level

The third is whether or not an order management system is just essentially a database that records what has happened, such what the current status of each shipment is, or whether it can tell other systems (or people) to do things proactively at specific times or in response to specific situations e.g. "these 10 customers should expect their sofa to be delivered tomorrow, so we will now send them a delivery information SMS".

The fourth is a more subtle I.T. architecture design issue. Which system is "in charge" of what? This is particularly important if the order management system needs to be interfaced to a warehouse management system. Can the OMS tell the WMS what to do? Who is responsible for making sure that you don't have too many orders to fit in the shipping company's collection van today?

Fifthly, does the OMS take responsibility for coordinating available-to-promise? As soon as your promise gets even a little bit complicated – such as shipping the same product from two different locations – you need something to do this job. The OMS is a prime candidate because it also knows the status of each order, including things like whether a customer has just cancelled and therefore some stock has come free.

Once you move from thinking about only a single channel (i.e. the website that this part of the book is primarily about) into multiple channels, a reasonably sophisticated OMS solution is going to be mandatory. Even a single website solution usually has some sort of customer service function, and the customer-service operators need somewhere to be able to view – and amend – orders; this inevitably impacts on the OMS, and some OMS solutions include a customer-service capability either by default or as an optional extra.

16.7 Search & Merchandising

If there is one component where a bit of extra complexity will quite probably lead to a lot of extra sales it is search functionality. Most packages come with a search engine in the box. Many are decidedly average. Experiment on a few mid-sized retailer websites if you don't believe me. Even very large retailers can make a bemusing job of it. My favourite example (I won't put the screenshots in here, read my blog if you want to find it[100]!) was a leading retailer running a promotion based around a charity link up, whose strap-line was a single "made up" word. I tried this word in their search box, and the top 3 results included a dictionary to help me with my spelling! Oh, and no reference to their charity link-up offer.

If you are at the "buying a solution" stage, have a serious discussion about whether a specialist component would be feasible. There are some good freeware solution possibilities, so this need not involve extra direct cost – although of course there will be integration requirements.

Search doesn't work well automatically – it has to be tuned/configured. There are search solutions which are self-tuning, but even these need a different kind of tuning, because they learn from experience (essentially they move the results customers most frequently click towards the top). Tuning search, in case you are wondering, means getting sensible, intuitively optimal, results to consistently appear at the top of the list of results, something which actually doesn't come terribly naturally to search systems(!). Include the lead-time to do this in your implementation plans, and remember that it can't be done until after your product data is mostly ready...

There is an armada of merchandising tools out there, all of which aim to do approximately the same thing: make it more likely that, out of your wide variety of products, you will display to your customers the ones they are most likely to actually want or buy. Many of the same comments apply as for search itself, and in fact there is increasingly a cross-over between the two, running under the banner of searchandising. They still need

---

[100] http://www.redsockmultichannel.blogspot.co.uk/2012/06/fix-cross-functional-before-you-try-do.html

configuring, monitoring and tuning – there is no such thing as a free lunch. (The most sophisticated of all come under the banner of personalisation – the topic of **Chapter 22**.)

The same challenges also apply: integration at the implementation stage, and especially measuring the benefits at the operation stage. If you plan to implement any such tool, try to phase it into your plans at a time when your business is otherwise fairly static, so that it becomes easier to identify any overall cause-and-effect relationships. Often the improvements directly attributable to the tool will be offset by reductions elsewhere (e.g. a tool that drives customers towards best-sellers, but then negatively impacts the long tail; it might have overall positive benefit, but of a two-steps-forward-one-step-back kind.) Most tools are not immediately effective, either because it takes time to tune them, or even if they are mainly self-tuning, it takes time for them to learn.

16.8   Security

Three simple words of recommendation: take this seriously. Listen to what your IT partner or department is telling you. If you are online, you are connected to the internet. If you are connected to the internet, you are connected to the wide world of highly skilled hackers. There have been plenty of high-profile cases where customers' details have been hacked, and it's expensive when it happens. Target, for example, estimated that the 2013-14 data-breach cost it $162M.[101]

The basic plan is straightforward:

1. Take reasonable precautions to deter casual or amateur hackers

2. You probably can't always keep highly professional teams out no matter how sophisticated you are

3. If they do get in, make sure the customers' data you store is securely encrypted, so it's useless to them

---

[101] See for example http://techcrunch.com/2015/02/25/target-says-credit-card-data-breach-cost-it-162m-in-2013-14/ Interestingly, when I tried to get this detail direct from Target's investor relations site, instead of merely from a press-report, the post on the investor site appeared to have been hacked...

16.9　Budget

Retailing is typically a rather thrifty sector when it comes to I.T. spending. Online, where the web-site is effectively occupying the budget-space that brick-and-mortar store estate would do, spending is relatively higher expressed as a percentage of turnover. *Figure 69* is an approximate synthesis of several reasonably consistent surveys[102].

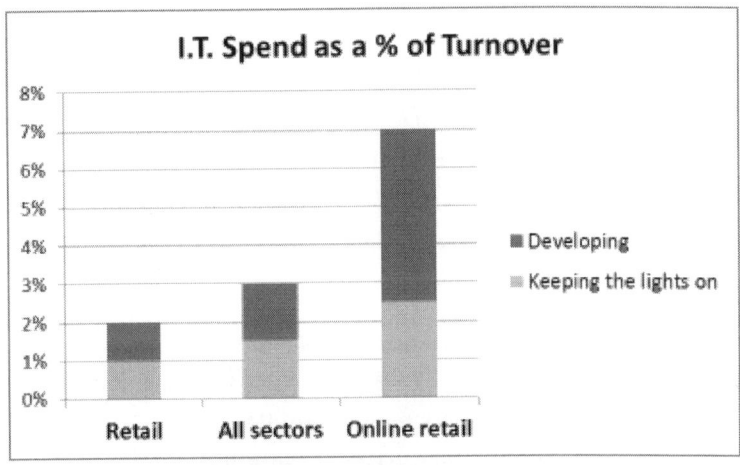

Figure 69 - Online retail I.T. spend

Unfortunately this is one of those areas where objective data is particularly difficult to source: very few companies are willing to break-out their IT spending in their published accounts. (Amazon published capital expenditure on IT of 0.6%-0.7% of sales in the last three financial years, but they have huge economies of scale, allowing them to stay much closer to a typical retailer average. Another published comparison is Ocado, the UK online grocery pure-play retailer, where it is estimated that IT costs represent 2.9% of revenues, split approximately 55:45 between running and developing[103]. Again, this is a large and fairly mature operation. The same study also quotes comparable figures for Asos.)

IT spend also an area where you can exercise a great deal of discretion in the start-up phase to which this part of this Handbook is directed: if you're happy with a less sophisticated or scalable solution in the early days,

---

[102] For example, see Forrester, State of Retailing Online 2009. Despite the old date, it still seems to be reasonably valid.
[103] Redburn: Ocado, Disruptor Disrupted, July 2015

and/or you're simply a more "standard" business, you can keep IT costs relatively low: just don't expect to be competing on customer features.

16.10 Top Takeaways

Online retail sites typically do a standard set of things: Help, My Account, Home & Category Pages, Search, Navigation, Product Pages, Cart, Checkout.

Variations from the standard set which typically might cause issues include: complex customers; complex pricing, especially customer-specific pricing; complex promotions which generate relationships between products and their prices; complex products, especially those which cause the calculation of ATP to be difficult, or which violate a simple model 'one item added to cart = one item to pick in the warehouse = one item to ship = one line on an invoice'

Advice for the small-medium player choosing IT solutions: focus on the differences from a vanilla book-store – the non-standard 20% will be 80% of the project effort; choose the supplier simultaneously with the software; clearly identify all expected inter-system integrations – integration is much harder than single system implementation; do a joint checkout design workshop *before* signing a contract.

Retail website design has adopted standard conventions. These are consistent within cultures. Break them at your peril.

Top considerations for site design: always remember the One Second Rule; page-load times consistent with expected customer bandwidth; no unnecessary mandatory logins/data; enclose the checkout; no nasty surprises; every page is a product page; clear calls to action; care below the fold; be conventional; provide help; never believe lists like this – test and measure instead.

Analytics is not optional. Everything online is measurable.

The need for a specialised Order Management System is determined by: scale; order complexity, especially split orders; co-ordination and proactivity in managing fulfilment; lead system; ATP coordination; multiple channels including customer-service.

Seriously consider a specialised search component, no matter what type or scale of solution you are otherwise implementing.

Search, merchandising, and searchandising tools all need time to be tuned or to self-tune.

I.T. spending as a percentage of sales is much higher online than for brick-and-mortar retail. It is a transfer of cost from store estate to technology. Benchmark planning figures are 2% offline, 7% online, but these are for guidance only. Published data points are few and far between and tend to be for more mature operations: c3% is more typical in these cases.

Take I.T. security seriously. Encrypt all stored customer data.

Chapter 17.   Summarising the Business Case

17.1   Introduction

In this chapter we will briefly summarise all the items identified in the preceding chapters in Part B, which as a reminder is defined primarily as the incremental cost of adding an online channel to an existing retail operating model.

This chapter is also a place to discuss a few P&L lines which don't merit entire chapters to themselves, of which the most important is...

17.2   Staff costs

More than any other topic, organisational size is the one where retailers most want to know "what others retailers like us" are doing. Unfortunately, more than any other topic, this is an area that is particularly difficult to make comparisons. No two retailers are alike, and in fact no two job descriptions are alike.

Because the question invariably comes up, I have eventually developed a sort of ready-reckoner, designed to suggest the <u>incremental</u> headcount required by a brick-and-mortar retailer adding online channel(s). It assumes that the organisation required to run brick-and-mortar retail is already in place, and therefore is not appropriate to headcount sizing for an online pure-play; it strictly considers incremental headcount only. I've based it on real organisations I've either worked with or received information from, and then tested it with others to validate it. It has proven surprisingly robust give or take 20% or so in either direction, but I would strongly warn anybody against using it as anything more than a very rough guide[104].

It is designed to work as a small spreadsheet lookup table and formula, so it's a bit clumsy when put into print. First take a look at *Figure 70*.

---

[104] I originally created this ready-reckoner in 2010, and refined it slightly in 2012 when preparing the first edition of this Handbook. It already seemed to be moderately robust; after another 3 years of experience it still seems to stand up surprisingly well, but do be aware that the sample size is nevertheless pretty small. It is denominated in Euros, so exchange rates might distort it a bit, and all other caveats against using it for more than just guidance remain equally valid!

	A	B	C
1	Sales Baseline, in millions of Euros	Base staff	Additional staff per million Euros of sales above baseline
2	0	2	0.6
3	10	8	0.4
4	20	12	0.3
5	30	15	0.3
6	40	18	0.2
7	50	20	0.16
8	100	28	0.12
9	200	40	0.067
10	500	60	0.04
11	1000	80	0.03
12	2000	110	0.015

Figure 70 - Incremental head count ready reckoner

Fairly simply, you first find the highest row whose baseline online sales you will exceed. So suppose you will have online sales of EUR 35 million, you would locate row 5, the one with the baseline figure of 30 in column A it. It suggests base staff of 15 column B. Then for each one million EUR of sales above the baseline figure, add that number of staff from column C. So in this case, you have 35 − 30 = 5 million of sales above baseline, and therefore require 5 * 0.3 = 1.5 additional staff, for a total of 16.5 altogether.

It excludes warehouse staff and for larger operations excludes customer-services staff too although for small-medium businesses this latter is something of a grey area.

17.3 Other costs

17.3.1 Product photography

We already discussed the need for high quality product *data* at length in **Chapter 12**. It's important not to overlook the corresponding requirement for product images. Quality really does matter here – just shooting badly lit pictures in your garage probably won't cut it. Obviously you'll need at least one per SKU; good practice tends to require several, typically three to five.

If you are fortunate, brands and manufacturers may provide these for you. Otherwise you're going to have to get them done yourself, which obviously has a cost. It's difficult to provide a benchmark because costs vary wildly by category, country, and the extent to which you can get it done in bulk, but you might start with USD 20 per picture as a budget line before investigating in more detail locally.

Don't overlook the extremely burdensome job of assembling product samples, getting them to where the camera is, and getting them back again in a condition fit for resale.

17.3.2 Content

A somewhat related cost might be additional content. Websites are surprisingly full of non-product related content, both exciting (merchandising) and dull (e.g. terms and conditions). Things like category-page banners, promotional banners and so forth all have to be created and maintained. You may be able to re-use existing skills or agencies, but the frequency tends to be significantly higher online.

Most sites just copy someone else's Terms and Conditions, Data Protection policies and so forth, until they get big enough to really justify their own.

17.4   Other income

It's always nice to finish a long list on a positive note. Just as in a store environment, it may be possible to generate additional income on a site, either via placement (if you're big enough), or via onsite advertising.

If the latter is good enough for Walmart, then it's probably good enough for the rest of us, although personally I find it quite disconcerting; I recently reviewed their site for a client, focussing entirely on pet-food categories, during which I was offered a new credit card, a new laptop, a flight to France, cable TV, and a sports-news subscription (*Figure 71*):

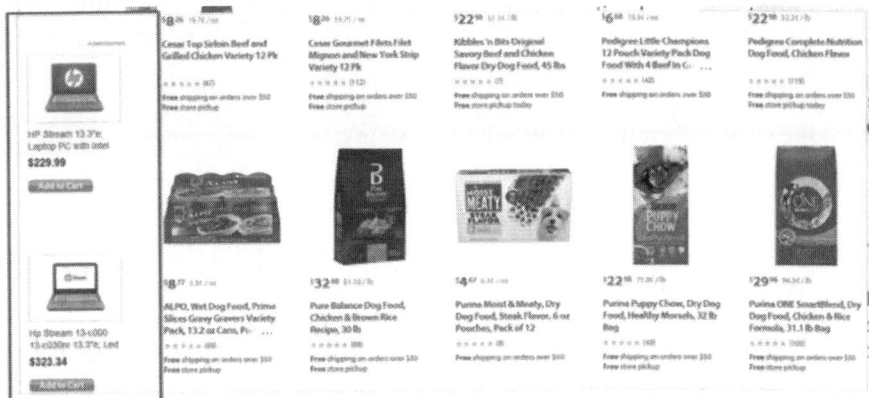

Figure 71 - A laptop with that dog-food sir?

17.5 Top takeaways

I'll take the opportunity to briefly recap and summarise all the income and cost lines that have been described in the preceding chapters in Part B.

17.5.1 Income

Gross margin – obviously your main income line will be the profit margin on the products you sell

Placement – if you are very lucky, you might be able to generate income from giving prominence to products or brands on key landing page such as category pages or your site home-page.

Advertising – detracts from your brand, and drives your hard-won visitors elsewhere, but maybe a worthwhile income line?

Services – e.g. installation, WEEE removal, on-site configuration, room-of-choice etc

Shipping fees – shipping fees excluding services, including options such as Express or Expedited

17.5.2 Costs

Warehousing and associated labour costs – as we noted, a specialised new facility, or specialised space within an existing facility may be required.

Stock – obvious; there may be a cost-of-capital associated with stock-holding which is over-and-above cost-of-goods contribution to gross-margin.

Packing materials – not an area to economise on.

Shipping/delivery – obvious.

Shipping insurance – depends on the shipper (and to some extent, country). It may be necessary to insure on a "per parcel" basis.

Returns shipping – depending on your proposition and/or country, it may be necessary to pay customers' return shipping charges.

Returns handling – customer-not-present returns are more labour, and issue, intensive than returns in stores. If you open the box and it contains a brick instead of the expected defective tablet, then there's going to be hassle…

Customer services – either FTE or cost-per-contact, depending on how you staff this area.

Payment processing – usually a percentage commission.

Payment processing, chargebacks (and related) – you should expect a relatively higher rate of these in a customer-not-present situation

Fraud – a provision is required and/or a cost for fraud-screening.

Cash-handling – if you are in a location where cash-on-delivery is a preferred payment method, there will be a cost for a delivery company to handle it.

Address-checking – if standard in your locale.

Marketing – typically this budget is broken down into costs of acquisition, conversion and retention, and then further broken down by channel such as SEM/PPC, eMail, SMS, affiliates and/or price comparison etc.

Product data maintenance – an initial cost plus a variable cost per SKU churn.

Product photography – maybe available from suppliers, otherwise a per product cost.

Other content – websites tend to trade on fast cycles, and therefore require more content than a store trading environment would.

I.T. – impossible to generalise. There will usually be an initial capital set-up cost, an ongoing running cost, and a cost to develop.

Staff – in addition to purely operational staff involved in warehousing, delivery and customer-service, head-office staff are required to manage the channel.

Part C – Operation

If you follow through on all the tasks outlined in Part B, you'll find yourself at "Day 1": new channel launched and ready to trade.

Part C considers what happens next. This will consist of two key tasks. Firstly you've obviously got to operate the new channel. Secondly, in a multichannel situation, you have to operate it in an environment where your existing store channel is already running. The purist version of this challenge is summed up in the question "are you multichannel or multiple channel?" In practice, it's not really a black and white question, and most retailers are somewhere in between.

Each chapter in Part C therefore starts with the single new channel context, and then looks at how this evolves towards a multichannel state.

Chapter 18.   Organisation

18.1   Simple Online Channel

In the previous chapter we look at the basic business case question: how many incremental staff do you need to operate a new online channel? In this section, we consider what they're all going to do.

A simple suggested outline structure for a small-medium "online" team within an existing brick-and-mortar retailer is shown in **Figure 72**.

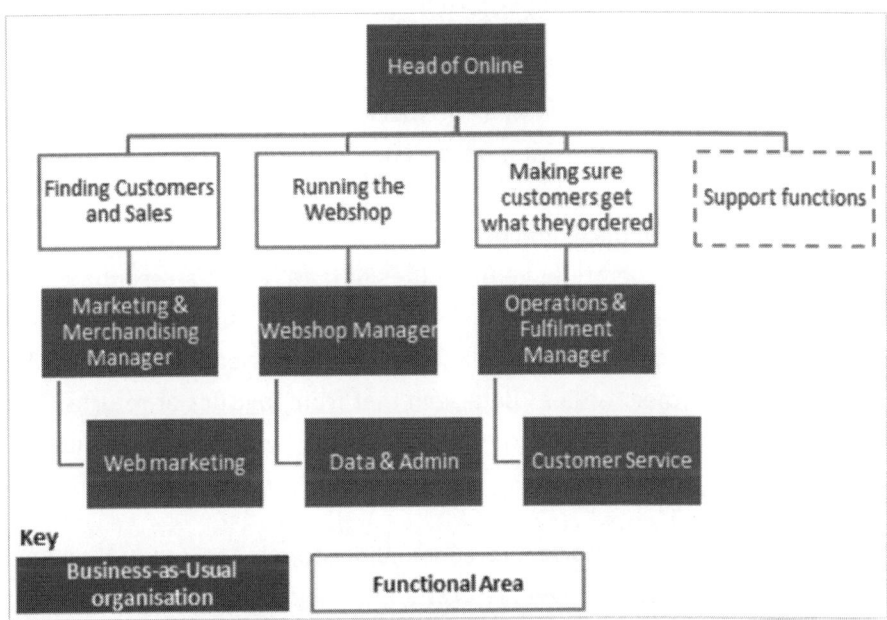

Figure 72 - Simple online organisation structure

Although I have used the word "manager" in some of the boxes, "management" would perhaps by more appropriate: there is no implication here that these are single jobs for a single person, or even just a single tier in an organisation. What follows is an extremely brief outline description of each suggested function. Anything more specific needs a detailed understanding of your particular organisation and chosen set-up; every retailer is simply too different when it comes to job roles and organisation design to get into precise job specifications in a general handbook.

18.1.1 Marketing & Merchandising

This area is responsible for the proposition: user-experience, design of the website and other online channels, promotional activities and calendar, and probably also high level assortment design. Its most important task is not directly online at all, it is ensuring that the offline and online propositions are consistent. While this once again leads us towards multichannel considerations, in its more basic form it means ensuring that things like trading and promotional calendars are synchronised, or if not, that this is a deliberate planned decision.

18.1.2 Web Marketing

There are a significant number of specialist technical competencies in marketing an online proposition, as outlined in *Chapter 14*, including SEO, SEM, affiliate management, email marketing etc. These require one or more specialists to manage and deliver.

Websites also generate huge quantities of data, and it's essential to be on top of it (see next *Chapter 19*). Web analytics is itself an essential discipline, and in practice analytics alone is insufficient: it needs to be correlated with other "offline" data such that from logistics or returns. This is a highly skilled technical job for someone with a facility with statistics.

18.1.3 Webshop Management

Just like a brick-and-mortar store, an online store is constantly changing: New products and prices, new features and functionality, new systems and seasons. Processes need to be defined and managed, and everything needs to be continuously tested. There is often a constant stream of associated IT development activities that need to be coordinated with the business.

There's a tendency to think of a digital channel as being, well, digital and therefore highly automated. The reality is quite the opposite: running a website is a very labour intensive task!

18.1.4 Data / Administration

You've read the lengthy chapter (*Chapter 12*). Someone's got to do it. It might as well be you. See later in this chapter for how to make sure it's someone else!

18.1.5 Operations & Fulfilment, and Customer Service

While a good proposition might generate sales, only a good fulfilment operation can keep costs down to a level where these sales are actually profitable. As suggested in the Order Lifecycle chapter (*Chapter 15*), this is typically sufficiently different from bulk activities supporting stores that new specialist roles are required.

18.2 Connecting to the existing organisation

In reality, such a team does not operate standalone in a vacuum, and so *Figure 73* shows its key relationships within a wider generic retail organisation.

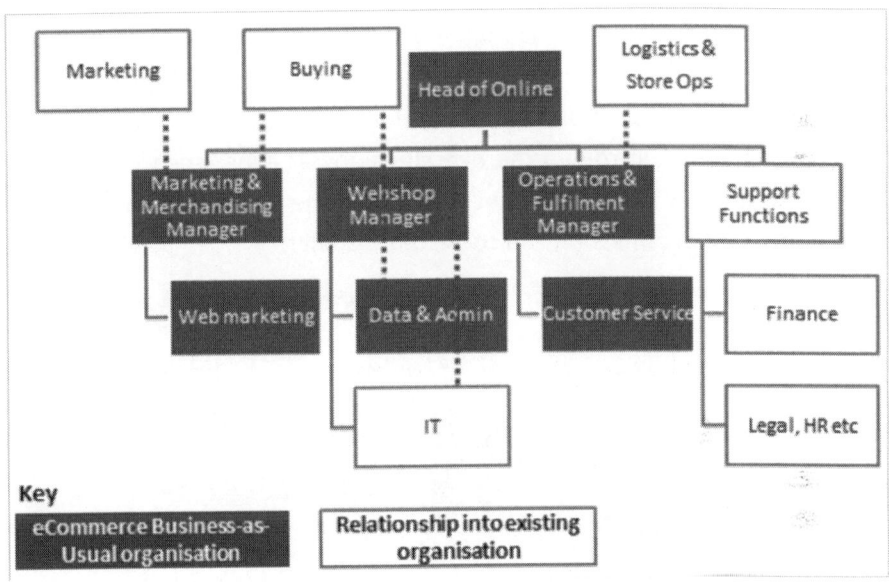

Figure 73 - Extended organisation

18.3 From multiple channel to multichannel

The organisation described in the previous sections is nice, but it isn't multichannel. It is probably the most appropriate approach for a retailer newly going online, and which temporarily needs a ring-fenced organisation in order to get started and build up some momentum. It is surprising, however, how many retailers still equate being multichannel with having a website, or even make statements such as "we have stores and we have multichannel", as though stores were in some way not part of being multichannel. (The easiest way to verify this is to look at job titles: is there a Director of Multichannel? Does he/she have responsibility for stores? The newly fashionable post of Chief Digital Officer tends to be a sign of an organisation further along the journey.)

Your customers certainly won't see it that way. As already discussed in the introduction (**Chapter 2**), they expect you to be present on all the channels they want to use and will penalise you if you are not. Trust is an essential element of any online channel (and of retail in general of course), and if your channels are inconsistent, they are untrustworthy. If you go one step further and start implementing self-evidently multichannel customer journeys such as click-and-collect, then inconsistency is not just untrustworthy, it is unacceptable.

Figure 7 illustrated a typical multichannel shopping journey: there are 14 touch-points in this journey, spread across six channels. **Figure 74** takes this to its logical organisational conclusion: although each of the touch-points has a different role in the overall customer experience, you want a consistent journey for a consistent brand, and the best way to deliver that is by consistent organisation in a consistent retailer.

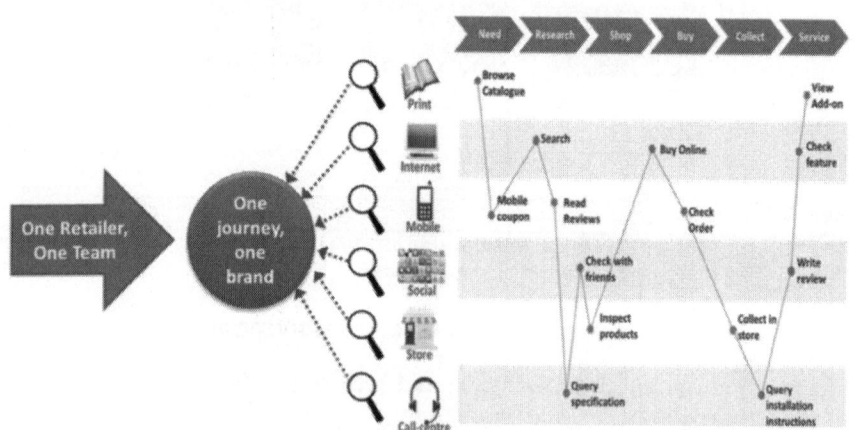

Figure 74 - Omni-channel: many channels, one experience

This is the kind of thing that it's easy for a consultant to write on a slide, but in reality it represents a huge change management challenge that most retailers prefer to defer until their online channel is at least well established and proven to be generating sales.

18.4   4-stage organisational maturity model

Not only is it preferable to phase in the challenge of organisational change, but in practice it would almost certainly be suicidally disruptive to try and get there in one single jump from camp zero. Four archetypal organisational stages characterise the transition (*Figure 75*); what is important is not awareness of such a model but having a conscious plan. Don't let any organisational cracks start to become visible to customers as disjointed gaps in their experience.

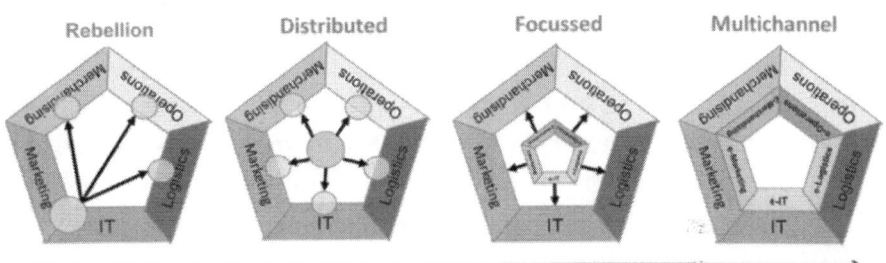

Figure 75 - Four-stage multichannel organisational maturity model

I'd like to say that the *Rebellion* model – where a small number of people, typically from I.T. and Marketing, conspire together to drag a retailer online – is already dead. In actual practice, a version which I'll call *Sponsored Revolution* seems to be alive and well. In its typical manifestation, there is indeed a general top-management mandate for adding new channels, but this does not translate into altering individual targets and KPIs in the existing and/or stores teams, and so the implementation project team has to spend a disproportionate percentage of its effort wheedling co-operation out of the rest of the organisation. To give a specific example, it is very difficult to persuade an individual buyer to devote 20% of his/her time to developing the range for online, or (worse) helping with product data management, when it is expected that only 3% of sales, and therefore 3% of his/her existing targets, will be met from online sales in the next 12 months.

The model recommended in the previous section probably falls into the *Distributed* class, and is where I would recommend that organisations should start out. A small dedicated team looks after driving the new channel(s), but has a clearly defined mandate to use certain resources from existing business teams. To use the same example, the pre-existing buyer would have a specific target for new channel sales, and a clearly stated guideline regarding the expected time commitment.

Whether you implement something like the *Focussed* model depends on your appetite for matrix-managed style organisation design. In this model the channel team is dispersed back out into its wider departments again, but the idea of managing specific (usually just new) channels persists, usually with a skeleton coordinating team. For example, the team responsible for online customer-service would now report into general customer-services, but would still retain a distinct identity and a strong affiliation with the online channels.

Finally, we reach the point where the distinction between channels ceases, a true *Multichannel* organisation. For example there are not two groups of customers, there is one group of customers – "our customers" – and so the existence of a separate marketing team makes no sense. Yes there may be channel-centric technical specialists, for example experts in SEM or Affiliate Marketing, but every discipline has its technical specialists, and the task of management is to coordinate them towards achieving the same organisational goals.

In practice, retailers make these transitions at different speeds in different areas of the business. It's not uncommon to see something like *Multichannel* buying, *Focussed* marketing, and *Distributed* logistics. It's important that this is a deliberate choice, not an organisational accident or worse still a kind of Darwinian struggle for channel supremacy.

18.5   Broader roles

Similar to the introduction of any other new business process, various roles need to broaden, and this brings the challenge of whether to take a horizontal or vertical approach. To take a simple example, endless aisles imply extended ranges, usually with somewhat different characteristics from a typical store range (*Figure 76*).

Extended aisle profile

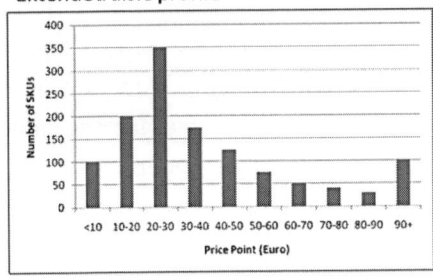

Store profile

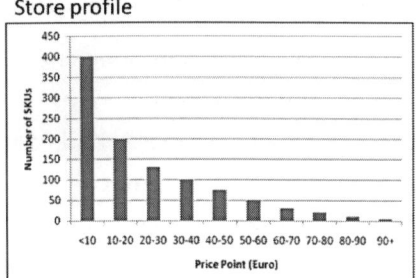

Figure 76 - Contrasting range profiles online and offline

In a well-designed multichannel proposition these two ranges will be complementary. Do you therefore make it one person's job to design the whole extended range, and perhaps therefore reduce the number of categories for which that person takes responsibility in order to re-balance the workload, or do you make it two separate tasks, risking losses of synergy (*Figure 77*)?

Option A – I liked 1992	Option B – 2 teams	Option C – 1 team
× lost sales	✓ simple organisation	× complex jobs
× lost customers	× planning in silos	✓ cross-channel plan
× long-term decline	× competing channels	✓ channel synergy

Figure 77 - Organisational synergy or organisational simplicity?

Doing nothing (Option A) is not an option. Option C is plainly the most "multichannel", but it is also the most complicated. The core competence, in this case range architecture design, has not changed. You could argue that it is still only one range to be designed but with an extra dimension to the task, but even then the task has still become larger. One option which I have seen successfully used during the transition through the *Focussed* model is to keep the role as one, but to add an "advocate" for the extended range into the team, who is subordinate but accountable specifically for the success of the extended components. Such an advocate might span multiple ranges have multiples bosses; it's very "matrix management", and therefore not to the taste of those who prefer hierarchically defined accountabilities and management chains of command.

18.6   Clicks in traditionally bricks jobs

Back to the exasperating challenge of product data management again. Take a closer look at it. What does it involve? Well, it's very business process driven, standards and compliance are essential, flow management is important, just in time delivery is a core competence, it's about getting something from suppliers, and you are always working to serve demanding sales channels... sounds very like logistics / supply chain doesn't it?

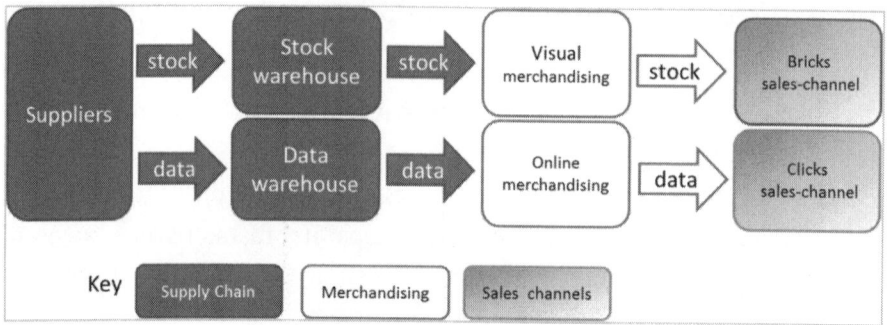

Figure 78 - Multichannel functions?

At first sight, product data management appears to be an additional competence, which arguably requires a completely new organisational unit to manage. There are lots of apparently new competencies which will be added to a typical retailer's team. SEM is obviously marketing discipline for example, but it isn't a traditional marketing skill. While keeping it separate might make sense in the early days, its budget very quickly needs to become part of the overall marketing budget – why should SEM have a ring-fenced budget? *Figure 78* extends this idea into product data management. Although the technical skills are quite different, the management competences are actually remarkably similar. ("Dear logistics manager, thank you for your letter of complaint regarding my suggestion that your team should...").

Whether you agree with this particular proposal or not (and I know of organisations who do indeed do this), the challenges of merging clicks skills like SEM into bricks teams like general marketing are another essential part of becoming truly multichannel in your organisation. Managing areas in which you do not yourself have experience and skills is one of the more difficult tasks for any manager. Seamlessly merging the old with the new to create a multichannel department, and ensuring that apparently competing demands of the new versus the old for budget, priority and resources are handled consistently with traditional old versus old debates, is a major but essential challenge.

18.7   Devolution

We've covered *Rebellion* and *Revolution*, so how about a gentler option?

We highlighted earlier some important trends changing the service expectation of customers in stores. Two stand out in particular: firstly customers arriving much better informed, after having spent significant extra time on research than compared to what they would have done in the pre-multichannel world[105], which in turns leads to a need for better informed staff engaging in more sophisticated sales dialogues; secondly the freeing up of sales staff from static sales positions enabled by the use of wifi and tablet technology.[106] Both of these changes imply a step-change in the role of sales staff in store, from mechanical cashiers to high-tech sales-people[107]. More on this topic in **Chapter 20**.

Here's one very multichannel retail talking about the benefits of such an approach:

"Our colleagues in store have benefited from our comprehensive training programme that allows them to be genuinely knowledgeable on all the latest product developments, so that when customers come in to our stores they can be sure they are getting the very best advice."[108]

Just in case you worry this might have a cost but no commercial benefit, the same retailer goes out of the way to make another very interesting point:

---

[105] See for example, http://internetretailing.net/2012/12/multichannel-doubles-the-time-taken-to-make-a-purchase-study

[106] While everybody knows about Apple, retailers like JC Penney, hardly a high-tech bastion, have made a series of high profile announcements of plans in this area: see for example http://business.time.com/2012/07/20/a-store-without-a-checkout-counter-jcpenney-presses-on-with-retail-revolution/

[107] 68% of customers in one survey expect the in-store staff to be experts on (all) the products in store; Customer Desires vs Retailer Capabilities, Forrester 2014

[108] Dixons Retail, Annual Report & Accounts 2012/13

"Increasingly, both our suppliers and our customers are showing us, tangibly, that this is valuable to them."[109] [my underlining]

Typically such changes are accompanied by a shift in emphasis from process to service, in terms of greater say in how things are done around here. This in turn potentially might lead by implication in flatter, more devolved, hierarchies.

It also leads in another critical multichannel direction: the need, and opportunity, to enhance the customer experience by increased personalisation... which is the subject of a later **Chapter 22**.

18.8 Culture Clash

Figure 79 - Multichannel culture clash?

Recently I helped a client select a new supplier to implement part of its new Multichannel I.T. platform. A noticeable feature of every single supplier presentation was a promise to use "hybrid agile methodology". Hybrid methodologies such as this example from I.T. are not caused by multichannel retail of course, but they are an interesting symptom.

A good reason for a retailer to consider holding their organisation at the *Distributed* stage is the culture clash, typically manifesting itself in differing expectations over the speed of change, between new (fast) and old (stable) channels. Partly this is a consequence of the differences in customer feedback cycle; tools such as online analytics mean that you can often see if a change to a website is working within 48 hours, and if it isn't you can reverse it. It's pretty difficult to do this with a brick-and-mortar store refit. The fact that it is so easy to use a suck-it-and-see approach in online

---

[109] Ibid. There is a persistent rumour, never confirmed or denied (which is generally taken to mean that it is true!), that this multichannel retailer enjoys better trade terms from its suppliers than online pureplays in the same categories, hence that fascinating word "tangibly" in the quotation.

channels means that planning is relatively a bit less important, and flexibility and responsiveness a bit more important, than offline.

The crunch comes when you start to implement genuinely multichannel propositions, such as click-and-collect (see **Chapter 21**), or endless aisle products which can be paid for at the same counter as in-store goods, and which therefore require change to be fully synchronised between offline and online. While such concepts can become a catalyst for organisational change, they are more likely to succeed if the change has been made first.

18.9   The whole business

Perhaps the key takeaway from all this is that being multichannel affects the whole organisation.

> If your multichannel strategy does not change the job description of every individual in the organisation, then you have the wrong multichannel strategy.

Back-office teams like HR and Finance just as much a part of multichannel as an obviously impacted area like marketing or I.T. Just as much as online orders need delivering, new KPIs need setting and measuring, which is the subject of the next chapter.

18.10   Top Takeaways

Incremental organisational headcount can be loosely predicted, but every organisation is different.

Incremental tasks include: marketing & merchandising, online marketing, webshop management, data administration, fulfilment, customer-service.

Running a website is very labour intensive!

Customers must perceive one brand, one experience. A proactive organisation plan is required to ensure that a customer experience always appears multichannel.

A four-phase maturity model describes retailers' evolution towards multichannel organisation: Rebellion (or Sponsored Revolution), Distributed, Focussed, Multichannel.

Rebellion: an organisational manifestation of channel conflict (See **Chapter 19** below).

Distributed: separate teams but with co-operating targets;

Focussed: joint teams but with channel-based targets;

Multichannel: one team, one target.

Practical challenges that may need to be overcome include: broader roles, clicks in traditionally bricks jobs, new KPIs, new budget relationships, blending different speeds of change and approaches to planning, more powerful roles at the customer-interface.

Clicks jobs may appear in traditionally bricks functions: product data management in logistics for example.

Store staff may need to become better trained and equipped to handle highly informed customers who have already done online research. There can be direct commercial benefits, both in terms of sales and trade terms, in doing so.

The culture clash, especially in terms of flexibility and responsiveness versus stability and reliability, between online and offline, needs careful management and should form part of organisational design.

If your multichannel strategy does not change the job description of every individual in the organisation, then you have the wrong multichannel strategy.

Chapter 19.   Measurement and Targets

19.1   Analytics

On a <u>single digital channel</u> such as a retailer website it is possible to monitor every customer through every page of their journey. Online you don't monitor them by name - usually, and especially not without permission! - but in aggregate (although see **Chapter 22** on personalisation and loyalty). Typically interesting is information about which products and pages get the most visitors, their effectiveness in doing what they are supposed to do such as "get the customer to add this product on this page into their shopping cart", and the transitions from one page to the next.

Analytics is built around the idea of measuring goals. The usual goal for a retailer is to get customers to buy something, and so a typical analytics report (funnel report) will look something like **Figure 80**.

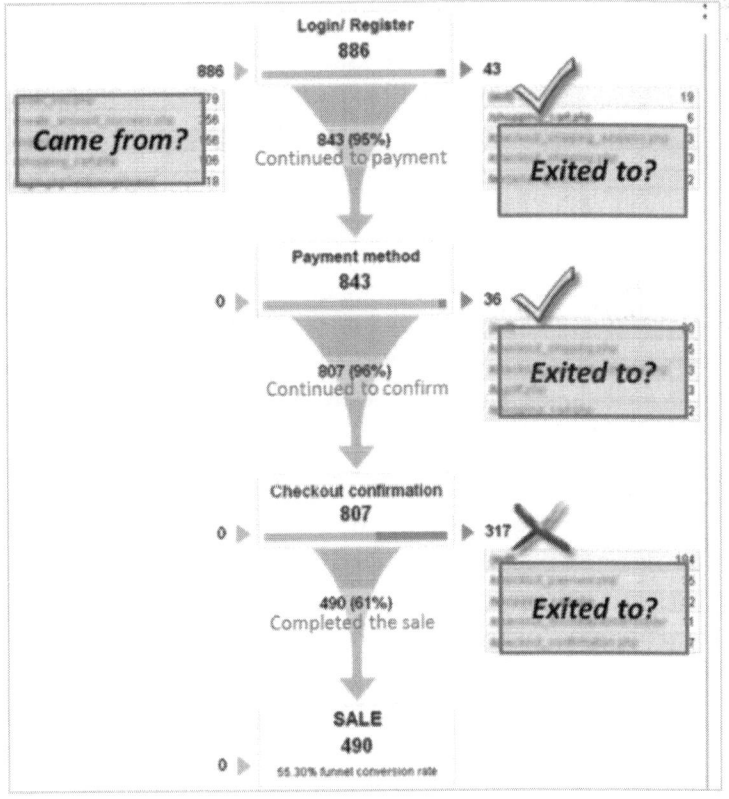

Figure 80 - Analytics conversion funnel

In this example the retailer has a good checkout in terms of retaining customers through it, but then some sort of problem with the checkout confirmation screen – at a guess this is probably a case of "sticker shock" unanticipated charges such as taxes or high shipping fees. Being able to quickly spot this kind of issue, and then do something about it, is one aspect where online retailing is much easier than brick-and-mortar, but also more data-intensive.

Failing to do all this is flying blind, a bit like running a corner-store without ever watching your customers shopping in it. Since there are even freeware tools available (such as Google Analytics – as always no endorsement or otherwise implied), there is no excuse not to monitor website analytics. It's one of the absolute basic disciplines.

19.2   A/B testing

A related use of analytics is for A/B-testing processes (or multivariate testing if you want to be an advanced user and change more than one thing at once). You try two different versions of something – say the special offer banner on the home page – and then measure which one is more effective in achieving your goals, be that checkouts or just visitors to the details of the offer. More sophisticated IT systems will let you do this testing simultaneously, by randomly serving up customers with the two different versions (typically in a 50/50 split for something like a new promotional graphic, or a 90/10 split for something scary like a new checkout process which might actually make things worse not better).

Because you can often get statistically meaningful results in less than 24 hours, it's incredibly powerful despite its apparent simplicity.

There are two schools of thought in this area: one is that you should make small incremental changes and measure-as-you-go, and the other that you should make bold large-scale changes, give them a while to settle in, and then decide whether reverse out or not. Personal experience tends to put me in the big-and-bold school but in reality this obviously depends on the circumstances of the particular change.

19.3   Online Channel KPIs

A consequence of everything online being so easily directly measurable is that almost every business process can have some sort of key performance indicator associated to it, and so you can end up with a huge list. At a high level, I suggest the following two short lists as a starting place. Although the list is very short, it includes at least one KPI which measures the most critical objective of each contributing function. It also includes those KPIs which most easily maintain a healthy tension between functions. For example, gross demand could be easily enhanced by making impossible shipping promises, which would then adversely impact OTIF and probably delivered margin.

Firstly, monitoring online marketing (*Figure 81*):

KPI	Description
Visitors	This is the simplest KPI of all, and is universally measured.[110] Typically it is broken down further via analytics to consider the different channels of marketing spend (did this checkout arrive via SEO, affiliate marketing, PPC etc)
Gross Demand	Total value of the orders checked out on website
Acquisition cost	marketing spend per "new" (the definition varies) purchasing customer, or more simply per checkout. Again typically this is broken down further via analytics to consider the different channels of marketing spend (did this checkout arrive via SEO, affiliate marketing etc)
Net Churn	New unique customers giving you enough information to market or re market them effectively *minus* existing customers who have not recently visited

Figure 81 - Website marketing KPIs

---

[110] ...and was accidentally omitted from the previous addition of this Handbook, sorry!

Secondly, monitoring trading (*Figure 82*):

KPI	Description
Net Sales	Value of orders net of returns and refunds (typically the equivalent target of gross demand but for buying)
Delivered margin	Gross margin + fees (delivery, services) – direct delivery/shipping costs
Conversion rate	Overall percentage of website visitors who checkout.
Conversion rate by ...	...category or product or price-range or promotion or banner or... I included this one just to give a taste for how quickly the volume of data and reporting can build up. A good case can be made for routinely monitoring any or all of these, depending on where your focus is.

Figure 82 - Website trading KPIs

Finally, monitoring the efficiency and effectiveness of the operation (*Figure 83*).

KPI	Description
Contacts per order	Ratio of customer contacts (phone, email, service desk in store, twitter etc) per order checked out
OTIF	On Time In Full. The % of checked out orders which were fully and successfully delivered to the customer within the published service levels
Assortment serviceability	The % of the published online assortment which is actually available for customers to purchase (usually measured at the start of the day).
Site availability	% of time that the site was fully functional for customers (this is often measured by an external "heartbeat monitoring" service, and/or in more sophisticated retailers by application performance management tools). It's best to try and measure this "externally" i.e. from the web, not from inside your own infrastructure.

Figure 83 - Operational efficiency KPIs

19.4 Multichannel Multipliers: The Halo Effect?

In the introductory **Chapter 2**, I quoted some studies which claim to show that multichannel customers spend more with you. The reality on the ground is that, while it seems to be generally anecdotally accepted, it's extremely difficult to prove. Almost all studies are methodologically flawed in a way that would make any first year student wince: they tend to assume correlation implies causality.[111]

The proposition of the halo effect is rather simple:

> **Argument A: Angels with Halos**
>
> 1. your multichannel customers can be proven to spend more - in total across all channels - than single channel customers
>
> 2. therefore being multichannel increases overall sales, because your customers will spend more

The trouble with this logic is that the whole argument can be turned around:

> **Argument B: Cannibals**
>
> 1. your best customers spend more with you
>
> 2. these same best customers are more likely to want to reach you via multiple channels
>
> 3. if you don't offer these additional channels, they'll go somewhere else

In this logic, it's still a good idea to be multi-channel, but it isn't really increasing sales, just preventing falling sales. Or put more succinctly, cannibalising yourself is preferable to being cannibalised by someone else. It's the macro-effect we discussed in **Chapter 13** transferred to the micro-level of the single customer.

In fact in some countries and/or verticals - probably most - the argument can be taken one step further:

---

[111] And, as with rather a lot of online shopping data points, they often conduct their surveys online (because it's much cheaper) – which is guaranteed to bias their samples

> **Argument C: Cannibals with Halos**
>
> 1. richer customers spend more
>
> 2. richer customers are more likely to have access to the internet, and/or to own multiple devices for accessing the internet - smart-phone, tablet, laptop, home PC, office PC etc
>
> 3. therefore customers who spend more are more likely to be multichannel customers
>
> 4. if you don't offer these additional channels, they'll go somewhere else

The challenge is particularly one of measurement. Very few retailers know at a customer-by-customer level exactly who is spending with them, especially in store. Doing so requires both a multichannel loyalty scheme (see **Chapter 22**) used by a statistically valid sample of customers which allows you to log who is spending both online and at point-of-sale in store, and a sufficient frequency of spending. Few retailers meet these criteria, and even fewer will willingly publish data if they do.

One that did, in early 2014, was Tesco. As noted in the comments on the validity of data in **Chapter 3,** it should always be remembered that retailers usually publish data points to make their case, not for general interest. In this particular case, Tesco was trying to prove the validity of its multichannel approach. So, caveat lector, here is what they showed (**Figure 84**).

So now *you* decide if this is cause or effect? Does using Tesco's online grocery service really *cause* customers to spend more in their stores? And taking this one step further, does purchasing from their general merchandise website as well as the grocery website actually cause a customer to spend two thirds more in store as well?

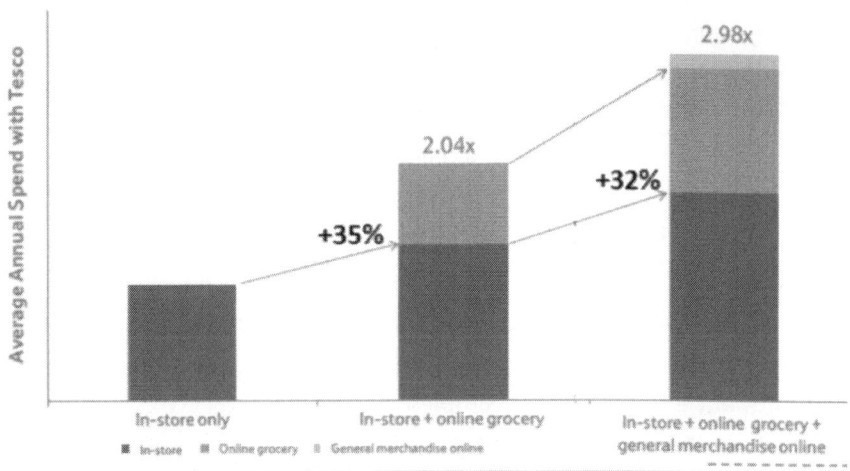

Figure 84 - Measuring the multichannel halo effect[112]

I like the idea; it helps justify the existence of jobs like mine. Judging from a Google search for the phenomenon, lots of other people with a vested interest in multichannel like the idea too. But does it really stand up enough to build a business-case from? Personally I'm much more comfortable with the Cannibals argument (B) above: you need to be multichannel because otherwise your best customers will go elsewhere.

19.5   Channel conflict

One group of stakeholders that is extremely unlikely to buy into the Halo effect quickly is your brick-and-mortar store managers. A general hazard facing any brick and mortar business which becomes multichannel is that of Channel Conflict.

19.5.1 Channel Conflict in practice.

In the simplest case, the (brick-and-mortar) <u>stores perceive that the non-store channels are "stealing our sales and customers"</u>. Taken to extremes, the multichannel retailer can end up creating entities which

---

[112] Tesco "Winning in the New Era of Retail", February 2014. Note that the percentage uplifts are mine, made by the not very scientific approach of counting pixels on their original slide. Tesco did *not* include a vertical axis on their original chart, and one has to question why not. They did, however, note that this behaviour was consistent across all customer affluence groups.

compete instead of collaborating. At its worst, this can lead to unfortunate behaviours such as store staff failing to steer customers towards the website, even when their store is currently out-of-stock or doesn't range the particular article the customer wants to buy but the website does.

As the trend towards true multichannel continues, this is unsustainable, and current best-practice is increasingly to integrate (see the previous chapter on multichannel organisational design), but this is not something that can be made to happen overnight.

Of course it is best if multichannel is implemented with full support from all stakeholders. The reality is inevitably that in a brick-and-mortar retailer introducing new retailing approaches, there are different levels of commitment and buy-in. The simplest way to ensure harmony in the early days of multichannel operations is to align KPIs and incentives, most especially in ensuring that stores are key supporters of all multichannel initiatives, whether these directly benefit the stores or not. (Typical contentious issues include increased rates of returns-to-store driven by non-store orders, handling costs of click-and-collect, reduction in takings at the store even while overall sales are growing, channel-specific promotional prices drawing attention away from the store).

19.5.2 Financial treatment options

The following basic accounting treatments are typical of new online operations added to existing brick-and-mortar retail operations.

Separate P&L: Both sales and costs associated with the non-store operations are captured into a separate financial structure. (Whether this needs to be a separate legal entity is normally determined mainly by esoteric tax considerations).

Lost in the wash: Non-store is not treated as separate at all. While this is theoretically ideal, in practice it represents a level of organisational maturity that very few multichannel retailers are yet ready for.

Virtual store: The sales are captured separately, as are the specialist costs (e.g. for fulfilment), but cost areas like category management are shared across the business. In practice this is a recipe for exacerbating channel conflict issues and I suggest it should be avoided.

Wooden dollars (recommended): Online costs are captured into distinct central (head-office) cost-centres. Online sales (and cost of sales, so therefore margin) are attributed to stores, sometimes depending on the extent to which stores have to participate in the selling, fulfilment and returns process.

19.5.3 Wooden dollars in practice

The principle is simple: *all sales are store sales*, no matter which channel they were actually transacted on. A basic implementation of this approach is as follows:

i) Each sale and cost-of-goods (and by implication margin) made to a non-store customer is <u>ALWAYS assigned to a store</u>. The algorithm for so doing depends on the retailer business model; if a "home-store" for the customer is available, that is used. An practical alternative is to use postal/zip code catchment areas

ii) The stores are allowed to count these sales/margin towards their KPIs

iii) Because stores are benefiting in this way, they are also expected to handle any returns from the non-store channels in a standard way, even if this means writing the occasional stock-loss into the store books. Because non-store sales usually generate a higher returns rate than brick-and-mortar, retailers with a big enough percentage of non-store sales (e.g. in fashion) will adjust their store stock-loss KPI.

Iv) All non-margin related non-store costs are kept in central cost centres attributed to non-store activities

v) The non-store teams get a normal P/L or KPIs, except that the sales & margin lines are "virtual" (thereby ensuring no double-counting). Sales, cost-of-goods (& margin) are written into this P/L so that the non-store team can be given business KPIs as though the eCommerce was a standalone business

A reasonable variation which is also sometimes seen is to pay stores a "commission" for handling non-store sales. This is especially common where click and collect type propositions exist (***Chapter 21***), and stores therefore have a cost of handling associated parcels and customers. As customer journeys get more complex, and concepts such as endless aisle are implemented, commission-type arrangements run the risk of becoming impractically complex – the basic rule that all sales are stores sales rule is much easier to manage and, equally importantly, to explain to staff. If your store-staff are on commission, it's also much easier to build an appropriate incentive structure. Here's an example where a large retailer has found such a change significantly beneficial enough to mention in its annual accounts:

"...our store colleagues are [now] rewarded for all sales in their catchment". [113]

19.6   Channel conflict and internal targets

19.6.1 New key performance indicators and targets

As the organisation moves through the phases of multichannel maturity, the ways in which internal channel conflict is resolved, and channel collaboration becomes the norm, will need to keep changing. *Figure 85* maps this evolution onto the 4-stage multichannel maturity model from the previous chapter.

---

[113] Dixons Retail, Annual Report & Accounts 2012/13. Another interesting published example by a retailer faced with the extra challenge that its stores are semi-independently owned franchises is the German-based multinational Media-Saturn: see their presentation "Media Saturn Group Online Strategy" July 2011

Organisation Phase	KPI structures
Rebellion	In conflict! The quickest way to control (and then sponsor) the Rebellion is by implementing targets along the lines described in the Distributed model in the next line. At the very least, incentivise co-operation with this new thing, even if a full set of duplicated "for the other channel too" targets is not put in place.
Distributed	There will typically be "parallel" departments in some areas – online marketing and offline marketing for example. Each should have its own targets for its main channel focus, but each should also be given targets specifically around supporting the other channel(s). For example an offline campaign will *also* be measured around online success, and an online campaign not just measured on additional visitors to the website but also on additional visitors to stores (or some indirect but equivalent method, such as the increase in take-up of the online store-locator – incidentally this example is quite a common one).
Focussed	One department, with (equally important) targets for each channel. Specific individuals or sub-sections, whose job might be heavily weighted or exclusively focussed towards a particular channel, should have targets structured similarly to the Distributed model, but the overall function and its senior management should not.
Multichannel	One department, one target. When you have reached the point where it doesn't matter which channel a sale (or any other activity for that matter) is made on, then you have come full circle, and are measuring yourself in a fully multichannel way. In the "ideal" model, all individuals are also similarly multichannel in their roles and targets. Inevitably in practice, of course, more junior jobs will always have some particular focus which may be channel specific, especially more technical roles. Such jobs should continue to have parallel targets as in the Distributed model.

Figure 85 - KPI structure by organisation development phase

19.6.2 New budget relationships?

Obviously it's not realistic to give people new targets without giving them the resources to deliver to them. While this might just be indirectly budgeted resources like headcount, it might also involve cross-overs in direct budget accountability. In **Chapter 14** in the section 'logistics is the new marketing', we considered a currently very visible situation; would you actually take this a step further and allocate some of that marketing budget to the logistics department, along with a sales-increment target to match?

Another real (i.e. some retailers have actually implemented it), but also illustrative example: a reasonably common accountability, and budgetary, switch along similar lines is in targets for returns rates in categories such as consumer electronics. A surprisingly high percentage of returns can be prevented by better information online (even if you don't have fully fledged eCommerce), access to better information in the call-centre, better information available to staff in-store – not just general information on policies, but specific information regarding product specifications, links to the online user guides typically available these days from most manufacturers, frequently-asked-questions. Maybe then the department accountable for product data management should also have the target, and associated budget, for waste? In some ways it is a very multichannel piece of organisational design: a function which at first sight looks like a new online function, actually responsible for a very old offline issue, and therefore targeted on building relationships with some of the most offline of all stakeholders – the traditional brick-and-mortar store management.

These examples also illustrate a secondary effect of multichannel: an increase in the number of *internal* organisational relationships that each stakeholder has. A potential benefit in accelerating towards a more genuinely multichannel organisation design is actually that the number of these relationships decreases again as a more conventional retail organisation model reasserts itself once more; in other words, although the roles get more complex, the actual organisation gets simpler (and possibly therefore slimmer and cheaper!) again.

19.7   Top Takeaways

Key KPIs for measuring online channel marketing: visitors, gross demand, acquisition cost, customer churn.

Key KPIs for measuring online channel trading: net sales, delivered margin, conversion rate.

Key KPIs for measuring online channel operations: contacts-per-order, OTIF, assortment serviceability, site availability.

The multichannel Halo effect is often demonstrable but difficult to prove causality: are you really seeing angels, or just cannibals with halos?

Internal channel conflict is a significant risk to retailer adding new channels to their operations.

KPIs and performance measurements should be aligned to reward inter-channel collaboration, not competition.

Multichannel affects the *whole* organisation. If your multichannel strategy does not change the job description of everybody in the organisation, you have the wrong multichannel strategy.

All sales should be considered store sales.

The Wooden Dollars approach is recommended as a starting point; measuring the success of new channels while simultaneously distributing its benefits to existing ones.

Internal targets need to drive channel collaboration, not channel conflict; these will reflect the progression along the organisational maturity model.

Wholly new targets, and interdepartmental relationships driven by them, may need to be created.

Chapter 20. Stores

20.1 Not so fast

OK, so you did everything in Part B, got online, and sorted out the initial channel conflict challenges. As we've already seen, you can reasonably expect to see a certain amount of cannibalisation of your real store sales, even if you camouflage that behind catchment-area attribution. Does that mean that the profitability of some of your store estate is now marginal and you should close some stores?

Well, some retailers have indeed initially drawn that conclusion. Best Buy is a good example. Best Buy announced the closure of 50 big-box stores in the US (as well as giving up on the lethal UK market altogether); the effects have – eventually - been profitable[114]. Tesco's CEO announced that "we've called time on the old retail 'space race'"[115]. Overall the effect was strong enough for the majority of analysts to predict an ongoing reduction in store rental space costs[116]. While this is bad news for landlords, it is extremely good news for multichannel retailers who will see an improvement in a key cost disadvantage compared to the online pure-plays. Does this then imply that a retailer planning its multichannel strategy should plan for a reduction in overall store numbers?

Not so fast.

Because that's exactly what your customers are going to be: not so fast. As online shopping has developed, the time a customer invests in making a purchase has increased by 33% (*Figure 86*):

---

[114] See for example:
http://www.trefis.com/company?hm=BBY.trefis&driver=idBBY.1368#
[115] Philip Clarke, Tesco CEO: speech to world retail congress, September 2012. This is one part of his generally ill-fated strategy that his successor has definitely *not* reversed, shutting further stores not long after taking over.
[116] See for example ING "the more clicks, the less bricks", October 2011

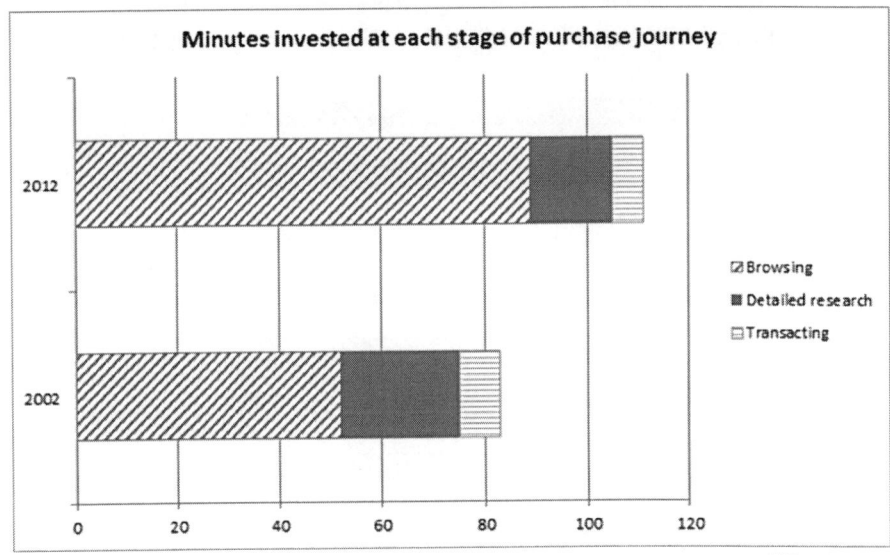

Figure 86 - 33% increase in time spent on a purchase[117]

The time spent on detailed research has reduced, because it's much easier to do detailed research online (familiar theme: provided that the product data provided is adequate). But the time spent on browsing has almost doubled. Some of that time will be spent browsing online, but actually much of this is incremental. Online is quite a bad place to browse, especially for touch and feel and sense categories: stores are still the best place for that, and the vast majority of customers in every country still do the majority of their browsing and researching in store (**Figure 87**); the percentage of customers doing research *only* online is small, even in very online countries.

[117] Conlumino, Thriving in a Multichannel World, May 2012

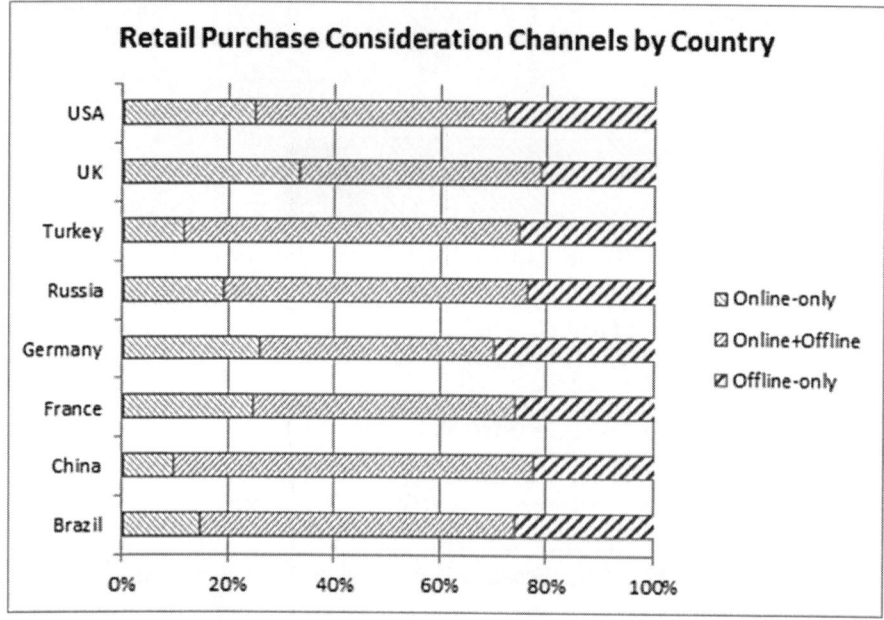

Figure 87 - Retail Purchase Consideration Channels[118]

The actual transaction might be made online, but it might not be made at all if you've closed the store that the consideration takes place in.

20.2 Changing places

If you are lucky enough to be a destination retailer, multichannel probably offers you the opportunity to have few stores, or to reduce the size of your store portfolio to flagships in major shopping areas plus multichannel catchment areas: a hub + online spokes approach. To use an obvious example, Apple covers its huge Chinese market with only 20 stores.[119] Even in the USA it only has 266, less than 1 per million of population.

For the typical retailer this might not be so clever. A clear illustration of why this might be so can be found in the published data from one of the most multichannel of all retailers, the UK's Argos (**Figure 88**).

[118] Google Consumer Barometer 2014
[119] www.apple.com/cn/retail/storelist/

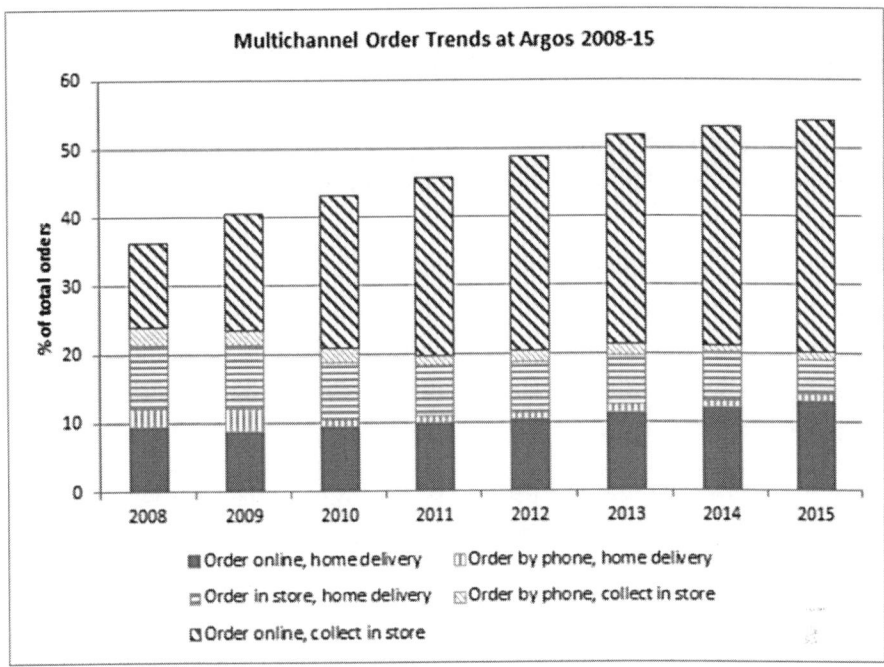

Figure 88 - Customer order multichannel trends at Argos[120]

One story is not unexpected, and consistent with equivalent channel shifts in other markets: telephone orders have continued to reduce steadily in importance, in the same way that, for example, German data shows a steady decline in mail-order that was traditionally strong locally[121]. Much more interesting, and far less predictable, is that the percentage of internet orders for home delivery has remained rather static for the last few years. In part this reflects mix (these orders are often for large items such as beds or white goods), but it sits in stark contrast with the relentless growth in order-online-collect-in-store (or Check & Reserve, as Argos calls it – the difference being that as a customer you don't pay online, you pay in the store when you pick up your goods).

So have brick-and-mortar store sales fallen as a proportion at Argos? Well, yes, initially as internet retailing was adopted by UK consumers, a percentage of the in-store business switched to internet home delivery, paralleling the ongoing switch from telephone/mail-order to internet

---

[120] Home Retail Group Annual Reports 2008-2015
[121] GfK data for Germany showed mail/phone-order sales falling by 25% in the period 2008-2011

ordering. But in the published data, certainly for the last 5 years, the percentage of sales that use the brick-and-mortar store channel in some way or other has remained rather static, *but the way in which customers use the stores has changed.*

The result for many retailers is a change in store profile, not a reduction in numbers. For example, while Best Buy closed 50 big box stores in 2012, it also opened 105 smaller format stores in 2013.[122] House of Fraser, a UK department store that you would think could reasonably adopt the destination plus catchment approach, has just opened its first new store for several years with the justification of "*a multichannel strategy to get closer to its customers*"[123].

> The key lesson: in a multichannel world, your stores might actually be essential for supporting your online sales channel.

Multichannel isn't a one-directional one-dimensional strategy in which store-sales gradually shift online, end-of-story. That's another reason why cross-channel measurements and KPIs, such as attributing online sales to stores by catchment-area are necessary: to ensure that your store estate contribution is correctly attributed.

Click-and-collect (pick-up-in-store) and its relatives might form part of this story, especially if you really are in the offline hub plus online spokes model, and is the subject of the next chapter.

20.3 From McJobs to iJobs

Take another look at *Figure 86*: customers are spending much longer in the consideration phases of their purchasing, despite the fact that the proliferation of the internet actually makes this an easier job: no more traipsing up-and-down the high street until you're reasonably sure where to focus for example. The consequence of this is that your customers will be much better informed once they actually arrive in your stores. And then, as *Figure 87* tells us, they intend to do still more research once they're through your doors.

---

[122] Best Buy 10K, 2013
[123] http://internetretailing.net/2015/06/next-step-in-house-of-frasers-multichannel-strategy-a-new-bricks-and-mortar-store/

With over 70% of all research taking place partially online in many categories, there's a big implication for store sales assistants, especially in "complex" categories such as consumer electronics: consumers are going to arrive in store already midway through their research and are therefore pretty clued-up about their candidate products. Sales assistants therefore need to be equipped to cope with such highly informed customers, the importance of which is attested by Best Buy's latest slogan:

In FY15, we articulated our value proposition around <u>advice, service</u> and convenience at competitive prices and started to use 'Expert Service. Unbeatable Price' as our signature"[124] *[my underlinings]*

In the UK, Halfords sounds a similar note when talking about its Reserve & Collect offer:

"Our product mix lends itself to a multi-channel offer as customers often want further advice, a demonstration or fitting. Online purchasing patterns reflect this, with 86% of sales on Halfords.com reserved and then collected from a store"[125]

Here the customer expectation that needs to be met is that store sales assistants will be more knowledgeable than the customer themselves, in this case not *before* the purchase during the research phase but *afterwards* when collecting.

Summarising, there is now so much information available online to consumers that they actually take longer to research purchases today than ten years ago. Channels might compete for the transaction itself, but the reality is that most consumers use multiple channels in collaboration to perform that research and make a purchase, including stores. When they visit those stores, their expectations are high: they will be well-informed consumers wanting to interact with well-informed staff. Retailers who understand this, and train their staff appropriately, see tangible rewards from doing so. Online is taking its share of the "process" steps in a retail transaction – for example taking money at the checkout – while at the same time raising the bar for the "service" steps. As a consequence,

---

[124] Best Buy CEO Hubert Joly's Letter to Shareholders, March 2015
[125] Halfords Group plc, Annual Report & Accounts, 2012. Their 2013 accounts state that this proportion increased further to 88%

retailers may need to change their store staff from simple processers to complex servicers... and their jobs from McJobs to iJobs.

20.4   Data

Increasing numbers of retailers are recognising this shift towards iJobs by giving their staff a more roving role, supported by tablet computers and/or more "intelligent" POS terminals. The tablet may provide many services, and might have a whole selection of features or dialogues, but at its most fundamental its purpose is to try and help ensure that the staff-member is at least as knowledgeable as the customer, and can actually add some value to the customer while he/she is in store. The added value, directly or indirectly, increases the chance of a sales conversion. Trustworthy data points in support of that assertion are scarce[126] by the way: there is plenty of anecdotal evidence, and it seems intuitively reasonable, particularly in retailers who employ large numbers of seasonal, peak-time or other temporary staff who inherently have little deep knowledge of their domain, and for whom a "wizard" in support can help them to step-change their ability to engage with the customer.

To achieve this, of course, you're back to the challenge of managing your product data (see **Chapter 12**), or more specifically, of deploying in ways that are useful to your store-staff (and other customer-facing operational staff such as your call-centre). Anecdotally, many head-office functions also benefit from the ready accessibility of product reference information, although it is difficult to quantify this in a business case. (Some retailers have experimented by going further and make (some of) their data available to 3rd parties to develop applications that in turn, drive sales for the retailer. At best this has rather mixed success.)

The next logical step is to enhance this basic data with rather less easily captured "knowledge". There are already some tools on the market which begin to attempt to interact with online customers in the way that a (human) sales assistant would, for example by asking a series of questions that attempt to drill down to the customer's need. These are essentially "knowledge based" and/or even self-learn dynamically (operating in a manner not dissimilar to the child's game animal, vegetable or mineral).

---

[126] Even more scarce than usual, that is!

Human beings remain a much better solution than IT for the true multichannel retailer, but even people still benefit from additional prompting, guidance and tools. Knowledge management systems are relatively well established – they are just better organised memories really – but screen-based conversational/interactive sales is still in its infancy, and any business case is likely to be speculative.

Sales channels operated by *computers* need to be heavily supported by additional merchandising data, including up-sells, cross-sells, taxonomies. Sales channels operated by *people,* however, need to equip their operators with tools to leverage the knowledge in an efficient way. *Figure 89* illustrates the flow.

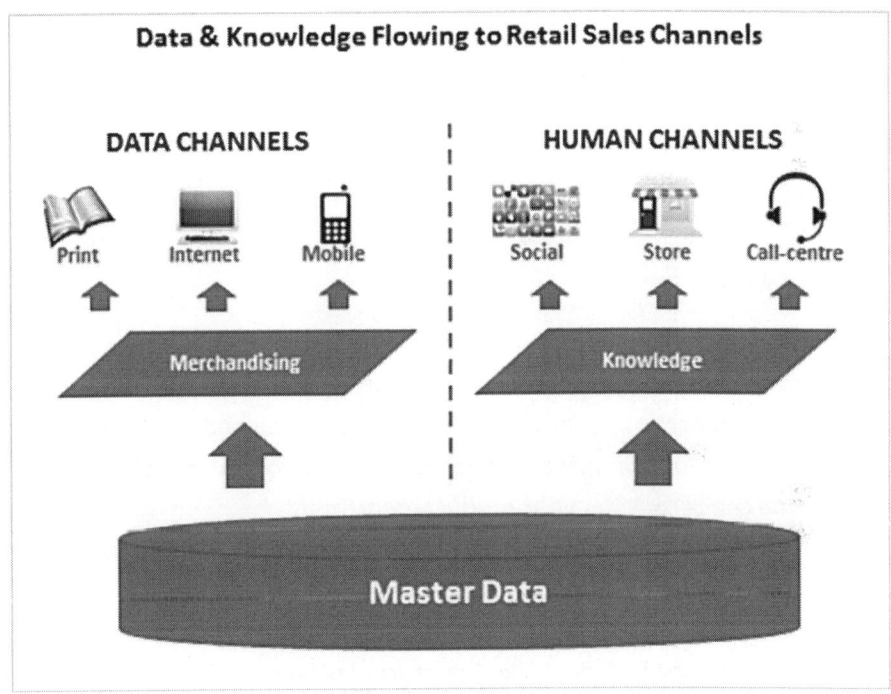

Figure 89 – Master Data & Knowledge Flow

Business cases for master data in data channels are probably most easily made on the basis of measures such as increased cart-size. Business cases for human channels most easily made on the basis of increased conversion or reduced costs (in various ways, from the straightforward e.g. reduced returns rates, to the more challenging reduced labour costs – cheaper people with better tools can replace better people with poor tools).

20.5   Wifi and the Time Dimension

Supplementing the sales-assistant-with-the-tablet is an increasing array of digital experiences in store (and in some case carried over into the online experience too), from virtual fitting rooms to massive TVs to gift-registry kiosks to... you name it. Interestingly the retailer with the clearest perspective on all this is an online pure-play:

"[we are] competing for a percentage of our... customer's <u>time</u> as well as an increasing percentage of their... purse."[127] *[my underlining]*

Besides all this gadgetry and wizardry to tempt and dazzle the in-store customer, retailers are increasingly competing for a percentage of their customer's time in a more direct way. Giving up on futile attempts to stop customers using mobile devices to check out their competitors while in-store, savvy retailers have now decided that offering free wireless broadband in-store at least keeps the customer a) happy and b) in there. Rather as click-and-collect leads to incidental purchases, simply extending visit times in a pleasant environment might lead to increased sales.

20.6   Mix

Finally, having re-sized your stores, reconfigured your store staff to make them more digital and service oriented, rearranged your stores to make them more of a leisure destination, redesigned your operating procedures and use of space to enable click-and-collect and endless aisle kiosks, you can reconsider your product assortment.

Developing the endless aisle concept, or even simply excluding "awkward" products from your store range, allows you to optimise your stores while still maintaining that critical Kompetenz discussed earlier. Some products are less than ideal in stores: pillows are a good example. They have a low price point, high space consumption (and logistics costs), and are unlikely to be a top-seller for most retailers. Nevertheless if you are operating in home-wares categories, you probably have to offer them. Some products are equally suboptimal in a non-store situation: mirrors and heating-oil are two examples.

---

[127] Asos.com, annual report 2011/12

Putting the right products on the right channels can be a good way of driving sales per square metre in store, conversions per visitor online, and profitability across all channels.

20.7 Top Takeaways

Destination retailers may be able to use multichannel to adopt a hub + online-spoke approach.

Retailers who are less of a destination are sometimes reducing the average *size* of their stores. In parallel, the same retailers are increasing the overall *number* of their stores, as convenience/proximity to the customer becomes more important.

Stores may still play an essential role in customers' shopping journeys: but that role may have changed; the transaction might now take place online.

The time customers spend on purchase-consideration has significantly increased, not reduced, with the growth of online retailing. This is despite the ease with which information can now be reached.

In most countries, for most categories, even very mature online markets, at least three quarters of customers do at least part of their research in-store.

Increasingly well-informed customers expect increasingly well-informed sales-assistants. The in-store focus may shift from transaction to information/service. The result is a change from McJobs to iJobs.

To enable this transition in a cost-effective way, retailers are increasingly supporting their in-store staff with knowledge-based technology. To do so, they need to enhance their product data flows with human-facing knowledge as well as digital-facing merchandising information.

Retailers are also recognising they need to compete for their customers' time, not just their wallets, and are supporting their use of technology in store instead of resisting it, for example by offering free WiFi.

Multichannel offers options to optimise the assortment-mix stocked in stores and online, to optimise sales per square metre offline and conversion online.

Part D – Enhancement

There is a valid truism that Retail is Detail. Successful retailing is often about getting the small things right, and gradually improving not violently step-changing. Once you have overcome the hurdle of getting online at all, it often makes sense to return to that step-by-step approach.

Nevertheless, there are some aspects of retailing where multichannel can offer profitable opportunities further step-changes in your operating-model and customer-proposition. Part D examines the most important.

Chapter 21.   Click-and-Collect

21.1   Why offer it?

Customers like click-and-collect (or "buy online, pick-up in store" as it's less euphoniously known in the US). Unfortunately one of the primary reasons they like it is to save on shipping fees (*Figure 90*). Click-and-collect in-store is almost always offered free; retailers who have tried charging for the service in store have found it impossible to explain to customers why there's a charge, and have quickly reverted to free[128]. However even retailers who routinely offer free shipping to home have seen high take-up of click-and-collect.

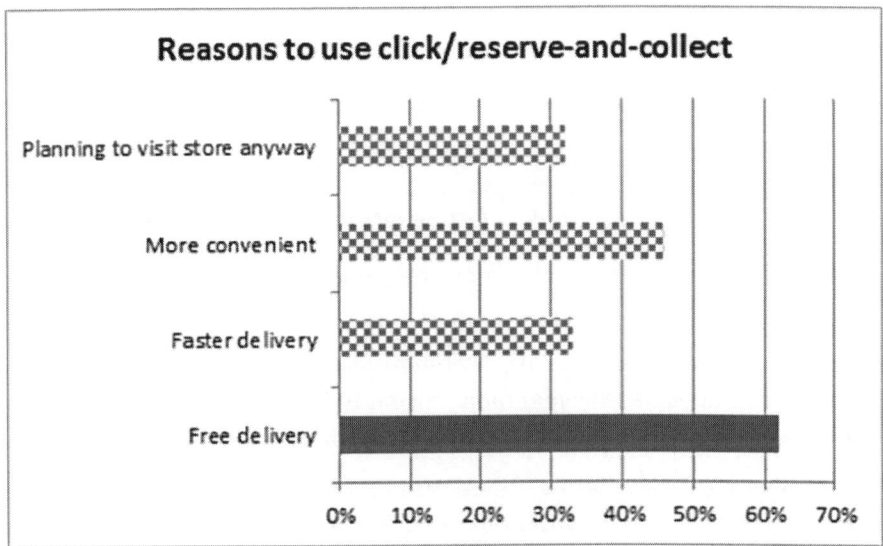

Figure 90 - Click-and-collect customer motivations[129]

"Trust" is one other that is missing from this chart but is mentioned by retailers themselves: retailers are trusted much better than carriers to get the goods on-time to the customer, especially prior to time-critical events such as Christmas or birthdays.

---

[128] Although John Lewis in the UK, a leader in this space, recently introduced a £2 collection charge for small-orders: those under £30, citing the economics of fulfilling very small orders for free as a motivation.

[129] IMRG eDigitalResearch eCSI Click & Collect Survey – January 2015

Reliable public domain data points remain elusive. I created **Figure 91,** about the take-up of click-and-collect in the UK, in mid-2012 for my blog, and then included it in the previous edition of this Handbook.

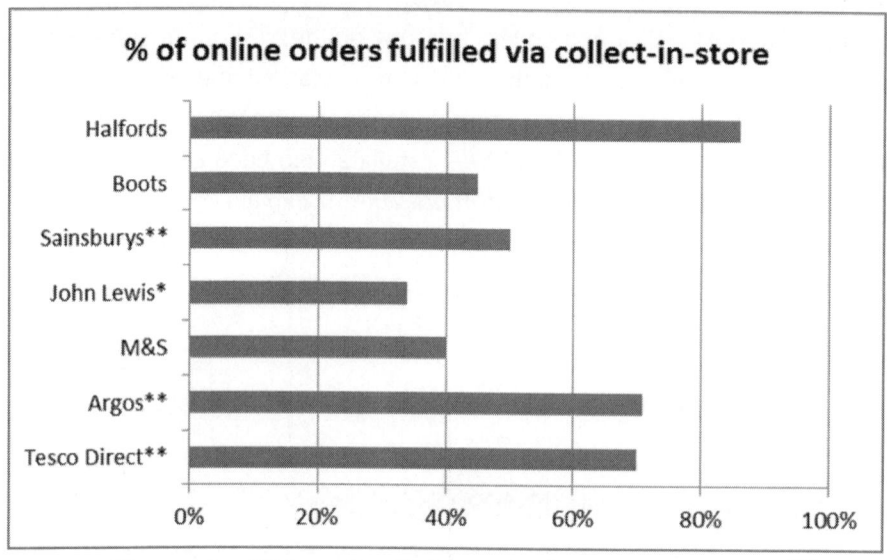

% of online orders fulfilled via collect-in-store

Figure 91 – Click-and-collect penetration by retailer, 2011[130]

It's been far and away the most referenced chart I've ever created, suggesting that it has probably appeared in a lot of internal business-case presentations subsequently. Its message has remained true, particularly because take-up is usually very rapid once it is offered (...for free). The 40% of Marks & Spencer's orders fulfilled in this way was a level arrived at after only around a year of offering the service.

The UK led the way in this space, but retailers elsewhere have seen the benefits and followed suit. Here's an updated version of the same chart[131] (**Figure 92**) showing an increasingly level of take-up in the US:

---

[130] Figures marked ** exclude "impossible" articles such as beds or large freezer cabinets and also exclude grocery; figures for John Lewis (*) were for orders placed on the John Lewis website but collected in sister brand Waitrose's stores, therefore actual John Lewis figures are much higher; there's a true data-point in the next chart. Sainsburys also observed that the percentage of general merchandise orders collected in store rises from 50% to around 75% during the Christmas peak.

[131] It's been noticeable that UK retailers have "moved on" in seeing click-and-collect as worthy of note; their annual reports used to proudly state the

Figure 92 - Click-and-collect penetration by retailer, 2015 update[132]

Not only do customers appreciate click-and-collect, but retailers do too[133]:

"35% of our orders are being collected in store, and even more than that from customers in a store catchment area. Of those we also know that a significant proportion are truly incremental, as customers would not have purchased from us without it. Add on the fact that 25% of people make an unplanned add on purchase when in the store..."[134]

Although it isn't quantified by any numbers, an observation in made the formal setting of the annual report is also noteworthy:

percentage of orders collected – this has markedly diminished as it has become business-as-usual

[132] Data mainly sourced from annual reports (UK) or 10-Ks (US). One or two are bit more elusive and so the sources are press interviews by senior executives

[133] The two quotations that follow are from UK retailers in 2012 and 2015. The following roughly equivalent 2014 data-point for the US "Over 40% of ... merchant in-store pickup orders result in additional sales when the shopper visits the store" suggests an approximately consistent behaviour in the 30-40% range might become a global standard as buy-online, pick-up in store rolls out. However it comes from a vendor of solutions in the space (Shopatron – as always, no recommendation or otherwise implied) who obviously have a vested interest

[134] Andrew Harding, Director of eCommerce at House of Fraser, interview October 2012 with eConsultancy

"...customers like the convenience of buying online, but also want to visit our stores for our expert advice and value-adding services. 91% of online sales were collected in-store, providing <u>opportunities for store colleagues to engage with online customers</u>" (my underlining)[135]

It isn't so often that you can find a service that customers actively like, that generates incremental sales, and that offers a chance to differentiate from online pureplays, all rolled into one!

21.2 Implementation

One extra stakeholder group that is fan of click-and-collect is consultants, because planning it can be used to illustrate many of the concepts and issues of multichannel retail. To begin with, it is a particularly clear example of proposition differentiation by convenience (**Chapter 9**), as well as something truly multichannel where brick-and-mortar combined seamlessly with online has a genuine advantage over either channel separately. In turn, planning its implementation brings together several of the essential concepts we have discussed in this book (**Figure 93**).

Figure 93 - Click-and-collect planning flow

21.2.1 Available to Promise

See **Chapter 15**. The most fundamental question to consider when planning a click-and-collect proposition is where you will pick the order, and therefore what stock (and by implication service level) you will promise to the customer. The immediate reaction – you've already shipped stock to your stores, surely you should pick it there – is not necessarily the right one. In fact many click-and-collect implementations pick their orders in a central fulfilment centre exactly like home-delivery orders, and then ship them to the stores. There a several reasons for this, at first sight illogical, choice including the following.

Confidence in the promise: most retailers have minimal or non-existent back-of-store warehousing areas. The best place for in-store stock is where customers can see it and buy it, out on the shop floor. If an

---

[135] Halfords plc Annual Report 2015

online order arrives in the store, can you be confident that the stock will be out there when you come to try and pick it? For many retailers, the answer is no: stock control accuracy or shrinkage might already be an issue; high velocity retailers can expect a percentage of stock to be in customers shopping carts and therefore neither available nor booked-out at point-of-sale; stock-control units might be in shipping units not individual items.

Picking process quality: a specialist fulfilment centre will devote a high proportion of its working time and business process investment into ensuring that orders are accurately picked. It is difficult to replicate this in store. Although in theory errors can be easily corrected in store, in practice many customers do not actually check the contents of their order item-by-item during the collection process.

Endless Aisle SKUs: if your multichannel proposition includes an endless aisle, then some or all of the products a customer might order will not be in store. If part of an order cannot be picked in the store, why not pick all of it anyway in the specialist fulfilment centre, where you are more likely to pick it right?

Reservation of stock: some retailers find it very difficult to physically separate out stock reserved for customer orders from stock generally on sale.

Paperwork: an online order, even one collected in store, requires some associated paperwork (see **Chapter 15**). Equipping stores to print this paperwork may be difficult.

If these issues can be overcome in your organisation however, then picking in store offers two important advantages. It's basically simpler, and it's definitely faster: you can make very aggressive customer promises – order online, ready to collect in an hour – which might be an advantage depending on your location and customers. Although it's not a retail example, takeaway pizza is a simple case-study where all the above issues are easily overcome and a timely promise makes a big difference.

It's also, at least theoretically, cheaper because you are picking from stock moved in bulk-store-replenishment. Remember that customers expect click-and-collect orders to be free of shipping fees. (See shipping below). In less geographically compact countries, such as the US or Russia, picking from store might be the more realistic option. Home Depot is the US, for example, operates both buy-online pick-in-store and buy online, ship-to-store, depending on the nature of the SKU and its membership of the core range vs long-tail.

21.2.2 Online checkout changes

If you are planning to pick from a central warehouse, then the changes required are fairly simple. There needs to be an option for the customer to locate and specify a collection store in addition to the existing dialogue to provide a delivery address. (If you are proposing to use a local collection partner service like Relais Colis in France, then these pick up points need to be included too. For most purposes, such services appear *to the retailer* almost the same as home delivery – they are not click-and-collect for the purpose of this chapter).

If you will also offer pick-up in store, then checkout becomes more complicated. Standard practice is to invite the customer to specify a location, and then display possible nearby pick-up destinations in a matrix of available-to-promise somewhat like *Figure 94*.

	Buda Store	**Pest Store**	
Product A	In Stock	In Stock	Click here to see other nearby stores
Product B	In Stock	X	
Product C	X	In Stock	

Figure 94 - Pick-up in store checkout availability matrix

The critical objective is to avoid the leading the customer into a never-ending journey of "no, not in stock there either, why don't you have another guess?" by at least displaying several plausible options on a single screen.

This is a relatively busy display, and so adapting it for smartphone display requires some care. Busy customers on the move – mobile customers – are the most likely to use a click-and-collect service, so this is definitely one screen that repays careful device-specific design (see *Chapter 23*). Having successfully persuaded the customer to navigate this, getting them through payment options may be a screen too far, which helps explain why pay-on-collection ("reserve-and-collect") might be especially suitable for smartphone users.

21.2.3 Shipping

If your choice is to pick in a central fulfilment location and then ship to stores, the shipping method becomes an issue. Mixing customer parcels with bulk distribution challenges is a step too far for many retailers' logistics; typically only those whose range consists of items which ship in large individual boxes or those who operate a cage-distribution network can easily blend bulk and parcel shipping together. The rest will use a similar shipping method as for parcel home-delivery, although of course it makes sense to try and negotiate some processes and discounts when several parcels will be consistently moving each day to a well-defined set of store locations: one consolidated fee per destination, not per parcel being the typical structure.

If you have chosen an aggressive promise – order today, collect tomorrow – then it may be necessary to be quite specific about timings. The order not only has to arrive in store, it has to be recognised, probably logged, and taken to a collection point. A closer look at many retailers promises reveals statements like "order by 6pm, collect after 2pm tomorrow", which gives enough time to pick centrally, ship to store during the morning, and register and file before a customer can come and collect.

21.2.4 Payment policy

If you already have a payment-on-delivery policy (see **Chapter 15**), then there's not too much to change. Amending this to pay-on-collection requires only minor changes to your order lifecycle. Ensuring that your point-of-sale is able to take payments for parcels of goods whose price was determined yesterday on the website may require some modifications. Most retailers do not scan individual SKUs at collection (and can't price them based on what the customer saw yesterday online in any case). Not only do customers not necessarily want to open up parcels already nicely packed for collection and transport, but for many retailers scanning this "non-store" stock would create unacceptable complications in replenishment or financial systems. If you don't want to start with a fully integrated systems solution, then answer is typically to scan a pre-printed whole-order pricing barcode on the invoice or parcel.

Collect-in-store orders have a higher risk of customer no-shows. If you just incurred all the costs of shipping the parcel to the store, without being able to charge a shipping fee, and the customer then fails to turn up, this can be expensive and irritating, doubly so if the products are from the endless-aisle range and therefore not easy to put back on the shelves. Payment-on-despatch or payment-on-order might therefore be preferred to payment-on-collection; a customer perception that they have already paid discourages no-shows, even though ultimately a refund would be forthcoming in any case.

Payment-on-despatch mixed with not picking in store requires a tricky technical issue to be resolved: when actually did the despatch happen? I'll risk a recommendation here: the despatch happens when the goods leave the central fulfilment warehouse, consistently with the despatch of orders for home-delivery. Moreover from the perspective of your financial systems, the goods are no longer "stock" once they leave the central warehouse nor when they are temporarily residing in the store. Instead they are parcels which the customer already owns. You are just a shipping agent and your stores now have a secondary role as post-offices. Set up your financial systems and processes accordingly.

Having a different payment policy for collect-in-store orders compared to home-delivery orders is really only practical if you will ensure that customers cannot place split orders – some goods to be collected, some to be delivered, altogether in the same order. This is less an issue of available-to-promise, more an issue of checkout usability. The most likely situation where this might arise is if you prefer pay-on-collection for orders from a smartphone while sticking with pay-on-order or pay-on-despatch from other channels. You have to balance between potentially lost sales by restricting the customer in this manner versus the complexity which would arise from split orders with mixed payment policies: simplicity usually wins this argument every time, not just in your IT department, but also in the interests of a checkout customers can actually successfully navigate.

21.2.5 Other order lifecycle issues

No-shows are the big downside of collect-in-store; they're like returns but with additional costs and complexity. Minimising their frequency is worth some investment. It makes sense to send frequent messages to the customer – this is one situation where the use of SMS is wholly legitimate – to remind them to collect.

The related question is how long to hold the items in store before treating the customer as a no-show. The minimum realistic minimum is seven days: the customer has chosen collection in order to choose a time convenient to them, and since most people's lives are built around weekly cycles, ensuring a complete week is available for collection makes sense. Good practice is probably therefore 14 days, allowing the customer to miss a week, assuming space constraints permit. In practice, the majority of customers will collect within 72 hours.

21.2.6 Fraud prevention

First the opportunity: a collecting customer who paid up-front needs to show some ID, solving lots of the multichannel identification challenges described in the chapter on personalisation (*Chapter 22*). In fact the collection process can be really omni-channel, with an online order from a PC being collected in a brick-and-mortar store supported by a mobile proof-of-order and a paper ID following a telephone reminder from the call-centre.

The corresponding problem is that proof of ID requirement. If your payment policy is pay-on-order or pay-on-despatch, then it is necessary to take steps to prevent fraud. All paid-in-advance click-and-collect propositions require both proof of order (confirmation message printed out or on shown on mobile) plus proof of ID to be shown. If you want someone else to collect, then either that person has to show your ID as well as theirs, or you have to specify exactly who will collect at the time you place the order.

21.2.7 Collection desk

The first question is location. There is obviously a minimum space requirement, including secure storage for parcels. Assuming you have some choice, then location is a choice between maximising convenience for the customer – preferred parking and a desk location near the door – versus maximising incremental sales for the retailer – usually a location requiring the customer to walk through as much of your casual takeaway assortment as possible. Incremental sales usually win this battle.

Secondly, remember that customer behaviour at the point of collection can vary. Some customers will simply take their parcel and leave. Some will (hopefully) bring additional purchases made in store to check out. Some will open their parcel at the counter; if there are issues with it, you are faced with instantaneous customer service requirements for replacement, refund or advice. In retailers where collect-in-store traffic is not big enough to justify a separate desk, a natural merger is between any existing customer desk and the collection desk, partly because the additional customer service skills overlap so much.

21.3 Cultural Differences

As we will explore further in **Chapter 26** about International and X-border, multichannel and eCommerce is *not* the same everywhere in the world, and in fact click-and-collect is one of those areas which display considerable cultural variation.

Collect-in-store is not the preferred model, even in the geographically compact and highly urban countries of western Europe, for example (*Figure 95*).

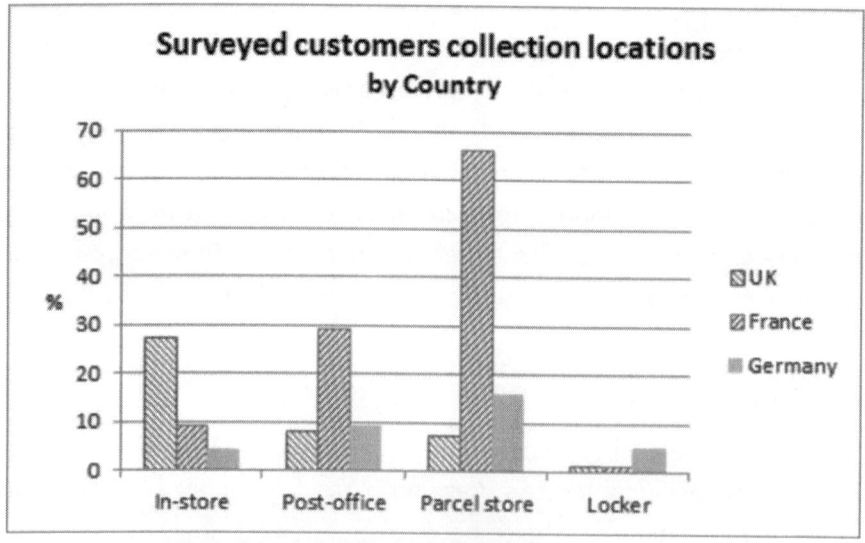

Figure 95 - Collection locations used, by country[136]

---

[136] Hermes Parcel deliveries usage and attitudes survey, 2014. Note that French numbers for parcel-stores are probably partially exaggerated by the prevalence of the "Drive" grocery concept. See Chapter 25 for more information.

Obviously if you don't bring such customers into your stores, you won't benefit *directly* from any incremental purchases made in them; of course you may well be benefitting already from incremental sales made due to the extra convenience you are offering by enabling nearby collection at a parcel-store, locker or post-office.

Some of these differences may be due to market-maturity, but some are genuine cultural differences: I can remember having great difficulty explaining to a German client that a British customer would use the website to purchase at their convenience *and then visit the store anyway* to pick-up the order.

In geographically less compact, or less urban, countries, the only logistical model that might make sense is picking-in-store; free shipping might otherwise be prohibitively costly. This in itself can restrict the applicability of click-and-collect. It is very difficult to operate a pick-in-store model in a fast-moving environment, challenging in fashion, and extremely awkward to execute in a concession or store-in-store environment.

21.4   Top Takeaways

Customers like click-and-collect. Take-up is usually rapid, and retailers who offer it typically see 30-50% of all online orders fulfilled via this route.

Unfortunately, the biggest reason for this customer preference is free shipping; much care is needed in the design of the operating model to offset shipping costs while still retaining internal simplicity and external convenience.

Click-and-collect generates genuine incremental sales in store. Two specific quoted data points from retailers: 25% and 40% of customers who collected-in-store made an unplanned additional purchase.

Planning decisions in implementation include: available-to-promise (pick in store/pick centrally); online checkout changes; shipping; payment policy; no-show policy; fraud-prevention and ID; collection desk location and processes.

Pick-from-store offers advantages in simplicity and customer promise. Its issues include confidence in the promise; picking process quality control; endless aisle (non-store) SKUs; stock reservation; paperwork printing.

Checkout dialogue needs be carefully modified to avoid infinite loops. A decision is needed regarding split shipping options (collecting only part of the order). Checkout can become complex.

Pay-on-delivery translates easily into pay-on-collection. However no-show rates will be higher, potentially exposing you to significant extra costs.

If you are offering the service on smartphone, you may choose to deliberately simplify the checkout, including switching mobile orders to a pay-on-collection policy.

A collection desk is required, which tends to be located at the back of the store. Customer handover processes, which may include ID validation and paying for additional purchases, overlap significantly with existing in-store customer service desk duties, and so many retailers double-up.

Cultural differences in take-up, and in collection models, can be very significant.

Execution can be challenging in certain environments, especially concessions and store-in-store formats, or when free shipping is impossibly uneconomic to due geography.

Chapter 22.   Personalisation

22.1   Introduction

Personalisation is not a new idea. Arguably it's been around since the invention of money and the establishment of the first shops; knowing your customers, offering them what they are most likely to want, and treating each as individually special to you, have always been essential elements in the recipe for retail success. Remembering Mrs Ancient Greek's preference for black olives over green ones was just as important for Old Athenian Olive Stores as knowing my reading preferences is for Amazon today. Industrialising this from corner-store to multiple-outlet is not a new idea either. As soon as the data-processing power became available twenty to thirty years ago, many industries, especially financial services, realised that the information they already kept about their customers could be used to tailor their offers to the needs of each customer. CRM has a lengthy history, and in many ways personalisation is just the retail application of it.

The first industrial-scale personalisation schemes in retail were loyalty cards, whose objectives are usually loyalty second, data-capture first. Big Data is a popular buzzword in retail right now, but once again it's an idea with a past. The big loyalty schemes run by (for example) supermarkets have been generating huge quantities of data for years. This data has been exploited for both general insight into customer behaviour at a statistical level and for more specific personalisation of coupons and offers.

For the multichannel retailer, personalisation is critical because it makes it possible to follow the customer across all those steps in the purchase journey – from research to purchase, from smart-phone to store. At every step, the customer leaves a trail of history, and this trail can be exploited. The idea of personalisation is not complex. The challenge is to translate these broad ideas about "knowing our customer and treating them as individuals" and turn them into concrete actions and implementation plans. There are various standard families of techniques.

22.2 Techniques of Personalisation

22.2.1 DIY Personalisation

Take a look at the home-page of your smart-phone or PC or tablet. There's a familiar collection of icons and widgets on it. Now take a look at home-page of the person sitting just along from you. It's most probably an alien landscape: why's she not got the standard email application, how can she possibly have all that space taken up with that rubbish, what *has* she done to that menu option, how can anyone use a device with a background set to that colour? Despite its popularity – there are a lot of PCs and smart-phones, all customised by their users – this is not an idea that has found favour with retailers. Slogans such as shop your way[137] really mean shop *our* way, preferably drilling down to the products and offers we're particularly interested in promoting to you. Even Amazon doesn't let you mess with the layout of the store.

There are several reasons why this approach to personalisation isn't used much in retail. Customers in general don't use most individual retailers' digital channels often enough to make it worthwhile customising the store. Retailers spend a huge amount of effort optimising the user-experience of their channels, and giving the customer the opportunity to mess this up is likely to produce sub-optimal results. Most importantly, it is surprisingly difficult to implement from a technical perspective online (I can't think of any standard software solution that offers this option), and impossible in a brick-and-mortar environment unless you are in the "personal shopper" category of luxury retailing.

In summary, it's probably expensive project which will only succeed in reducing sales.

22.2.2 Simple Segmentation

The Old Athenian Olives Store in the introduction to this chapter was able to deduce its customers' preferences for colour of olives. Being able to deduce anything about a customer relies on being to identify that specific customer and also remember and subsequently analyse his/her actions. The olive shop proprietor would do so by knowing his/her customers personally, watching their shopping over a few visits, and drawing a simple

---

[137] Used for example by Sears in the US or Marks and Spencers in the UK

conclusion about customer segmentation – black only, green only, or both black and green olives.

In modern, multiple-outlet brick-and-mortar retailing, it isn't possible to know every customer personally. The typical solution is a loyalty card. A loyalty card involves a trade – the customer gets some sort of reward, in exchange for which the retailer gets to collect data about them. The retailer can analyse this data by itself, and in many countries can also purchase supplementary information (usually at street or postcode level, rather than individual customer level, for data protection reasons, but this granularity is generally sufficient). From this data, the retailer can make deductions about the customer – rich/poor, old/young, black/green-olive-eating – and place them in a segment. The segment can then be marketed to. For example by a coupon can be issued for a new premium, juicier, flavoursome variety of green olive targeted at the richer, green-olive-preferring segment.

If you interact with your customers two or three times a year via brick-and-mortar channels only, this is probably about as good as it gets. You have to deduce the customer segments and then pro-actively market to them; too many segments are impossible to manage, and the effectiveness of the marketing becomes impossible to measure. This kind of simple pro-active segmentation can be surprisingly effective, but the key word is *simple*.

To go beyond simple, you need more data.

22.2.3 Complex Proactive Segmentation?

Creating a loyalty scheme which is worthwhile enough for a two-visits-per-year brick-and-mortar customer to join is something of a challenge (if you only spend twice a year, how long will it take to save up for a meaningful reward?), hence the existence of multi-branded loyalty schemes. The value for the customer multiplies as the participation of retailers (and other sectors of course) increases, and the deductive value of the data may increase for the retailer, although possibly its value may be limited by terms and conditions or local data protection laws.

Other retailers are fortunate enough to have much higher customer frequency. An average family might purchase several *thousand* items a year at a supermarket and visit weekly. Clearly a lot of segmentation is theoretically feasible, but how practical or commercially useful is it? And what relevance does all this have to Multichannel? Here's a lengthy quote from the former CEO of Tesco:

"correlating the data we have with [other] sources of data – social networking data, mobile phone data, payment methods... and use that understanding to deliver an <u>even more personalised</u> offer... We're now making changes to our UK website to highlight promotions that are relevant to the customer who is browsing the site. Using Clubcard [loyalty card] data, we would show, for example, offers of our Everyday Value range to price sensitive customers, and offers of our Finest range to more upmarket customers. The power of this approach was born out by a test we did to sell mattresses. When a customer visited our website, we would use Clubcard data to tell us if the customer was more swayed by price or quality. We'd then display the type of mattress that best reflected that shopper's characteristic. <u>Sales grew by 10%</u>."[138] [my underlinings].

This quote encapsulates several important points. Firstly, the data sources are multichannel themselves – not just purchase history but social networking, mobile, and probably many others. In other words, even Tesco, with one of the most sophisticated purchase-history based analytical databases in the world ("you are what you eat" as they put it, which is itself a pretty succinct personalisation statement), feels the need to supplement this information. And a rich source of additional data is customers' online behaviour. Just consider the numbers briefly. A typical retail website might have a conversion rate of 3% to 3.5% - say 30 visits per purchase – and a typical mobile site will be even higher, up to 100 visits per purchase. A customer in the research phase of his/her purchase might consider dozens of candidate products, each generating several page-views. Actually making a purchase and steering it through checkout requires further page-views (and explains the success of 1-click checkout). I have data from various retailers which suggests an average of around 200 page-views per cart, although of course it varies a lot by category. A customer making just two or three purchases online per year will leave a trail of several hundred data points.

---

[138] Tesco CEO Philip Clarke, Global Summit of the Consumer Goods Forum, Istanbul June 2012

Secondly, even armed with all this data, the proactive segmentation described basically just splits customers into cheap or posh. Doubtless Tesco's actual strategy was rather more sophisticated than a brief speech by the CEO at an executive conference can truly describe, but nonetheless this does illustrate an unavoidable limitation of this proactive segmentation approach: you can only realistically work with a handful of segments. The numbers quickly get out of hand. Cheap or posh, old or young, kids or childless, pets or none, drinker or teetotal, indigenous or immigrant... that's already 64 segments. Now invite your marketing or merchandising teams to come up with 64 different offers each time you want to do a campaign!

Thirdly, it works: a 10% uplift in sales should delight any retailer.

Fourthly, multichannel correlation of the kind suggested in the quote is only possible <u>if you can identify the customer consistently across all these channels.</u> Tesco here claims it is taking brick-and-mortar data, augmenting it with social networking data and mobile data, and then deploying this usefully to its website channel (**Figure 96**).

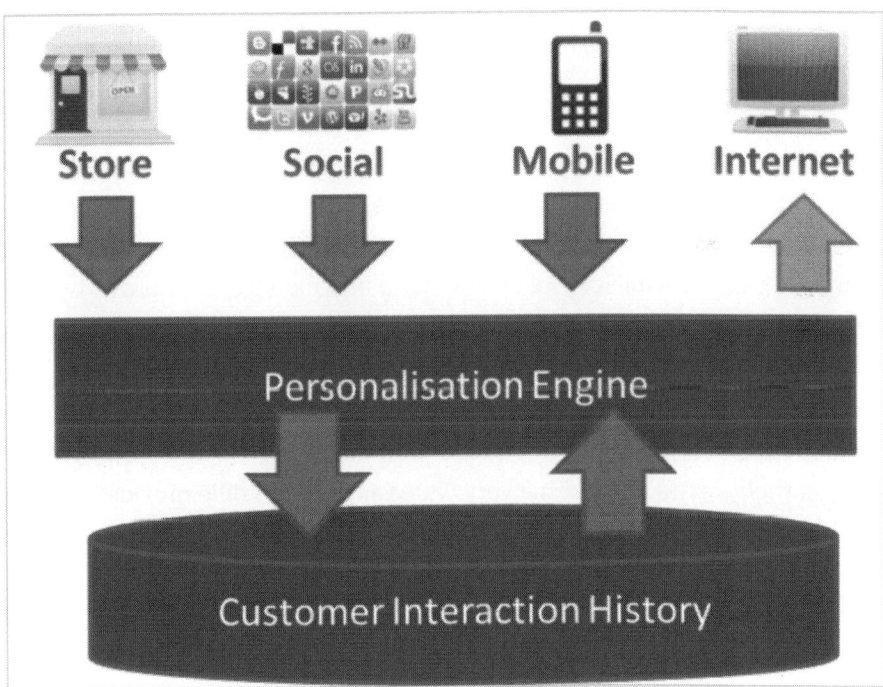

Figure 96 - Example Personalisation Data Flow

Tesco can do this effectively because it can use its loyalty card as an identity stamp on every channel the customer is interacting on, and has made it sufficiently worthwhile to the customer to take the trouble identify themselves (login/register online, present card offline). For many retailers it is difficult to offer sufficient advantages to the customer to identify themselves across channels in this way, and then technically very challenging to combine the data even it is available. A "single customer view" is an attractive concept on consultants' slides, but a very difficult implementation journey.

Lastly, being a supermarket with a loyalty scheme, Tesco already has a huge amount of essentially offline data available. For most retailers, the bias of data is the other way around – they can potentially capture a large amount of online data from website or smartphone, which they need to deploy at the right moments to influence the customer.

A 10% sales uplift is a big advantage. However the difficulties and disadvantages of this complex proactive technique – data bias towards online and/or limited data sets, reliance on customer identification, limitations in segmentation, huge databases – lead many retailers towards techniques which are single online channel specific and which are, in an apparent oxymoron, effectively anonymous personalisation.

22.2.4 Product associative personalisation

It is every retailer's dream to predict what their customers most want to buy, and offer it to them directly. Quite how difficult this is to do is exemplified by the famous Netflix prize[139], in which the online movie rental company offered a million dollar reward to anyone able to improve by 10% its existing algorithm to predict which movies a given customer would rate most highly. A read of the (mathematically) interesting papers describing the winning solution reveals the critical obstacle to such predictions – very small datasets about most customers' viewing/rating histories available to predict their satisfaction with a very wide range of possible movies.

The simplest strategy to overcome this is obviously to have bigger datasets. The problem for most retailers is that putting this simple strategy into practice requires a lot of purchasing history of reasonably characterising products, already stamped with some sort of customer-ID. Even if this data is available, then in practice this technique only really

---

[139] See www.netflixprize.com

works very well in some categories such as media (books, movies, music downloads etc) and possibly fashion. In its simple form, it is just another variation on the simple customers who bought X also bought Y, just with a bit more complexity – customers who bought X and Y and Z over the last few months might like A or B. Importantly, this approach requires knowing nothing else about the customer except their purchasing history (which of course the customer has inevitably disclosed) – it is anonymous.

It's noticeable that Amazon themselves appear to have de-prioritised this kind of product associative personalisation which was once one of their flagship marketing tools. Instead they now tend to adopt a more route-one approach. If you are ever unwary enough to browse a category without purchasing, for example, you will swiftly receive numerous prompts for products from that category, both via mailings and "next time" you access their site. Yes, these are still cleverly personalised, but the basis is your expressed interest in the first place.

22.2.5 Real time personalisation

If "next time" seems a bit sluggish, how about "during"? It's important here to distinguish between engines which are genuinely profiling customers based on a history of activity over multiple visits, and those which are merely segmenting visitors based on information disclosed during a single session. That isn't to say both techniques may not be effective, but the latter applied to retail tends to drift back towards the rather easier (and cheaper) "customers who looked at X subsequently liked Y" techniques.

Dynamic visitor segmentation, based on information gathered during a single visit only, works especially well in sectors like travel. Deductions are made – for example have you expressed a preference for family holidays or not, long-haul or not etc – and the customer placed into some sort of segmentation tree (*Figure 97*).

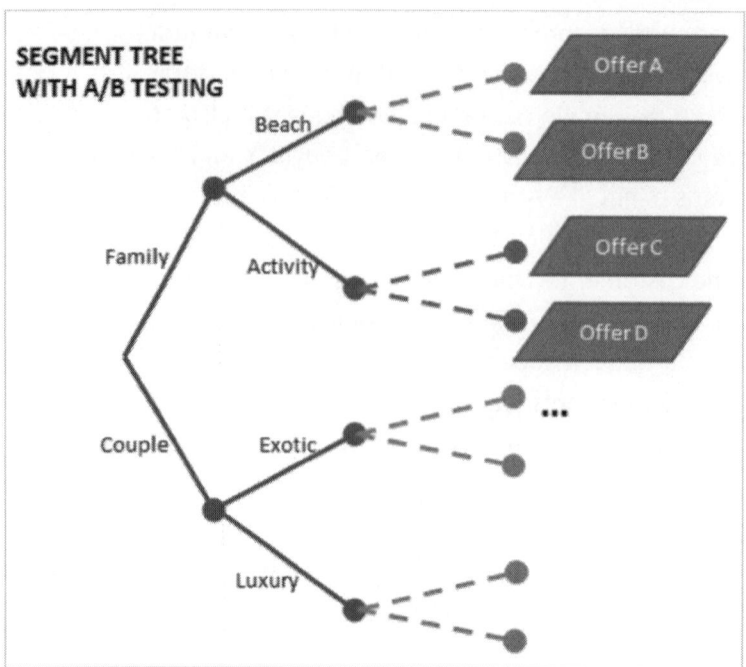

Figure 97 - Segmentation Tree Personalisation + A/B Testing

The segments are pre-defined during configuration, as are the possible offers. As with all A/B testing approaches, offer A or offer B is served at random to visitors who are classified as falling into that visitor-segment, and the site is dynamically tuned to favour serving the one which generates most favourable responses (the real-time nature may constrain this to simpler definitions of the response, such as just click-through, rather than the more complex goals typical of analytics such as actual checkouts).

On retailer websites, the most familiar form of this technique is those "you may also like" panels. The solutions that populate them are variously referred to as personalisation engines or recommendations engines. They can be very effective; you'll probably be presented with case-studies showing sales uplifts in the 10%-30% range if you talk to a supplier. Here are three things to explore when considering them.

Firstly, make sure your product range is suitable. For them to be fully effective, you need either a range with many natural substitutes between products, or better, an assortment which contains many "secondary" products: ties for shirts; cement for bricks; cases for laptops; whose price point is c20% of the primary article price.

Secondly, consider how you will change your UI/UX up-front, and preferably actually do that change, using "dummy" recommendations. You might be surprised how much sales up-lift you see simply because this process forces you to reconsider and update the customer experience anyway.

Thirdly, structure the commercial deal very carefully to make sure that only truly incremental uplift is measure – see below.

22.2.6 Extended dataset personalisation

Personalising based on one visit to your website, or even on multiple interactions over several channels, might still leave you with an inadequate dataset about each customer to make meaningful deductions about them. Why not, then, use their interactions with other retailers – or in fact other interactions in general – to supplement this data? The best known users of this data-aggregation approach are the online advertising networks – a successful business model depends on displaying to users the adverts most likely to generate revenue for the ad-network i.e. the ones the user is most likely to click. The same logic works just as well for retailers – you use the same technique to predict what your customer is most likely to add to his shopping cart.

Such techniques aren't only valid for online advertising. They can also be used within a retailer website, for example to serve different banners, or to respond to particular search terms differently for different customers.

Strictly speaking it isn't the customer who is profiled by such data aggregation, it is the device (PC, smart-phone, tablet etc). In practice since the majority of customers don't share their device widely outside their close family, the effect is much the same. In fact, the reputable solutions in this space go to great lengths to avoid collecting information which could be considered genuinely personal - such as name or address – or jeopardise security – such as payment card details. Of course this is to avoid legal issues with data protection, but it is also because they simply don't need it; the technique is powerful enough at device level without trying to link the device back to its human user.

(Many of these data aggregation solutions rely on browser cookies, and the use of cookies is the subject of legislation in many countries, for example the EU cookie directive requiring sites to inform their users of the existence of such cookies and offer an opt-out. In practice only around 3% of users opt out, so the practical impact of legislation on the effectiveness of these techniques is extremely limited).

22.3   Issues

22.3.1 Into brick-and-mortar

The above account highlights the biggest issue with these techniques for the multichannel retailer – personalisation which is effectively anonymous or based on the device rather than the individual is all very well online, but rather less so when a human customer walks into one of your stores. There are two sides to this issue. On the one hand, many of the online techniques use sophisticated mathematical analysis to deduce facts about the customer which are totally self-evident face-to-face; most of us can tell whether someone is young or old without advanced technology to help us. There's nothing to then stop you propagating knowledge gleaned online – this type of customer prefers that model of product – into the brick-and-mortar environment, via training, promotional material or increasingly via tablet-applications which help in-store sales-assistants.

On the other hand, a customer coming into a store after leaving a trail of online footprints is probably getting close to making a purchase decision. The rise of the ROBO-customer (research online buy offline) is one of the phenomena of the Multichannel age. Ideally you want your sales assistants ready-briefed to focus their efforts into dialogue and demonstration of products your personalisation algorithms have already predicted this customer is most interested in. Asking the customer to login to an in-store device to identify themselves, and then suddenly demonstrating a detailed knowledge of their browsing history might possibly be great customer service, but equally likely it might be perceived as creepy big-brother-like snooping. It might work on an in-store self-service kiosk, but in general self-service kiosks in store have a very poor track-record. It might possibly be an option on a sales-assistants' tablet device with very careful staff training. But the one time you can reliably ask the customer to identify themself is during checkout, and probably the most likely incentive for them to do so is the tried-and-trusty loyalty scheme. It's a case of better late than never, but it might create the opportunity to cross-sell at a time when the customer is at least in buying mode. (You also need an operating model in your stores that will allow an assistant completing a checkout to be free to also accompany a customer somewhere else to consider an additional purchase.) All roads tend to lead to Rome, in this case back to a loyalty scheme. Note that this does not necessarily mean a loyalty *card* – especially in the age of the smart-phone.

Alternatively you can take the broader multichannel view. A customer in store will most likely have researched any significant purchase online first. This means that any personalisation solution in your online channels should have two sets of goals: firstly (of course) driving online checkouts; secondly, and possibly more importantly if you still have 90%+ of your sales taking place over the counter, a personalisation solution should be leading customers towards the product, or product options, they are most likely to finally evaluate and purchase when they arrive in-store. The latter is difficult, but definitely not impossible, to measure and should be an element of the business-case for any multichannel retailer considering personalisation strategy and solutions.

22.3.2 Not your data

So you've collected petabytes of data, analysed every customer in depth, personalised your online and offline experiences, and surmounted some minor legislative issues. What happens next? The answer in several countries is major legislative issues. Two quotes from the British government's Midata initiative:

"[Midata is] aimed at giving consumers access to the data created through their ... internet transactions and high street loyalty cards."[140]
"Midata will allow consumers greater insight into their everyday consumption and lifestyle habits by using applications and intermediaries to analyse their actual behaviours and thereby <u>*empower them to make better spending choices and secure the best deals.*</u>*"*[141] *[my underlining].*

One view of this the idea is that you surrender all that personalisation data back to the customer, and the customer then uses it to beat you up, especially on price. A more interesting longer term take is the notion that the customer will create their own personal profile of aggregated data, and

---

[140] UK government, department of business innovation & skills
[141] www.bis.gov.uk

make it available to you - the retailer – to allow you to customise the deal you want to offer them (*Figure 98*).

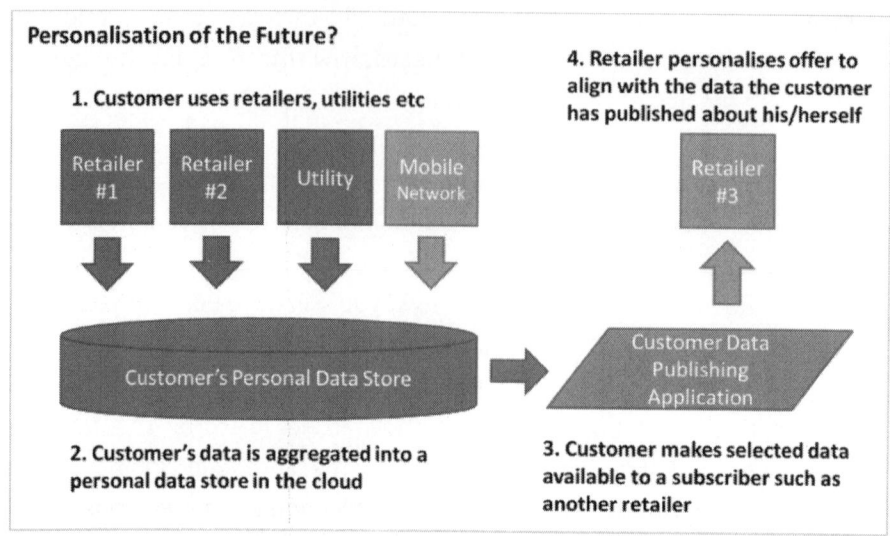

Figure 98 - Personalisation of the Future?

Although it might appear merely speculative, when there is a government initiative behind it, many possible partners already signed up, and retailers already beginning to advertise positions such as "Product Manager (My Data)", then it's certainly a trend to consider carefully when planning a personalisation strategy.

2016 edition retrospective: the above sub-section was written for the previous edition, and I deliberately left it unchanged. The reality is that this concept is currently only getting traction in areas such as banking. Some retailers seem to have flirted with it, and then quietly buried it as just a digital bridge too far.

22.4   Implementation

Is a personalisation strategy worth all the effort? For the online pure-play retailer, the answer is almost certainly yes. Inevitably the data points are confusing, conflicting or self-serving, but a reasonable planning benchmark is that good online personalisation will increase sales overall by *at least* 15%. Actual gains might depend on how much you are already doing, since many sophisticated solutions also include simple features such top-sellers or basic recommendations that might come out of the box with your website.

Helpfully, and as usual with anything online, it is possible to measure the benefits directly. Furthermore, all the plausible suppliers of software or services will provide straightforward A/B testing tools to compare your existing default approach with "their superior" results. Do NOT be seduced by reporting allegedly demonstrating that "X% of your sales came from our recommendations." All too often, this is just measuring the effect of adding a new feature, such as cross-selling, to your site.

> Measurement *must* demonstrate that additional sales are delivered compared to a proper control-group of recommendations generated by simple business rules, occupying exactly the same spaces on your site.

Make sure any commercial deal is either based on a percentage of any measured uplift, or has an exit clause if a measured uplift is not achieved.

It is actually feasible to build simple segmentation solutions yourself, and in fact if you are new to personalisation, you might find it effective to begin this way. Quite a lot of the eighty-twenty rule benefits of personalisation can be gained from very simple segmentation of the cheap-or-posh kind. To go beyond this, it probably makes sense to purchase a service or solution. Delivering into multiple channels (including online channels such as email), personalising in real-time, complex algorithms, extended data sources, etc, are all challenges for which it is unlikely to make sense to reinvent the wheel.

For the multichannel retailer, any strategy needs to consider brick-and-mortar. As we have already seen, this might well imply a loyalty scheme of some sort in order to generate the data and identify the customer, which may not otherwise be a priority for your business. The benefits of confining personalisation only to digital channels, via anonymous or device-based approaches, might well have sufficient positive benefit by itself, especially if online personalisation can also be proven to deliver sales uplift in stores.

22.5   Top Takeaways

Personalisation – changing the customer experience individually to draw each customer's attention to the things he/she is most likely to purchase –

is not a new idea. When industrialising it, there is a family resemblance to CRM.

Reasonably reliable statistics suggest setting benchmark expectation of sales uplift at 10-15% at least.

Sales uplift should be directly measurable; when implementing a vendor solution, consider a shared-success deal. Make sure that there is a true control-group, not just a before/after measurement.

Six technique families are identified here: DIY, simple segmentation, complex multichannel segmentation, product associative personalisation, real-time personalisation, extended dataset personalisation.

Personalisation techniques divide into two basic strategies: segmentation and anonymous personalisation.

Anonymous personalisation is more applicable to devices rather than individuals, and relies on devices not tending to be shared outside family groups.

Anonymous techniques depend on data volumes. Sources of data may include gathering data about the product set purchased or browsed, demographic or preference information supplied in real-time by the customer, and external sources information. The latter resemble the methods used by online advertising networks. In general, the more input data, the better the outcome.

Even simple segmentation with just two segments (e.g. cheap-versus-posh) may have significant benefits for small effort. Personalisation drawing on multichannel sources may only be appropriate for the biggest players with high participation loyalty schemes.

Recommendations engines are an effective technique on retailer websites. Preconditions for success include: an appropriate assortment with natural swaps or cross-sells; UI/UX changes; a commercial deal based on measurable incremental sales up-lift against a proper baseline-control.

Letting the customer personalise his/her own experience (DIY) is not a technique that has found favour in retailing.

The biggest challenge for the multichannel retailer is always how to connect back to the human customer in the brick-and-mortar store. Loyalty schemes are one such option. Personalising only online channels via anonymous techniques may be the best option for those without a loyalty scheme.

Open-data ideas, such as MiData, have not generally gained traction with retailers in the 3 years since the first edition of this book was written.

Chapter 23.   Mobile

23.1   Mobile First?

It's seriously questionable, in a 2016 edition of this Handbook, whether Mobile should have a separate chapter devoted to it, and even more questionable whether it belongs in a part of the book entitled "enhancement". Even writing the previous edition in 2012, I felt able to introduce the equivalent chapter with the words: "While a personalisation strategy might be optional, a mobile strategy is not." For this edition, I seriously considered replacing that with the words: "While a personalisation strategy might be optional, a desktop-PC strategy is not" instead!

Mobile is the currently the fastest arena for change in retail, and is inescapable for retailers, even if you do not actually have, or even plan to have, an online sales channel. This is particularly true in the developing world where fixed-line infrastructure is typically relatively sparse, and if it exists at all access to it is expensive relative to average incomes. Take a look at this chart of device usage in a sample of countries (**Figure 99**). In places such as China, India or the Phillipines, mobile dominates.

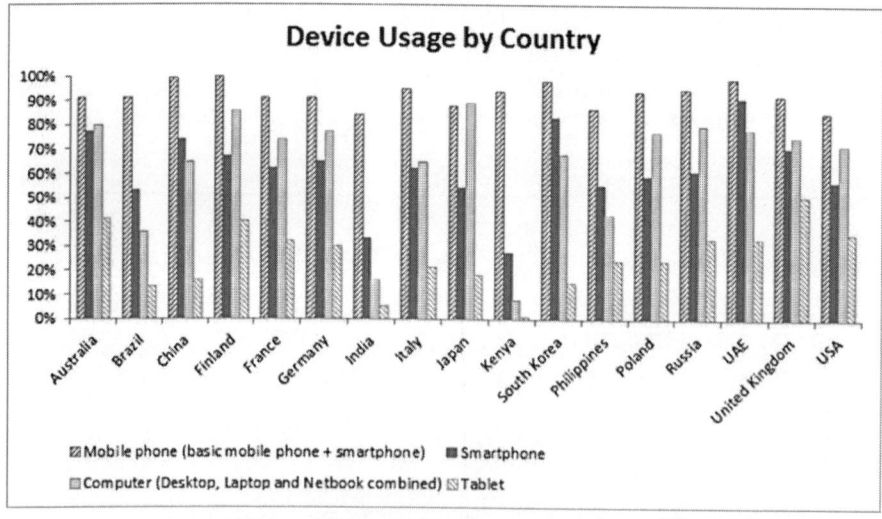

Figure 99 - Device Usage by Country[142]

---

[142] Source: Google Consumer Barometer 2014

A currently fashionable mantra is "mobile first"[143]. This advocates that your online experience should be designed *first* for mobile customers, and then retro-fitted for desktop-PCs and laptops. There is a great deal of validity in this argument[144]. An objection is sometimes raised that conversion on mobile is less than on desktop, but although this is true in a strictly "per visit" sense (it's typically around 40%), it isn't really true when you look big picture (**Figure 100**).

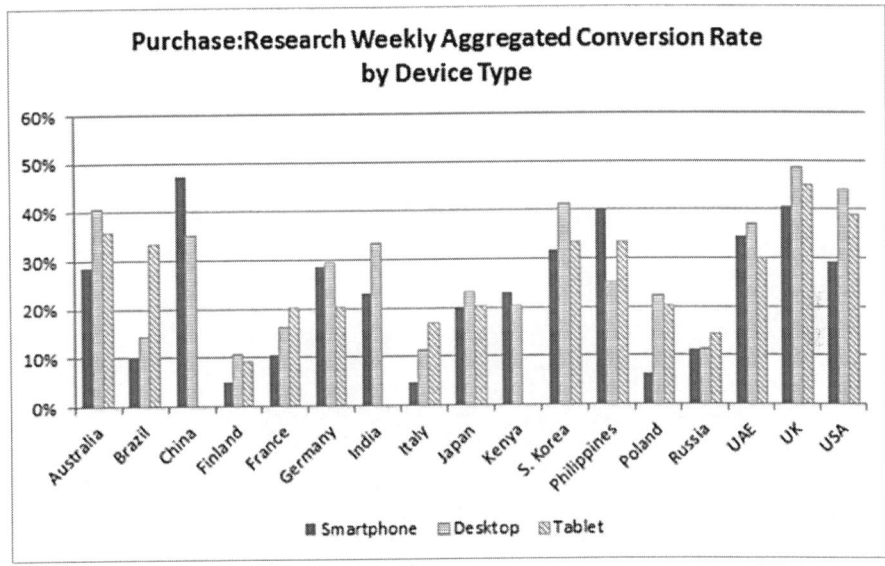

Figure 100 - Aggregated Conversion Rate by Week[145]

Once you step-up from a "visit" to a longer time period, more aligned with how consumers actually use their devices to shop, the differences between device-types mostly disappear, at least in countries where properly responsive (see below) sites are in place for shopping on. Using a smart-phone is typically a more staccato process – many short visits – than

[143] As I write this, I am perusing an article discussing "mobile only" as an approach, in the particular context of online shopping in India. Even the quoted advocates admit this is pretty radical (at the time of writing...)

[144] And even more validity from a technical design and build perspective.

[145] Data source: Google Consumer Barometer 2041. For a more detailed discussion of this idea, see https://www.linkedin.com/pulse/conversion-rate-mobile-really-equal-desktop-chris-jones . They key idea is that measuring conversions per visit is wrong, and that what you should measure instead is conversions per unit of information gathered by the shopper.

the legato experience using a laptop. Viewed over a week, instead of a visit, this smooths out. In countries such as China, where mobile-first is definitely the story, smart-phone conversion is actually higher.

"Mobile" is often a catchall term used to include basic phones, smart-phones, and tablets. In practical terms for retailers this is an unhelpful division. It is generally much more useful to consider large-screen devices versus small-screen devices. Take a look at this schematic from an "old-fashioned" (i.e. desk-top) online retail screen - I took a screenshot from the category page of a retailer's website directly from my laptop and then overlaid it to capture the essential features of the page layout (*Figure 101*).

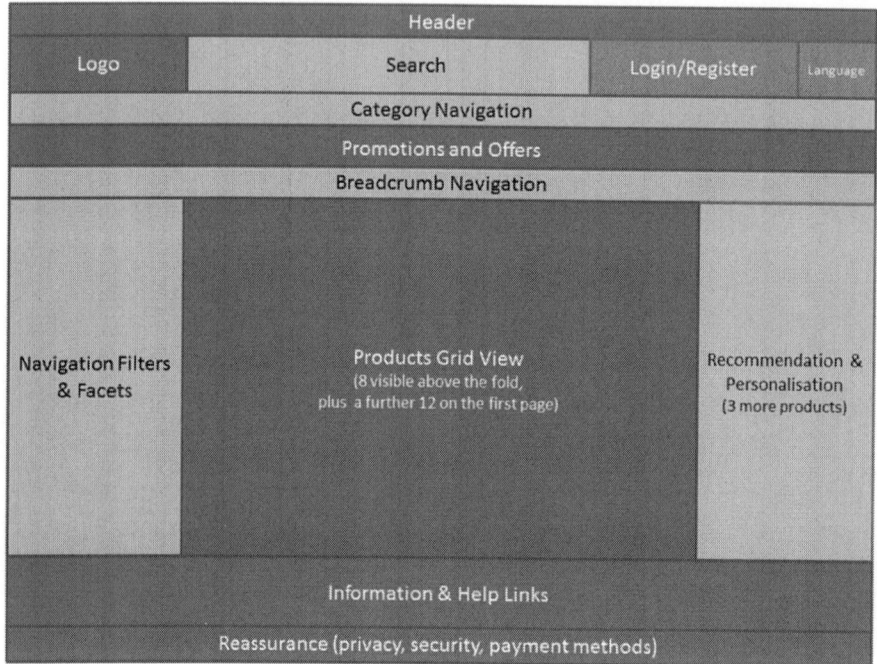

Figure 101 - Typical B2C desktop-site category page schematic

There are thirteen different basic sections, each of which contains multiple items of information. Eleven different products are fully or partially displayed before scrolling, including photographs and star-based ratings, plus further promotional items. I selected the retailer to use for this screenshot from amongst those whose online user-experience is generally considered to be best-practice. Translating this desk-top best-practice to a large-screen tablet is clearly not much of a leap; the same thing on a smartphone would be completely unusable.

The same retailer has a very good-practice smart-phone user-experience too, but the experience is fundamentally different (*Figure 102*): information has to be presented in a much more compact, much more impactful way; space for merchandising and personalisation is more limited; there are far fewer products shown per screen; "clutter" in the header has been moved to the very foot of the page; even fairly important stuff like reassurance-messages have been sent to the bottom.

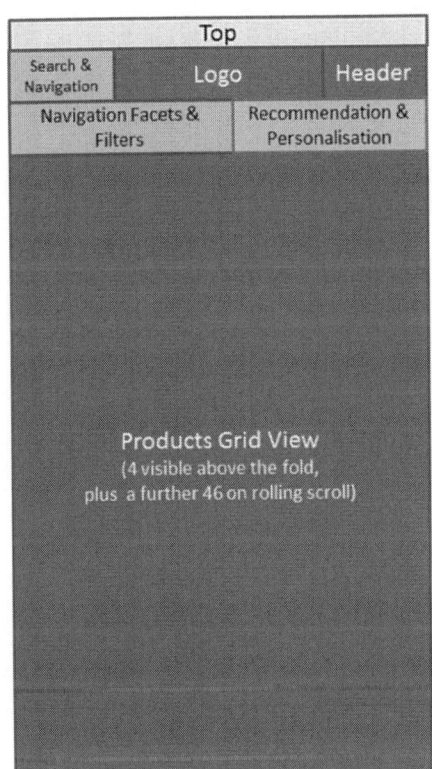
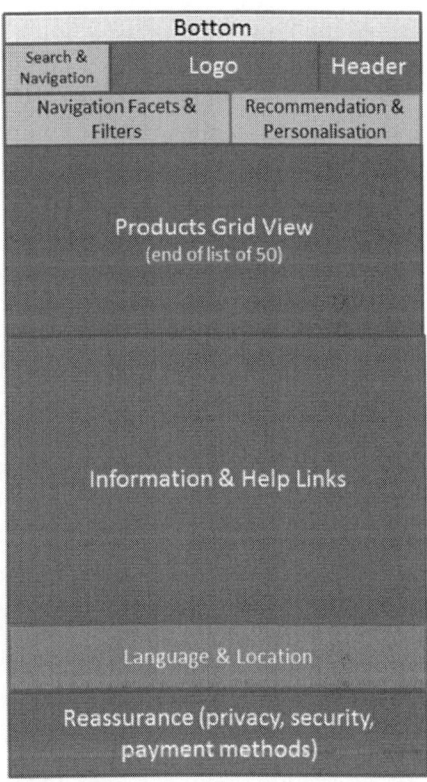

Figure 102 - Typical B2C smart-phone site page schematic

This is especially important when it comes to check-out. An online check-out is a complicated thing, typically requiring a lot of data to be keyed-in, multiple steps and options to be completed, and a nagging feeling that someone - or something - might be watching when you enter your credit-card details. In most countries, customers are still a bit more reluctant to undertake check-out on mobile.

The small-screen format demands much more careful consideration of what is most important. Since focussing on the needs of your customer is the key task for designing a website anyway, this is another reason why "mobile first" is a good paradigm to follow during your design: it forces you into those importance-decisions.

23.2   Mobile second

23.2.1 Introduction

If you're lucky enough to be starting from scratch, or perhaps totally redesigning your customer experience from ground-up, then "mobile first" is indeed probably the best approach. Many retailers are not so lucky: they already have a legacy desk-top site, and need to add mobile to it. This section considers that journey.

The next section reverses that perspective, and examines what it means to be "desktop second."

23.2.2 Customer objectives: identifying relevant tasks in your customer journeys

As always with anything multichannel, the right place to begin planning is with your customers. Who are they, which ones have mobile devices, and what do they want to use them for? The same approach as already described in *Chapter 11* is still applicable for mobile: what are your preferred customer journeys, and what steps along the journey might *best* be served by mobile? That word "best" is very important: mobile purely for the sake of mobile is likely to cost more than it earns. Mobile for the sake of enhanced customer experience, however, drives sales, either directly or indirectly.

Once you have identified a set of potential customer uses, then next few subsections outline a basic decision tree to follow when laying out your mobile strategy.

23.2.3 Location and Time-of-day

Mobile is exactly that: mobile. The opening question to consider is *where* the customer might be carrying out the potential tasks you have identified. Broadly these fall into five different spaces.

At home (or equivalents, such as in the office but using the device for non-work reasons): most probably the customer is using a mobile device for exactly the same tasks that they might use a PC, or especially a laptop, to perform. Your existing website, if you already have one, suitably optimised for mobile devices (see below) might well do the job. Tablet usage peaks mid-evening, for example: it's the device people use in a social setting.

At work for work-related reasons: many people have jobs on the move, and many of these jobs require on-the-spot research which might lead to a retail purchase decision. A niche example might be a plumber who needs to look up the right spare part to repair a broken boiler.

Generally on the move: sitting in a traffic queue or on a train is mobile time. Some directly retail purchasing activities, such as the weekly grocery shop, are ideal uses of this dead time. Otherwise, customers become just people: they want to be engaged and entertained.

In your stores: customers will be in mid-purchase research mode. Checking specifications, comparing products, and of course – unavoidably, so you may as well embrace it – comparing prices.

Near your stores: think mobile, think local. In fact the most popular use of a retailer mobile site or app is for its store-locator function. You probably put a lot of effort into driving traffic to your sites or stores – don't forget to plan to literally drive traffic!

A related, but rather critical question, is whether or not the task in question needs a real-time connection to the internet. If you are building up the weekly grocery shop, for later checkout, then no. If you are looking through a downloaded encyclopaedia of boiler-parts, then no again. But if you want to compare prices across multiple retailers, then definitely yes. If so, how fast does this connection need to be? Page-loading time matters just as much, if not more, on mobile as it does on conventional internet.

23.2.4 Your objectives: marketing and/or transaction support?

What stage in the purchase funnel are you attempting to engage the customer? A mobile strategy can often logically split into two separate threads. The first thread will be aligned with your marketing strategy with separate elements associated with attraction, conversion and retention; the second more directly associated with transactions: information, price comparison, cart, checkout.

Mobile apps can be particularly effective at the attraction stage. Retailer mobile apps run the risk of being downloaded once, opened once, and then consigned to the lengthy list of scarcely used apps lurking on every mobile device. Engaging apps, that just happen to feature your brand and products, by contrast are likely to get a reasonable amount of re-use. Avoid the mistake of forgetting to give them some retail utility - showcasing your products, locating your stores, driving retention or reactivation - in favour of being purely entertaining.

Coupons and vouchers are an excellent use of mobile to enhance conversion. Unlike their paper equivalents, mobile coupons don't get lost, are difficult to forge, and with the right technology can be validated at the point-of-sale in store. They can be issued dynamically in real-time based on trigger events such as customer near the store, excessively quiet Tuesday afternoon for general footfall, competitor event. Their redemption can be tracked afterwards for subsequent measurement and retention remarketing.

Purely mobile payment methods as a conversion-enhancing option appear tempting at first sight, but this is *very* country specific. For example in China, it is already mandatory, but then China is probably the most mobile market in the world. Some surprising developing countries such as Kenya have SMS-based schemes with impressively high take-up. The landscape of payment schemes and standards in many countries could best be described as confusing, which drives a vicious cycle where consequently consumer take-up remains rather low, and so it would be very easy for a retailer to make a significant investment betting on the wrong horse.

Transaction-enhancing mobile as a whole requires overcoming an additional challenge: the complexity of the user experience that can reasonably be delivered on the device.

23.2.5 Complexity

Take another look at *Figure 101*. That web-page is a surprisingly complex thing, and that's just one sub-stage in an overall purchase journey. There might also be home-pages, product pages, information pages and most complex of all, cart and checkout pages. On each page, the user has a choice of many ways to proceed. If your target task, location and purpose expect that the customer will be using their smartphone, then such complexity is often impractical. Interaction with a smartphone needs to take place in bite-sized chunks, with only a few diversionary options available, on simple screen layouts. A moderately greater level of complexity is possible via an app than via a smart-phone web-browser, but realistically the complexity-bar remains low even on an app.

There are further implications to this. Your existing online presence will require modification for smartphone users. Your website is still accessible via a smartphone web-browser, and you cannot afford it to appear unusable. You will have invested significant time and effort in making an existing website optimal for your customers, and you don't want to throw that away just because many of them are now using their smartphone instead of their PC or laptop. Inevitably, this leads to a need for responsive or adaptive design (see below); the site needs to detect the type of device being used to browse it, and change its presentation accordingly.

You may also decide that some interactions which are appropriate via a PC browser don't belong on a smartphone. This is particularly true of checkout and especially the payment sub-step. A classic customer journey change is when click-and-collect (see **Chapter 21**), implemented with pre-payment during the checkout on a PC browser, is changed to reserve-and-collect with payment in-store when translated to a smartphone. There are two benefits to this change: the checkout journey is simplified to help it through the smartphone; it overcomes the continuing reluctance of customers to provide payment details to mobile devices[146]. There is, however, a corollary – associated business processes have to be changed. Continuing the click-and-collect example, a payment step may now be required during the collection process.

23.2.6 Omni-channel

Reserve-and-collect is one situation where mobile plays a part in a longer, truly omni-channel multistep connected customer journey. Another common example is the omni-channel shopping cart/basket. Mobile is a great channel for research, but a difficult channel for final checkout. A

---

[146] See for example http://www.paymentssource.com/news/Mobile-Payments-On-Rise-But-Many-Consumers-Wary-About-Security-3009979-1.html although be warned that published statistics in this area are particularly variable, changing continuously and often more-than-usually country-specific

brick-and-mortar checkout like reserve-and-collect is one option. What about online?

Connecting online channels typically requires two things. The first is a common login. Implementing a shared login benefits the customer some, but benefits the retailer more: it helps solve a key challenges in implementation your personalisation strategy (see *Chapter 22*). The second is typically a shared-channel shopping cart. Customers don't just use shopping carts as a checkout vehicle; even on sites with helpful features like wish-list or save-for-later, customers often prefer to use the cart itself as a scratchpad to save items of interest for further research, and then eventual selection and checkout. Ensuring that the cart can be shared between mobile (research) and PC/laptop (selection and checkout) is an essential step to capturing customers on this particular journey.

23.2.7 From requirements to implementation

The link from requirements to implementation strategy is summarised in *Figure 103.*

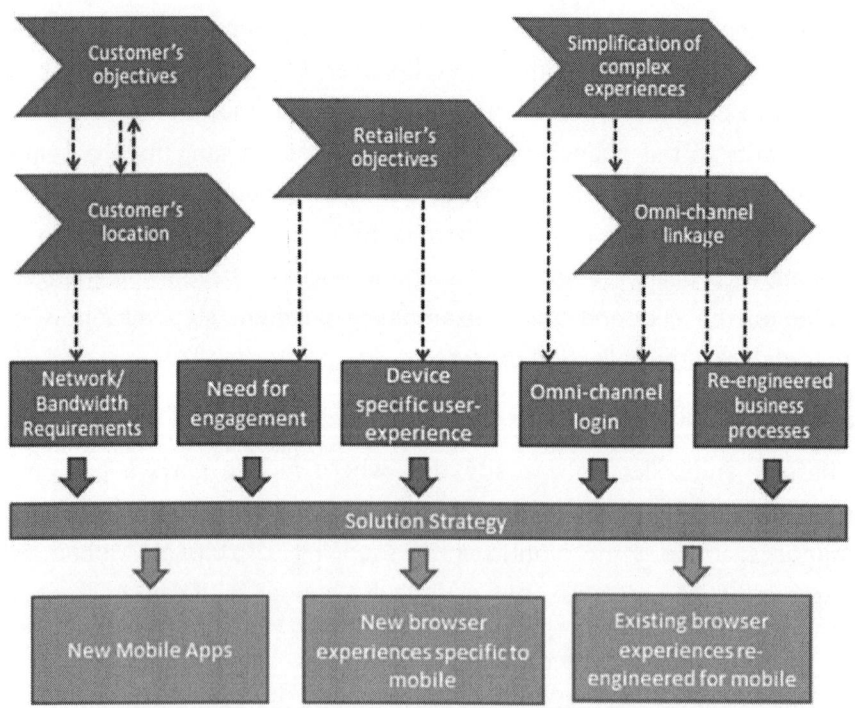

Figure 103 - Mobile strategy, schematic

Having mapped out your candidate set of customer requirements, including changes to your existing proposition or business processes, you are then in a position to consider them from an implementation perspective.

23.2.8 Do you need apps?

An issue to be addressed early in planning mobile implementation is whether or not you propose to create any mobile apps, or whether a browser-based approach alone will be sufficient. I would suggest that your approach *as a retailer* is to take a default position that you will not create apps, and then seek to justify whether any exceptions are appropriate. An individual retailer should start from a position that it is not inherently compelling or useful enough to justify special place on its customers' mobile devices. The challenge to any proponent of a retailer-specific app should be to demonstrate that this is wrong.

What criteria might an app proponent employ in support of the need for an app? A starting list should include:

Necessary **complexity**. Complexity which is merely desirable is almost certainly complexity which is unnecessary and which you should be considering how to engineer out of your multichannel proposition in any case. Necessary complexity might arise if you have, for example, sophisticated configurable products with many options. Working through these within the confines of a smartphone screen will be challenging for your customers, and subjected to the limitations of browser capabilities will be doubly so. In fact an app may well be a better solution altogether than any browser, including those on a laptop or PC as well as mobile.

Compelling engagement. If your chosen objectives are less transactional and more focussed on engagement, and by implication entertainment, then an app is probably a better option. Nevertheless you should remember that the average lifetime of an app, from download to neglect, is brief; some reports suggest it is under 30 days[147]

---

[147] See for example: http://techcrunch.com/2009/02/19/pinch-media-data-shows-the-average-shelf-life-of-an-iphone-app-is-less-than-30-days/

Offline operation. Self-evidently, if your customer task is expected to be performed when an internet connection is unavailable, then an app is probably the only option. Continuing the example used above, when someone has his/her head – and phone – inside a boiler while validating the specification of possible replacement parts then a high-quality connection is unlikely to be available.

Complex memory. Logged-in browser sessions, and cookies, can of course remember things. But if your task requires a large amount of option setting and personal configuration, then an app is more likely to be the right option.

Developing an app is probably a more expensive option with less likelihood of customers using it; you need concrete reasons of the kind listed to justify the additional investment.

23.3   Desktop Second

23.3.1 Tabula Rasa

No, not the name of the next generation mobile tablet, but Latin for 'clean slate'. We now look at the opposite logic. Suppose you are in the fortunate position of genuinely being able to be "mobile first". What, then, do you need to consider when extending back to the laptop/desktop PC?

As we've already seen, the reality is that this question probably also extends into the realm of tablet: the key difference is big-screen versus small-screen.

23.3.2 Customer objectives

If you're mobile first in mindset, you might wonder why a customer could conceivably want to use one of those old-fashioned desktop devices! What part of the customer journey might *best* be served by desktop?

There are typically three answers:

Depth. The large-screen is the preferred format used by customers who want to study something in depth. Some nice statistics published for a non-retail site – the New York Times – illustrate this point nicely (*Figure 104*):

NY Times Data	Avg Pages per Visit	Avg Session Duration
Mobile	2.55	1 min 43 secs
Desktop	3.58	17 mins 31 secs

Figure 104 - NY Times reader behaviour by device type[148]

What this data pretty much says is that customers read headlines on mobile, detail on desktop. This is particularly important if your products are complex, have detailed specifications, multiple feature-options, or your customers find side-by-side comparison features particularly important. Connecting to the next topic, if your assortment in a category is huge, and filtering by a set of features important, then desktop is a better place to do that too.

Complexity. Some processes are inherently complex. In online retail, that's often not so many in reality, but check-out is definitely one such. How difficult checkout is really is rather culture specific. It depends on the payment options available locally, and the extent to which customers are comfortable with you saving their data.

Security. Related to the previous point, this is largely (some might say purely) a perception issue. Mobile tends to get used on wifi connections of possibly dubious provenance. Smart-phones are much easier to lose than desk-top PCs, which is unfortunate if your personal details are stored on them.

23.3.3 Location and Time-of-day

Another kind of security might matter to your customers: job security. If your customers are buying or researching in the workplace, and particularly if this is for genuine professional reasons, then they might prefer to use the official equipment. This is still usually a PC or laptop. If it isn't for professional reasons, they might still prefer to do so: in Europe at least, many sites see a temporary peak in sales in the lunch-hour and just before the end of the working day.

Most tablet access is via wifi, not true "mobile", and therefore typically takes place in some sort of communal setting: home, office, coffee-shop.[149]

---

[148] (Data source: SimilarWeb/Clickz)
[149] Consumer Electronics Association holiday purchase patterns study, November 2013

Tablet usage peaks mid-evening, even on retail sites and not just for watching movies. Tablets are good for sharing, and they tend to get used at the "are you sure" stage of the purchase. In the US and UK at least[150], there's a strange surge in purchasing online around midnight.

23.3.4 Retailer objectives

Obviously the most important retailer objective is to be available to your customer wherever and however they want to access you. If you're in a culture where that means a mixture of device-types, then that's where you need to be.

Over and above that generic statement, there are indeed some objectives that might be better served on a large-screen device than on a small-screen one.

Merchandising: quite simply, you can fit more information on a large-screen. This gives you more opportunities to propose alternatives to your customers, including *much* more space for merchandising activities such as cross-selling.

Checking out: as noted above, in many countries, especially those that *do* have an extensive fixed-line infrastructure, customers prefer to check-out on a device with a bigger keyboard and a higher perceived security rating. A particular technical challenge that then needs to be overcome is known as *persistent cart*. What this means is that when a logged-in customers adds an item to their cart on one device (usually the smartphone) then if they log-in on another device (usually the desktop) they find these added items in their cart ready-and-waiting to be checked-out. This is technically a bit more tricky than it sounds to implement: ask your IT provider.

Demographics: if you're targeting 18-24 year olds, then you might even contemplate mobile-only, not merely mobile-first. But if you are targeting silver-surfers, then this isn't so sensible. In fact if you're targeting me it isn't sensible either (and no, I'm not that old)!

---

[150] Data sourced from IMRG data blended with various published analyses of device usage by hour e.g. those by Demandware, Comscore and Mobile Marketing

23.4   Implementation considerations

One of the happier aspects of being a web-developer in what we might call the "desktop years" was the uniformity of the user-interface device that needed to be supported. When aiming only at PC/laptop browser sessions, it was generally acceptable to target a maximum of two or three display sizes. Furthermore, although the idiosyncrasies of the different browsers – and their apparent inability to adhere consistently to standards, especially CSS and DOM model – can occasionally be exasperating, it is rarely more than a nuisance. Enter the smart-phone and tablet. Now even a simple browser interface may have to cope with multiple screen densities and sizes, from cramped early smartphones to the latest tablets, which might then be operated in either portrait or landscape mode (or worse, in both modes), support widely variable features and capabilities, while still continuing to successfully support PCs, laptops and notebooks.

23.4.1 Two site solution

For early adopters of mobile, a frequently chosen approach was to route the customer through to what was effectively a separate site, detecting device type and re-directing the customer. Sites whose names suddenly change from 'www.xyz.com' to 'm.xyz.com' when accessed from a smart-phone, or even 't.xyz.com' from a tablet, are typical of this approach.[151] If you are currently living with a rather old implementation of a desktop site, it might be the quickest (if not necessarily best) strategy. The upside of this option is that it usually does not require significant technical changes or reskilling of IT teams, and implementation is reasonably quick-and-dirty. Two approaches are typical. The first is the obvious build two (or more) parallel sites. The second, which involves much less up-front labour but has significant downsides including potentially poor performance and compromised user-experience, is to use a supplier/tool which will (semi-)automatically re-render your site for mobile.

23.4.2 Responsive design

The more strategic solution is to implement *responsive design*. This is a technical term basically means ensuring a single page caters for the layout

---

[151] Homedepot.com is a nice such example at the time of writing.

– essentially shape and density – of all the devices that might access it by responding to the needs of each device. Longer term this offers many advantages, not least that a particular page (a product or promotion for example) retains a single url for external sites such as social media to link to.

If your website has been built properly, it will have a strict segregation between the part of the programme-code that decides what the site *does*, and the part that decides what it *looks like.* This latter is the styling, technically known as the CSS (cascading style-sheets). With such proper segregation of duties in place, responsive design is surprisingly easy to implement.

I've generally avoided too much technical detail in this Handbook, but this is one place where it's worth delving down just a tiny bit, if only for the reason that it might save you an awful lot of costs. Here's a very small sample of CSS code just to give the idea (**Figure 105**). Without getting bogged down in exact syntax and meaning, what this fragment of CSS is saying is "by default ['mobile first': smallest screen-size first], I want the 'menuBox-style' areas of the screen to have a small font and be 2 rows high. On a mid-size device whose screen is between 520 and 700 pixels wide, I'd like a medium font and 3 rows high. On a larger screen than 700 pixels, I'll go one bigger again."

```
.menuBox {
    font-size: small;
    height: 2em;
}
@media all and (min-width: 520px) and (max-width: 700px) {
    .menuBox {
        font-size: medium;
        height: 3em;|
    }
}
@media all and (min-width: 701px) {
    .menuBox {
        font-size: large;
        height: 4em;
    }
}
```

Figure 105 - Responsive CSS

Pretty easy huh? The trouble is that on older sites this nice clean separation tends to have become blurred (if it was ever clean in the first place), and some parts of the styling are buried in the 'what it does' part of the code. If that's the case then arriving at a proper responsive site is much more disruptive than the two site solution approach because your existing site probably has to be rebuilt at the same time, possibly by IT teams/suppliers who also need to adapt to a different way of doing things.

If you're in the lucky position of starting anew, do lay down the law here to your development team: any departure from the segregation of functionality from styling needs to be signed off by you personally (or your boss's boss...)!

23.4.3 Adaptive design

For the advanced, there's *adaptive design*[152] to consider: what capabilities does the device have? For example do you want to use the inbuilt GPS, does your interface want to support pinch-gestures on the touch-screen? If so, what happens on devices without this particular capability? This is typically a rather bigger issue for apps than browser-based interfaces although it applies to both; users have lower expectations of a browser interface, and a minimum-standard is probably acceptable.

23.5   Top takeaways

A mobile strategy is not optional. In developing markets, mobile devices are already the primary means of accessing the internet. In more developed countries, this cross-over either just happened or is just about to.

For many purposes, the key distinction is not mobile vs static, it is large screen vs small-screen.

Your existing website is already visible on mobile devices. If it doesn't look good on a small smartphone screen, you have a problem.

---

[152] Both responsive design and adaptive design are generally understood terms, but which lack a formal accepted definition. Adaptive design, in particular, is a term whose meaning can vary more widely than the suggested description given here. Responsive design, by contrast, is now well established, although technical specialists can of course argue forever about the best way to implement it.

If you are starting from scratch, consider a mobile-first, desktop second strategy.

Where is your customer? At home, at work and using a mobile device for work reasons, on the move, in your stores, near your stores?

Consider what steps in the customer journey might *best* be served by mobile. And then consider what steps in the customer journey might *best* be served by desktop!

Five important factors to consider when planning mobile strategy requirements: customer objectives, location, engagement-versus-transaction, complexity, omni-channel link-up.

Three important factors to consider when planning desktop requirements in an otherwise mobile-first approach: depth, complexity, security (and job security!).

Three feature-sets where you might prefer your customers to still use your desktop site: merchandising, check-out, targeting silver-surfers.

Engagement marketing might need a separate mobile strategy thread from transactional support.

Mobile payment take-up is very variable by country. Mobile coupons or vouchers, however, may already be an excellent tool. Solutions which validate them directly at the checkout and make their redemption available for analysis and re-marketing are already available.

Interactions on smartphone screens must necessarily be simpler than on large-display devices. This may necessitate amending some of the flow of the customer journey – for example deferring click-and-collect payment-step from click to collection.

Five important factors to consider when planning mobile strategy implementation: connectivity and bandwidth requirements, engagement level, device specific experience, omni-channel (especially login), re-engineered business processes.

Browser versus apps: a retailer's default should be browser. Apps might be justified by the need for: *necessary* complexity, compelling engagement, offline operation, complex memory.

Temporary re-engineering of an existing website may be achieved by duplicating/redirecting, or by tools which re-render. Such solutions typically produce URLs of the "m.xyz.com" structure.

Longer term, responsive design should be implemented, and should definitely be the default for any new solution. Demand that your IT provider makes a strict segregation between code functionality and styling (CSS).

Responsive design (suggested definition): ensuring each page caters for the layout of any device that might be accessing it, by changing itself to fit.

Adaptive design (suggested definition): adapting the user experience to fit the capabilities of the device. For example does it support GPS, or pinch-gestures? For most retailers, this is optional.

Chapter 24.   Clearance

24.1   Background

A frequent problem facing retailers of any kind is in clearing old stock. There is an inevitably unpleasant write-down to handle, and probably an adverse impact on margin targets. The challenge, then, is to find an efficient channel to clear the stock, and minimise the margin hit and write-down impact. Many retailers implement clearance tabs on their websites via a separate parallel taxonomy branch. These can be linked to seasonal sale events and can be excellent drivers of traffic and cross-sales.

However an alternative, implemented by many retailers, is to use eBay, Amazon, Allegro or other online marketplaces – to use another additional channel as part of their overall multichannel approach. This keeps the clearance stock out of stores/off the main website, reduces negative brand messages, and also potentially allows an efficient route to clear "second quality" stock. The catalogue retailer Argos, for example, is one of the biggest Sellers on eBay UK – driven in part by its constant need to clear supply chain space to make room for the next catalogue.

At first sight, however, marketplaces look like expensive channels. On eBay for example, by the time eBay listing fees and commissions, plus probably PayPal fees, have been charged, the total commission will average around 11%. Amazon Marketplaces, for typical sales volumes, is comparable or more expensive. Other marketplaces such as China's Tmall/TaoBao - which includes its own PayPal equivalent in Alipay – or Poland's Allegro are not much cheaper. Why would you want to use a channel taking a further 11% in fees against products where you are already taking painful margin hits, and when you've already investing in implementing your own online sales channels?

24.2   Analysis

24.2.1 Pricing efficiency

For products which are reasonably in demand, sold via an online marketplace which has a sufficiently large number of Buyers (i.e. any that you might reasonably choose), the marketplace will operate fairly close to optimal price-efficiency.[153] In plain English, on a busy marketplace things sell for what they are worth.

A concrete example will help (and I'm going to refer to eBay, rather than the generic term auction marketplace, in the interests of simplicity). Suppose you have an article originally priced at $100 but which you are now obliged to put into clearance. Evidently it wasn't "worth" $100 after all in the eyes of your customers. Feed a steady supply into eBay, without flooding the market, and you might reap an average selling price of say $70, with minor variations around this average. eBay will then take its various fees out of this, leaving you with an average net price of perhaps $62. Suppose instead of using eBay, you decide to use a clearance section on your own site. What price should you ask for the same product? The answer of course is somewhere between $62 and $70, a kind of goldilocks zone where the price is not too high, not too low. Price it above $70 and you'll be undercut by the marketplaces and your rate of sale will be low; customers prepared to buy clearance goods are probably also marketplace customers. Price it below $62, and you will make less money than you would have done via eBay (*Figure 106*).

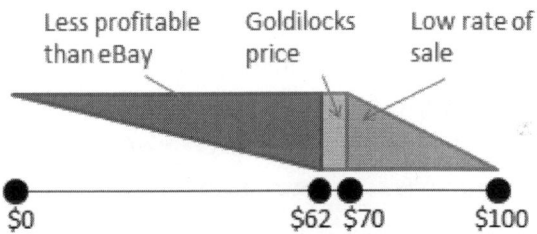

Less profitable than eBay   Goldilocks price   Low rate of sale

$0 $62 $70 $100

Figure 106 - Goldilocks price range for clearance

The problem is that you can only know this optimal goldilocks price after seeing the auction price for this product before placing on clearance. How easily can you predict it, and therefore do better via your own clearance?

---

[153] eBay, formally defined as a Second Price, English Auction, Fixed End-Time marketplace, is the subject of numerous (mathematically) interesting academic studies. See for example www2008.org/papers/pdf/p925-huA.pdf. A general summary of their conclusions is that marketplaces are not quite properly efficient in a purist sense, but for products in common circulation whose value is reasonably understood by enough bidders, then they are sufficiently price-efficient for the purposes of this book!

Well, firstly you might be able to do so by watching similar items auctioned on eBay. Of course eBay is not absolutely a perfect market, so you would have to watch a series of auctions and take a reasonable average. For most retailers, this is impossibly labour intensive.

Secondly, you might just price the item at more than $70 anyway. In fact, if you have a very small stock-holding of this item, and reasonable traffic to your clearance channel, this is a sensible policy. Not every customer is a "perfect" customer in the sense of optimising price, and in fact experience in non-price transparent retailing environments shows that the prices paid by a customer are (more-or-less) normally distributed. So if you only have a small stock-holding, and can wait long enough for a non-price sensitive customer, you can maximise your clearance this way. (Discussions of buy-it-now pricing on eBay generally recommend that this should be 15-25% higher than you expect to realise via auction).

Thirdly you might be skilled enough to price in the goldilocks zone – exactly between $62 and $70. This is unlikely at the first attempt, but if you have the systems and processes to monitor rates of sale and dynamically vary prices accordingly, then although you might make a few under-pricing mistakes early on, if you can react to these fast enough, then you are better setting your own price via your own clearance channel. Note that "fast enough", in an online environment with a bargain to be spotted and circulated quickly via social media, might be a matter of hours.

Otherwise, you are, in fact, better off paying eBay, or some other auction site, their commission in exchange for their highly liquid, "perfect" market, optimising your return on the sale. Alternatively, you could use non-auction retailer marketplaces like Amazon Marketplaces. Amazon operates, in effect, a reverse (or Dutch) auction. Sellers bid down, until a lowest consensus price is reached. In the clearance scenario envisaged, this is in fact quite bad for you as the Seller. The problem is that this Dutch auction takes place, with complete transparency, and without a committed purchaser at the end of it[154]. So the buyer can cherry pick. The optimal buying strategy is, in effect, to wait for a seller to make a mistake. As a seller, you are bound to do worse than you would via eBay, unless your commission advantage is significant on Amazon. In practice the difference

---

[154] Formally, It is not fixed end-time

may be more theoretical than practical, as eBay buyers may well base their buying valuations on Amazon marketplace published prices anyway.

24.2.2 Cost of servicing

However there is another factor to consider before finally selecting the best channel for your clearance: the secondary incremental costs of marketplace selling. Many apparently "additional" tasks, such as listing, can be automated, and others, such as photography and product description can re-use the assets you already created to sell these articles online in the first place. The same logistics processes can probably be reused with only minor modifications.

However some differences generate truly incremental costs, most especially customer contacts. Marketplaces switch the bias of customer-contacts from post-sale to pre-sale. Moreover the customer-contacts-per-order ratio for a marketplace sale is typically between three and five times greater than the same ratio on a conventional B2C site, albeit mainly via the cheaper channel of email. Success on a marketplace is strongly correlated to reputation, which means you also need to respond promptly to all these additional contacts. Marketplaces are extremely unforgiving of sellers who attempt to economise on service.

24.3   Top Takeaways

Marketplaces offer an alternative clearance option, at a high cost in fees. Many retailers, however, find them an effective option despite the apparent cost.

Should your retailer use a marketplace for clearance?

Yes: if the quantity of stock of a particular SKU is relatively high;

No: if you only want to clear a small quantity of stock, have an alternative sale channel, and can afford to wait for a less price sensitive customer to come along;

Yes: if you do not have the time to invest in finding the goldilocks price in advance;

Yes: if you cannot afford the systems or time to highly-dynamically price yourself;

No: if you cannot handle 3-5x the customer contacts-per-order you normally expect, albeit by email;

Yes: if your brand strategy finds a marketplace channel acceptable;

No: if the additional traffic generated from the clearance section on your existing online channels generates significant cross-sales.

Chapter 25.   Online Grocery

25.1   Background

At first glance, online grocery should be a huge opportunity. Grocery represents a huge sector of retail in most of the countries where online retailing has already achieved significant general penetration. And yet this online penetration hasn't stretched very into the grocery sector.

Even the in UK and France, by far the most developed online grocery markets in the world, penetration of online grocery is only around the 5-6% mark, far below that of non-food (especially in the UK where non-food penetration is up over the 20% level). Theoretically there is a still huge potential for growth worldwide. A closer look at the business model, however, demonstrates why penetration is not greater, and why an apparently untapped opportunity remains to a large extent just that - untapped.

Webvan was perhaps *the* iconic failure of the dotcom bubble. Google for it and you'll find lots of analysis of what went wrong, but they could all be summed up fairly simply: online grocery is very difficult to operate profitably on a cart-by-cart basis, economies of scale are limited, and so pursuing a growth strategy is liable to just grow losses on a cart-by-cart basis with no end in sight. Consider for a moment a typical shopping cart from another online retailer who pursued a growth strategy with more success: Amazon.

They don't publish average cart sizes, but let's take a reasonable example of a £25 cart (I'm going to keep the currency in this chapter consistently in GBP, for reasons that will become apparent shortly) with two or three items in it. Gross margin on books is typically 40%. Let's assume the worst possible case – free shipping and no other fee income. The £25 cart is generating £10 of gross profit, out of which all the costs of handling the cart have to be paid. Shipping might be £2.50, packaging materials £0.50, labour costs in picking three items another £0.50, and a whole bunch of miscellaneous additional costs such as payment processing, contacts-per-order, returns handling etc, perhaps contribute another £1.50. That leaves £5 in net profit. In other words, the <u>delivered margin</u> (see *Chapter 18*) is around 10% (this helps illustrate why delivered margin is such a critical KPI for an online business).

It's possible to repeat the delivered margin exercise for online grocery with some level of confidence, because helpfully there is an online grocery pure-play, Ocado in the UK, which is a publicly quoted company and which publishes sufficient statistics in its annual reports to permit its business model to be approximately reverse engineered with some intelligent guesswork.

Having talked about Webvan and Ocado, both online pureplays, what is this chapter doing in the section of the book on multichannel? The answer lies in taking a look at what changes could be made to the Ocado business model to move it from break-even to profitability. Many of them, and in fact those mainly adopted most retailers who are genuinely able to operate online grocery profitably, especially in France, rely to a large extent on multichannel. Before investigating these further, let's take a more detailed look at the Ocado model.

25.2   Ocado Case Study

Before heading into the analysis, I'd just like to get the caveats out on the table. Ocado publishes a lot of data[155], but there is still a great deal it does not publish. A big dollop of approximation and guesstimation is still required in order to derive meaningful conclusions. Although I've shown figures to the nearest penny in order to make up the picture and get totals to add up to 100%, they should certainly not be regarded as accurate to the nearest penny. There is also a risk that details of the calculations are simply wrong, and/or that some key factor is omitted. However, having tested this cart-by-cart approach to online food on some client assignments, I believe the broad conclusions are still valid, and I'd request that you look at the top-level picture without getting too bogged down in the precision of the calculations. I've supplied details of the calculations to assist anyone who wants to build their own model, and because some of the reasoning helps illustrate key points about online grocery as a proposition.

I've deliberately stuck with 2011 as the model-year, because subsequently Ocado started acting as an outsource provider to another UK supermarket, Morrisons, and this confuses their published figures (some

---

[155]   See   http://www.ocadogroup.com/investor-centre/results-and-presentations/pr-2011.aspx. All quotes in this section are taken from the 2011 annual report

might say deliberately); Ocado-only data is no longer fully broken out. This case-study isn't supposed to be an investors' guide to Ocado, it's an illustration of the challenges of online grocery as a business model, and so the purer data from earlier is generally more helpful.

25.2.1 Delivery fees

Ocado told us they delivered an average of 110,000 orders per week, equating to 5.73 million over the full year 2011. The first piece of missing information, and therefore the first approximation, is the delivery fee income. Differentiation in online grocery is primarily about convenience, and Ocado rises to this challenge by offering very precise delivery slots; as a customer you can be sure when to wait in for your groceries. These slots – a customer-selected one hour window booked up to 3 weeks ahead – are variably priced like airline tickets: a popular slot is more expensive.

When I first made this analysis, just after the annual results were published in March 2011, I estimated that the average delivery slot charged a fee of £4.75. As I write this sentence in October 2015, I've just logged into their website and I can now see that the majority of delivery slots are free-of-charge. Like many other online pureplays, Ocado is seeing the attractions of offering free delivery; delivery charges are one of the top reasons customers don't complete a checkout. We'll see what impact this might have on the challenging online grocery model later in the chapter.

Note that free delivery is something of a come-on offer; repeat customers can find themselves paying, and the estimated average fee is around £2. However since 2011, Ocado have become much better at leveraging secondary media income, which contributed an additional £1.34 to the average cart in 1H2014[156]. For the purposes of this analysis, and for consistency, I'll stick with the £4.75 estimate that was roughly valid in early 2011.

One other significant data point here is from Amazon Fresh. Amazon's online fresh grocery service costs an incremental $200 per year (over and above the price of its standard $99 Prime offer) for membership: even Amazon thinks free shipping is prohibitive for this particular proposition,

---

[156] Ocado plc half year results, 2014

despite its general willingness to subsidise shipping in general. The problem for all online retailers is that customers don't share that perspective!

25.2.2 Margin

Although Ocado published gross margins of 30%, these include delivery-fee income. Once this is stripped out using the above estimate, gross margins are around 26%. By food retail standards this is still a pretty respectable number.

It's worth briefly considering whether higher margins might be achievable online than in store. Online grocery shoppers are primarily motivated by convenience first, price second. The stereotypical persona is a middle-class working mother with two or more young children - cash-rich, time-poor – who will buy at least some premium products. Online grocery carts also typically include a larger percentage of the sort of bulky items on which margins may be higher.

25.2.3 Overview of average cart sales and margin

Bringing the previous two calculations together into an overview of the income half of the story, we find the picture shown in **Figure 107**, for an average order cart after sales taxes.

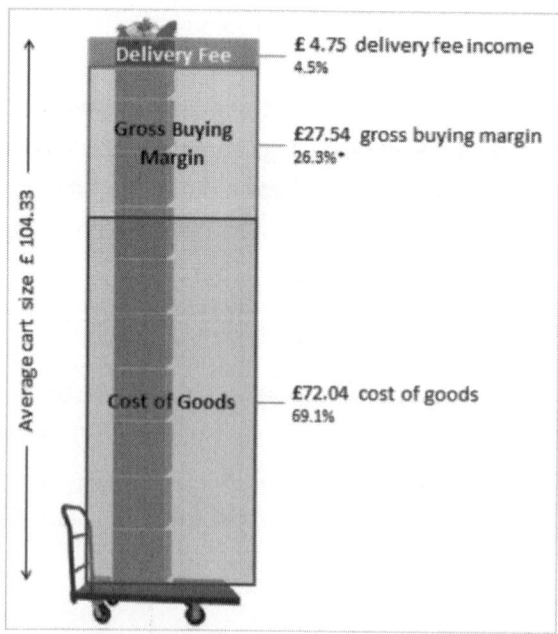

Figure 107 - Ocado cart, income breakdown

25.2.4 Costs introduction

Now for the costs side of the same average cart. We'll use the definition provided by Ocado themselves:

"Distribution costs consist of all the cost incurred, excluding product costs, to the point of sale, usually the customer's home. This includes the payroll-related expenses for the picking, dispatch and delivery of the product sold to the point of sale, the cost of making those deliveries, including fuel, tolls, maintenance of vehicles, the operating costs of the properties required for the picking, dispatch and onward delivery operations and all associated depreciation, amortisation and impairment charges, call-centre costs and payment processing charges."

Ocado told us that altogether this cost them £151M in FY2011. How does this break-down?

25.2.5 Last mile delivery

A major complication for an online grocer attempting to offer customers a complete online weekly-grocery-shop is the multiple product storage requirements. Fresh, chilled, frozen, bakery, super-fresh (seafood for example), room-temperature products are all involved. Ocado, in common with other such home-delivery services, uses specialist delivery vans equipped for these multiple product types.

A very useful statistic they published was the number of deliveries made by each such van: 145 per week. Their deliveries operate from 6:30am to 11:30pm seven days a week. Making a few allowances for operating processes, we can estimate that an average delivery requires around 49 minutes, including both travel time and handover time on the doorstep.

A lot more approximation is required to turn this into financials, including factors such as the hourly cost of drivers, likely distance between drops (a figure that unfortunately is not published) based on average road speeds, fuel prices, and the likely cost of specialised vans. My estimations are that the costs per order for Ocado are £1.81 for fuel, £1.31 for other vehicle costs, and £6.57 for drivers' time. Deriving these figures requires long chains of assumption and estimation. Anyone making a model for online grocery themselves, rather than reverse engineering somebody else's, will be able to make much more accurate models. The critical factor in countries with high labour costs is the time between deliveries, and in countries with lower labour costs it is the distance and consequent fuel consumption and vehicle wear-and-tear. More generally, drop-density is the key KPI. All successful online grocery propositions for home-delivery concentrate first on densely populated urban areas (that also contain enough cash-rich time-poor consumers). Any rollout strategy should be planned on a district by district basis.

Before the assumptions get too risky to be credible, fortunately Ocado also published a statistic for the total cost of deliveries:

"Trunking and delivery costs fell as a percentage of revenue from 13.2% in 2010 to 12.9% in 2011"

If the above estimates are accurate, then the remaining cost - trunking - equates to £3.76 per order. Even if all these assumptions mean the previous individual data points are somewhat off the mark, this published benchmark provides an overall sanity check.

25.2.6 Warehousing and picking

Ocado helpfully told us the overall operating cost of their central warehouse: 11.3% of revenues. They operated in 2011 from a large, highly automated, single central warehouse[157], and then if necessary trunk the picked orders to spoke depots from which the specialised vans make the last-mile deliveries.

Even more helpfully, they provided a labour efficiency measure for this central warehouse: 111 units picked per hour per man-hour of labour[158]. And they told us how many items are in each order:

"...picking an average of over 50 items per order from over 20,000 SKUs across three temperature zones with different product life (ambient, chilled and frozen)."

---

[157] A second warehouse was subsequently opened; however this partly supports their outsourcing deal with Morrisons, and so again confuses the data, another reason to stick with the "purer" 2011 model.
[158] This is an area where they are driving considerable efficiency improvements. However various studies suggest that overall picking-efficiency is not that much better than the best-in-class pick-in-store operations

So roughly it still takes <u>half-a-man-hour to pick a grocery order</u>, even in a highly sophisticated and automated warehouse. With some reasonable assumptions for the hourly costs of labour, again it's possible to estimate the costs-per-order at £3.80 per order, and the remaining costs of the central warehouse at £8.04 per order.

25.2.7 Other costs

Other costs per order are relatively insignificant. Online grocery generates less contacts-per-order than most other models, partly because items are very standard, but mainly because queries are typically resolved on the doorstep. I estimate around £0.38 per order.

Fraud is a relatively insignificant in online food, and so payment processing costs are generally low. I estimate around £0.83 per order.

25.2.8 Overview of average cart costs

Bringing all these calculations (and assumptions!) together, we end up with the picture in *Figure 108*.

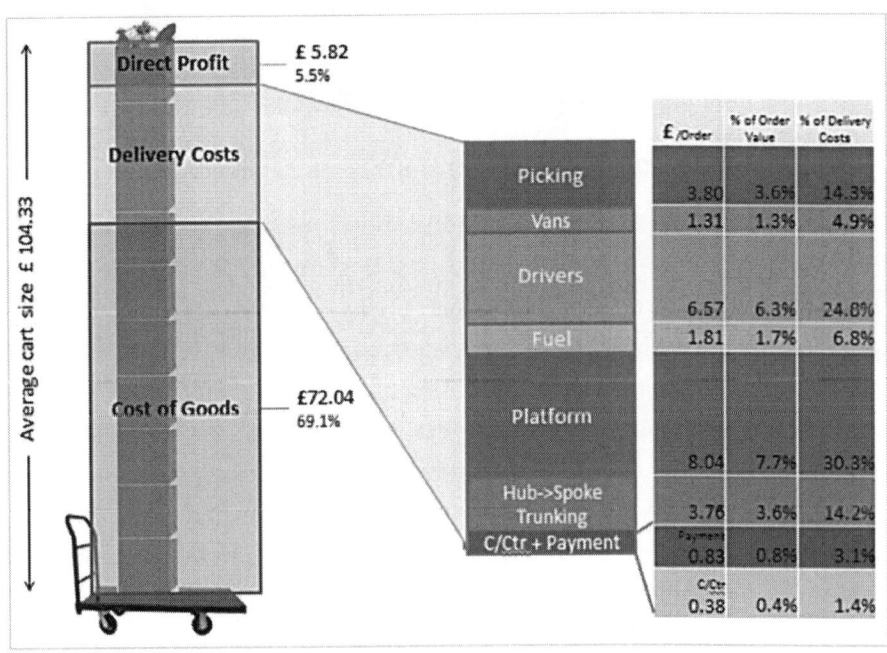

Figure 108 - Ocado cart, cost breakdown

25.2.9 Summary: the online pure-play perspective

The challenge of online grocery profitability is most clearly illustrated when we set Ocado's costs and income per average cart side by side (*Figure 109*).

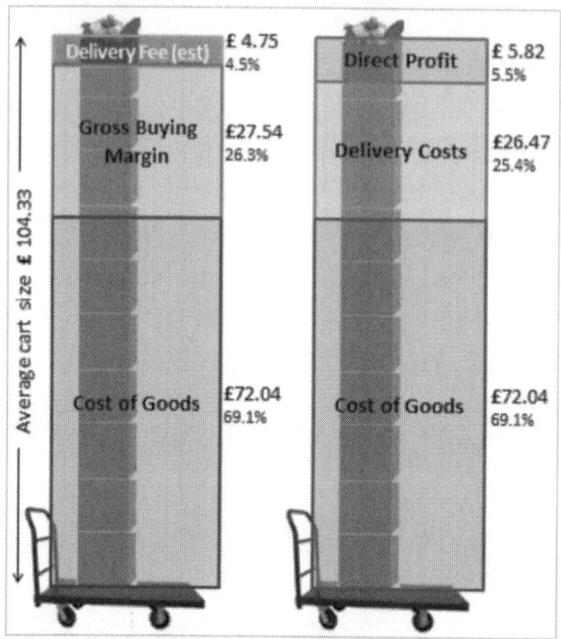

Figure 109 - Ocado, costs and income per average cart

Direct Profit of 5.5% is measured before non-cart related expenses (head-office costs) are taken into account. Once these are added to the mix then an average cart with a tax-inclusive cost to the customer of £112.15 generated a net profit of £0.18, equivalent to 0.16%, in 2011; this was after over 10 years of optimising the operating model.

A critical limitation in this business model is that carts smaller than £82.50 are actually unprofitable. Suddenly the size of the potential market decreases violently – how many grocery shopping carts are larger than this number? If we estimate that only 25% of grocery sales by value are in carts larger than this threshold, then the penetration of online into overall UK grocery restricted to above-threshold carts changes from 5-6% to 20%, which is magically just about consistent with non-food penetration.

Ocado's approach to improving the situation includes increasing cart-size by increasing their assortment, reducing trunking costs by adding another central warehouse in another part of the country, and continuing to drive the efficiency of their platform and picking. Ideally they'd also like to drive up that crucial KPI last-mile drop density, but against stiff local competition that isn't so easy to do. As an online pure-play, their options are somewhat limited.

25.3 Multichannel perspective

Now take a look from a multichannel point of view. A lot more of those unpleasant costs can be attacked in some way. The most obvious option is to get rid of all those difficult last-mile delivery costs, by simply not offering last-mile delivery. In food it potentially allows the customer to blend their order by picking those difficult fresh items themselves during a store-visit to collect their order, rather than writing hopeful – and time-consuming for the retailer - notes to the picker. (An anecdotal story, which I can't resist repeating here: a customer who specified that a turnip should have a skin with a pattern like a smiley face. Her home delivery duly arrived with a turnip just as specified, with a handwritten annotation from the picker "glad to be of service.")

25.3.1 France

The country where multichannel grocery probably works best is France. They've generally avoided setting the precedent of offering delivery and then allowing a race-to-the-bottom on shipping costs, for the simple reason that most online grocery in France is collected. The result is very rapid growth, without impossible challenges to operating profitability (*Figure 110*).

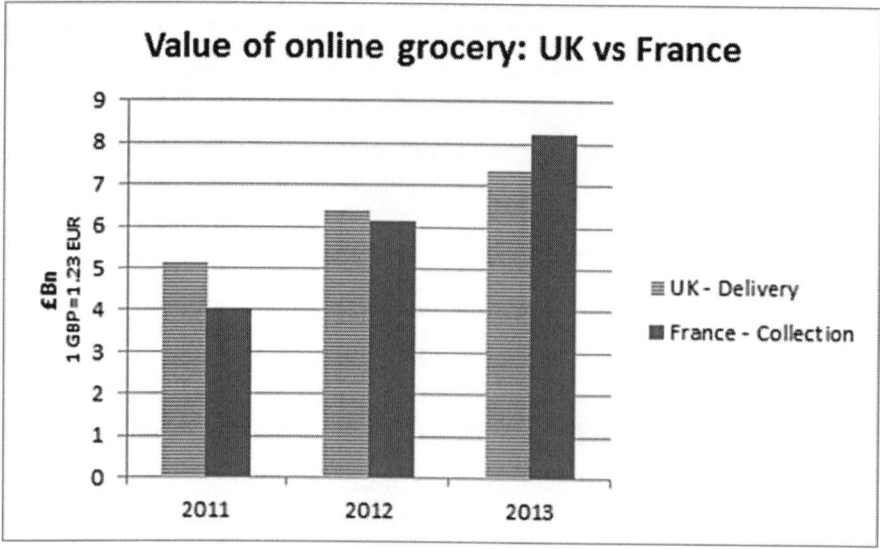

Figure 110 - Online grocery, France vs UK[159]

The model is known locally as "Drive" and is fundamentally based on the idea that it has to be local: 80% of the French population has a Drive location within 10 minutes of their home or work address.[160]

25.3.2 Pickup and Picking

There are a few basic flavours of the Drive offer. The first key distinction is in the pickup process. Does the customer get out of their car (Casino, Intermarche, System U), or is their role basically confined to opening the boot (Carrefour, Leclerc, Auchan)? In either case the total target collection time including all steps in the process is sub 5-minutes. The difference is largely accounted for by the sophistication of the customer-facing I.T. solutions at the point-of-collection.

The second, and probably more important, distinction is whether orders are picked in store or in some sort of nearby dark-store – and also whether customers come to the supermarket or a dedicated location (which might be the dark-store itself). Apart from obvious issues like store capacity, parking space, planning regulations and so forth, the most important criterion for this decision is probably the service-level offer to the customer. Online grocery is pretty much *solely* about Convenience. Other

---

[159] IGD, Developments in Click and Collect for Groceries, 2013
[160] Olivier Dauvers "Le Drive, Une affaire qui roule", 2013

considerations that might normally apply via the P.R.I.C.E. model (**Chapter 5**) are still relevant but are entirely subordinated to the challenge of minimising the inconvenience of the tedious weekly food shop for your customers. (In the UK Tesco has stated that a third of grocery orders were placed via mobile in 2014; customers are dealing with the tiresome task while doing something else, such as sitting on a commuter train or in a traffic queue.)

One way in which French retailers are addressing the convenience challenge is via ever shortening lead-times. For example the offer from Casino Express requires the customer to wait a mere 2 hours between placing their order and collecting it, an ideal option for the on-the-move customer ordering via mobile and then dropping in to collect shortly afterwards. To provide such a service-level in a pick-from-store environment is very challenging, not least because Drive order-pickers will get in the way of real customers at all the most important times of day i.e. those times when customers most want to shop and stores are busiest. Realistically a dark-store solution may be the only option. (The main downside of dark-store is the size of the assortment: can you justify stock-holdings of notorious slow-movers like vanilla-pods?)

Store-picking has another advantage. An online grocery fulfilment centre is a specialised affair, with its multiple temperature zones and difficult to pick-for-customer items (think loose tomatoes or fresh fish). Non-food fulfilment is fairly standard, and so it is relatively easy to scale warehousing space to match the volume of business. Not so for food if you follow the Ocado central-warehouse model; a new specialised fulfilment centre is a major step-change. Store picking, by contrast, is relatively easy to scale. Platform costs are not zero – modifications are required to the store for marshalling and loading orders – but they are modest on a store-by-store basis. If you are offering a home-delivery service, store-picking also acts as an automatic incentive to drive the critical drop-density KPI by localising it.

Where online grocery is currently growing without large capital investments, for example in the USA and Netherlands, it is almost always based on a store-picking model that reuses existing assets. There is now a trickle of software solutions specifically for this business model that are reasonably cost-effective, whose presence in the market of course depends on there being enough clients.

25.4   Other differences from non-food

There are various other differences between online grocery and non-food which mean that "standard" online solutions, especially IT packages, are challenging to apply. In no particular order these issues include:

Large carts: a typical non-food shopping cart will have two or three items in it, and will rarely have more than a dozen. A typical food shopping cart, at the sort of minimum size necessary for profitability, will have over fifty items. Many standard software packages, and also user interfaces, will find this stressful to handle.

Substitutions: if a customer orders a Sony camera, you are out of stock, and so you instead supply a Canon camera of a similar specification, your customer is unlikely to be very impressed. The opposite applies to food. If you are out of stock of the 500g pack of butter, 2 x 250g packs or an alternative brand will almost certainly be accepted instead, and in fact the customer would rather experience this situation than be out of butter. Picking processes, and other related operating processes, need to take this into account. Substitutions represent a time consuming and costly part of picking, and yet a 50 item cart requires better than 98.6% stock availability to be picked at less than an even chance of at least one substitution, a very challenging target indeed. Many online grocery sites also have specific interface areas for the customer to indicate what policy they would like applying in the event of an out-of-stock.

Loose-weight and catch-weight products: many customers prefer to add apples to cart by the apple, not by the kilogramme, even though they may still be priced by weight. Meat or fish is almost always priced by kilogramme, even though the customer may simply want a whole joint or whole fish. Alternatively if the customer does prefer to buy by the kilogramme, they typically want a fraction – 0.2Kg for example. The user-interface, and supporting software, needs to be capable of operating in alternative or fractional units.

Price-after-pick: because of substitutions and weight-based products, an online grocery order typically cannot be finally priced until picking is complete. The following two quotes show an example policy, and are especially interesting because the proposition is actually B2B not B2C – Booker, whose website these are taken from[161], is a food wholesaler with a £500M+ store-picked online food delivery business:

"The guide prices shown online are the prices that are currently valid in-store, albeit these prices are only a guide as to what your total order may cost at the time of processing. Prices charged will be the cost of products you have ordered at the time of picking and processing your order, and as a result they may be different to the price shown on the website at the time of order."

"All of our promotions and special offers are displayed on the website as soon as they become available. Please note however that the invoice price will be applied at the time of picking and processing your order, and not at the point of ordering. You should therefore ensure that you check any validity periods of promotions and offers…"

Delivery scheduling: offering, as Ocado does, specific one-hour delivery slots three weeks ahead with dynamic pricing by slot-capacity requires some sophisticated – and therefore expensive – scheduling software and systems.

Favourites: the first time you try and online grocery shopping site can be enough to put you off for ever. As a simple illustration of why, please think of a canned product that you routinely keep in your store-cupboard (and not beer!). Now, without going and looking at it, tell me if you usually buy the 141g/5oz can, the 198g/7oz can, or the 255g/9oz can. Oh yes, and how many mangoes make up 1.6Kg/3lb? The equivalent on Amazon would be if I asked you to purchase your 60 favourite books of all time, but I insisted on specifying exactly which edition you had to choose. An average unaided first-time user of a grocery site will take over 45 minutes to place an order for a weekly shop. Having completed this awful task once, given that the proposition is supposed to be all about convenience, a customer will expect it to be

---

[161] www.booker.co.uk

easier next time around. The sites therefore remember what each customer has bought recently – their favourites - and offer a tick-cross shopping list facility. A nice multichannel extension of this is listing favourites from loyalty card data gathered offline, in order to help overcome the first-time shop barrier. Once again, this is specialist functionality which is largely irrelevant to non-food categories.

25.5   Alternative models

Given the foregoing, it's perhaps less than surprising that multichannel penetration of the grocery sector lags behind other categories globally. The full weekly-groceries-shop model is both complex and very far removed from "standard" models of online retail. Some alternative food models, therefore, seek to avoid the majority of the complexity and/or operate in a more nearly standard way. A large proportion of the complexity is caused by the need for mixed temperature zones, and consequent specialist warehousing, picking and delivery vehicles.

A plausible alternative is adopted by online stores offering organic or local produce, such as Aussie Farmers Direct in Australia or Riverford in the UK. Warehousing and picking costs are minimised by offering only a very limited assortment, often "fixed" weekly box-sets – one item for order management purposes, although containing many different pieces. Difficult temperature zones like frozen are excluded. In general the proposition is that you get high quality fresh staples from the online offer, but still go elsewhere – less frequently – for your other needs. Distribution costs are reduced by franchising, which has the side-benefit of incentivising drop-density. Long duration doorstep handovers are minimised by few items-per-cart and by generally avoiding specific substitutions.

25.6   Top Takeaways

Online grocery is a potentially very large opportunity. Penetration of online into food is very limited in most countries. However it has a challenging operating model. Analysis of online grocery models should proceed on a cart-by-cart basis.

A case-study, Ocado, illustrates a finely balanced business model. The costs of highly convenient last mile delivery combined with multi-zone (fresh, super-fresh, frozen, chilled, bakery, room-temperature) product management and fulfilment can soon eat up gross margins. Drop density is an extremely critical KPI.

High order lifecycle costs demand very large average cart-sizes to reach break-even; this limits the size of the potential market.

Other features of online grocery models which are different to non-food models include very large numbers of items in carts, substitutions, loose- and catch-weight products, price-after-pick, favourites, and complex delivery scheduling.

A multichannel approach can eliminate or reduce some of the cost burden, making it profitable, especially by eliminating the prohibitively expensive last-mile delivery element of the model with a collection-based proposition.

France has a well-developed collection ("Drive") model, which is growing rapidly. It is very strongly based on convenience: 80% of the French population has a Drive collection location within 10 minutes of home or work.

Alternative models can also be successful, such as regular boxes of fresh and/or organic produce; they reduce costs by simplifying delivery and not handling a complete range.

Non-capital intensive growth of online grocery is usually based around pick-in-store, collect-from-store models. This model is starting to gain significant traction, for example in the US.

Chapter 26.   International and Cross-Border

26.1   Size of Prize

It's easy to forget sometimes that WWW stands for *world wide* web. In theory, if you sell online, the whole world is potentially your customer. Whilst we looked at domestic customers swapping purchase channel to online (**Chapter 13**) cannibalising your store-sales, you can be pretty confident that international customers are wholly incremental.

It's already big business. 34 million Americans spent USD 40.6 billion on overseas websites in 2013, and 14 million Germans spent EUR 7.6 billion[162]. One way to look at this type of data is as a threat: why are those customers not spending domestically with you?

But a much more positive way is to consider the opportunity. The UK, for example, is a very developed online retail country. 74% of adults, 36 million people, bought something online in 2013[163]. But more non-UK customers bought something online from a UK website in 2013 than did UK customers (they don't buy as often as locals of course[164]). **Figure 111** considers only the named countries: when you add in France, Netherlands, Scandinavia, Russia and Ireland, the size of the opportunity becomes clear.

---

[162] Paypal Modern Spice Routes, July 2014

[163] Office of National Statistics: "Internet Access, Households & Individuals", 2014

[164] It's estimated that around 18% of UK online retail sales are shipped to addresses outside the UK

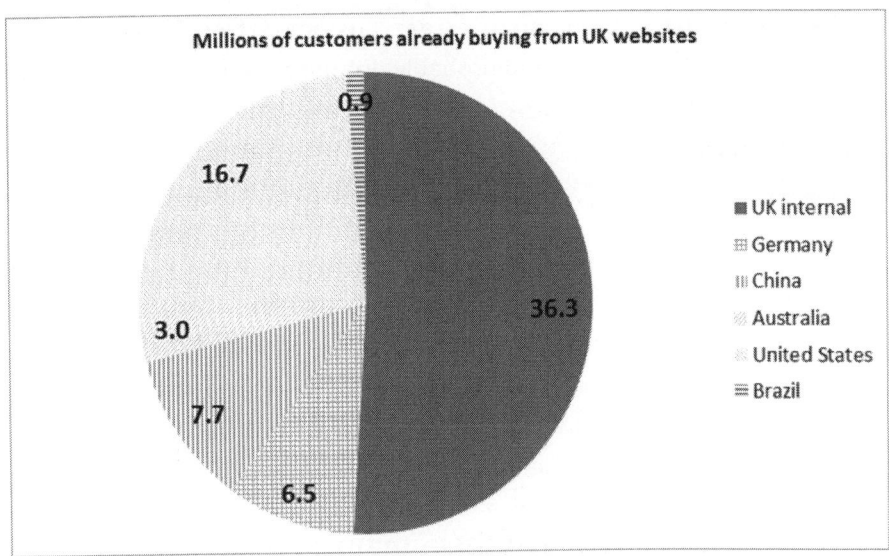

Millions of customers already buying from UK websites

0.9
16.7
3.0
7.7
6.5
36.3

- UK internal
- Germany
- China
- Australia
- United States
- Brazil

Figure 111 - Domestic vs international customers, UK[165]

Particularly within some sort of free trade-zone, such as the EU, or where bilateral agreements exist or customs-barriers are not prohibitive, a "fire-and-forget" approach to international customers – let them shop on your site, ship to them, don't worry much beyond that – can generate some incremental sales quickly and with remarkably little change to your existing operations.

To take the full opportunity, however, may need more extensive changes, and the rest of this chapter considers them step-by-step. Unlike the main flow of the Handbook, which considered the strategy and opportunity and then the challenges in taking it, the flow of this chapter is the opposite. We'll start by looking at the challenges, and then the strategy. The reason for choosing this sequence is that it's much easier to decide on strategy in this particular space when you have a clearer picture of the challenges you'll face.

26.2 Products, content and translation

26.2.1 Introduction: translation is not localisation

Maybe this is obvious? Full localisation is a complete scope of activities – shipping, payment, returns, festivals and events, language, customer

---

[165] Combining the previous two sources to make the chart

service etc – that makes an overseas customer feel fully at home. Translation is just one part – and probably not the most important part – of taking your site international.

It's also optional...

26.2.2 The customer perspective on translation

So who needs translation?

The obvious answer is "your customers", and the obvious answer is partially correct. As so often, however, the real answer is "it depends" – not all customers are equal, and just because British and Americans shoppers are no good with foreign languages doesn't mean that holds true for everybody. Here's an EU perspective (*Figure 112*):

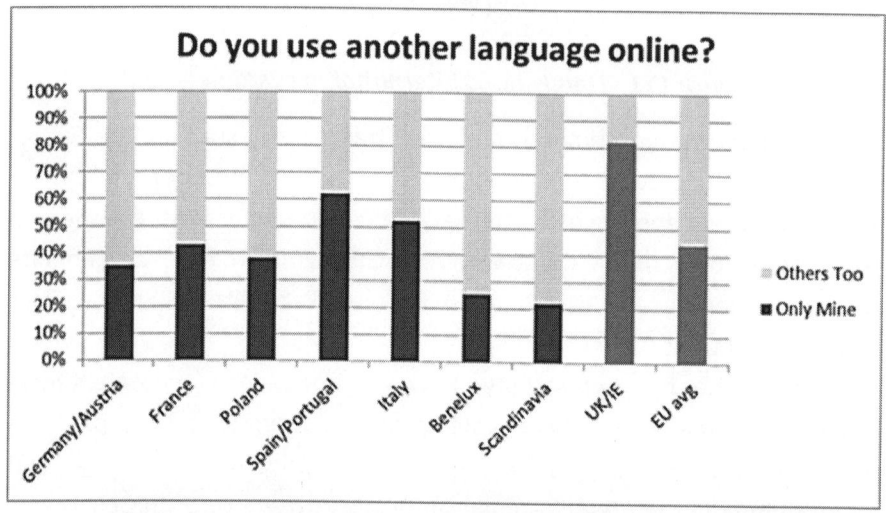

Figure 112 - EU web-users willing to use foreign language[166]

Across the EU, more than half of internet users are willing (and able) to use a second language online (compared with only 15% of British users incidentally) and the language they use is, unsurprisingly English: 85% of EU internet shoppers who are using a second language online are using English.

This behaviour tends to be even more pronounced in markets outside the EU. 'Good' customers – those in high income groups able and willing to

---

[166] Data Source: European Commission Flash Eurobarometer, May 2011. Interestingly the research was conducted from Hungary, but unsurprisingly Hungarian isn't the language the results are publicised in!

consider purchasing from overseas sites – tend to be those who are better educated. In many interesting areas of the world filled with potential customers, China or Brazil for example, 'better-educated' tends to be strongly correlated to 'good skills in English'.

Not only will customers use the internet in a second language, but they'll buy products in a second language too (**Figure 113**).

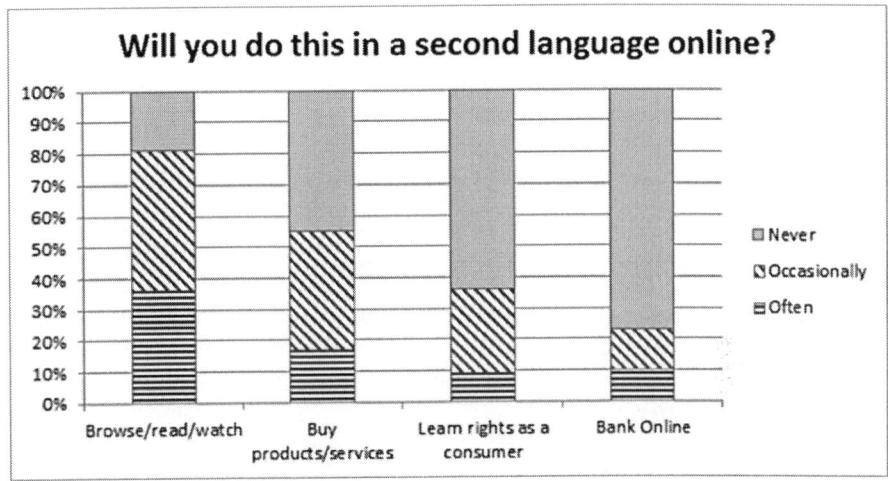

Figure 113 - Would you do this online in a 2nd language?[167]

One final statistic helps to complete the picture:

74% of people would buy again from the same brand if the aftersales care is in their local language.[168]

Bringing this all together, where should translation start *from the perspective of the customer*? The answer is in the areas that the consumer is least comfortable. Happily this tends to be those areas that are lowest cost to translate (**Figure 114**):

	The checkout and its prompts/help
Highest priority	This does NOT (necessarily) mean fully localised payment methods, a topic we cover later. But it does mean making it clear what to do for a customer unfamiliar with your existing local conventions. Address formats is a good example. To create alternative forms

[167] ibid
[168] Can't read, won't buy: The Common Sense Advisory, 2014

for different countries is technically moderately complex and probably not a top priority. Just showing customers from your preferred overseas markets how to format their address to fit onto your existing template, in their native tongue on a pop-up help prompt, is a simple quick-win.

P.S. and do make sure that phone number fields accept characters like +()- , not just digits. 'Anti- localisation' of your site also matters!

Delivery and returns information ("rights as a consumer")

Many retailers tend to treat the 'help' areas of the website as a bit of a tiresome afterthought. The result tends to be pages heavy on text, low on easy-to-understand pictures.

For an overseas buyer, this is probably the most important page on the site. There isn't much of it. It isn't going to be expensive to translate into your key target languages.

Website prompts and error messages

It's easy to overlook this. All those messages such as 'this promo code is not valid' need to be translated (NB: there were over 1,200 of these the last time I was involved in such an exercise, just on a fairly standard website).

Customer service

We'll come back to this point a bit later.

Marketing and merchandising communications

By definition these need to have rapid, high impact. Second-language communication simply does not "catch the eye" in the same way.

Your products

Lowest priority

Before taking the rather counterintuitive proposal that products are the lowest translation-priority at face value, it's worth reading the next sub-section: the customer perspective isn't the only one that matters here. But products tend to have pictures, unambiguous titles, clear descriptions that are either easy to understand or simple to attack with Google Translate; second language customers can have the most confidence here.

They are also by far the highest volume part of your site, by implication the most expensive to translate, and (see below) their translation will have the biggest impact on your existing internal business processes.

Figure 114 - What to translate?

26.2.3 The search perspective on translation

Before any of the above is relevant, prospective customers need to find you. The importance of translation diverges very strongly here between 'brands' and 'others'.

Typically a brand site will see the majority of its traffic being driven in some way by the brand term – direct entry to the brand-named site, search-terms including the brand-name. In this situation, translation may well have lower value – translated terms simply aren't how the customer arrives at your site. Apple is certainly not going to translate Apple iPhone into Apfel Handi for the German market, for example.

By contrast, if a significant percentage of your traffic arrives via generic terms – "men's jacket", "cheap laptops", "ethnic carvings" – then translation of your products, and even more critically your categories, page titles, and other landing pages, becomes a much more urgent priority.

Similarly, of course, if you plan to target a country via a marketplace (see later) rather than an own-website, then you will need to translate your products, otherwise they'll literally get lost in translation.

26.2.4 The process and cost of translation in money... and time

Rule number one is: do NOT use Google Translate! Here are a few examples, just to illustrate the point, where I've put some slogans via Google Translate into Chinese and then back into English (*Figure 115*):

Before	After
We are never knowingly undersold	We never sell intentionally
Live well for less	Live less well
Vorsprung durch Technik	Technology by-product
Soft, strong, and very long (for non-UK readers, this is the local slogan of a well-known brand of toilet-paper)	Soft, long and solid

Figure 115 - Soft, long and solid

To avoid your offer appearing soft, long and solid to a potential new customer, translation is first of all going to cost some money. How much money is a how-long-is-a-piece of string question: on the one hand professional translation is a very competitive market which keeps costs down. On the other hand it's going to depend on how complex your products are to explain. (I remember hearing an online retailer of sex-toys mention a figure ten times higher than what I would consider a norm... but then their products need a *lot* of explaining). Don't forget that this is going to be a (partially) recurring cost. Most sites have significant product churn: new seasons, new ranges, new technologies.

Secondly, and maybe more importantly, translation is going to cost some time, in two different ways.

When you begin to translate your site, the translator will need to build a dictionary, and you will need to work through it. Surely that's what you are paying them for? Well, unfortunately, almost all sites include:

- specialist terms whose translation needs to be validated (e.g. "last" in the shoe-sector)

- phrases, especially about things like style and colour, where awkward decisions need to be made about how to translate them. Some random examples from just a single page of a leading fashion site include "sweetheart necklines", "staycation", "lulu kennedy for indigo collection"

- brand words. Again picking a couple of phrases from the same fashion site: "Fitbit Charge" – the word "Charge" probably shouldn't be translated; "Autograph swimwear" – we certainly don't want "Autograph" translated

Once through that initial set-up process, there is a much more important *elapsed* time requirement to deal with. This sounds harmless until you consider the impact on your product launch critical path. Most brands prefer to launch new product near-simultaneously in all countries. I've yet to work with a brand or retailer that creates its new-product copy and content comfortably ahead of time. And now the translation process will demand several additional weeks be squeezed in between the final local copy and the proof-read translated copy. This can have a profound impact on your whole organisation and the change needs planning well ahead (*Figure 116*). Remember that just because you created a new language version of your website, that doesn't stop customers still browsing the local original.

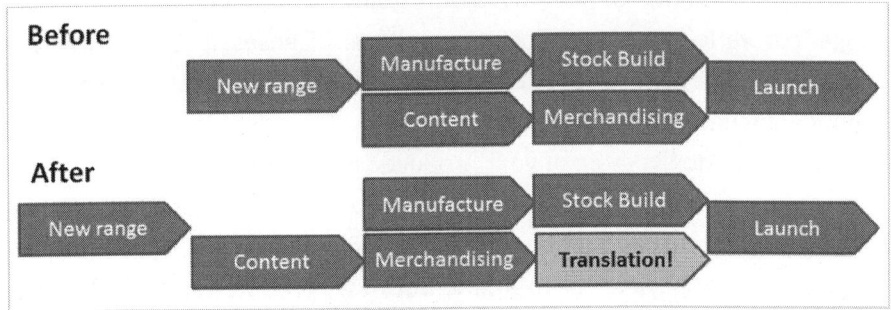

Figure 116 - New process, new critical path?

The same considerations apply at a smaller scale to content and merchandising. Typically this is a very responsive process, often on a daily or weekly cycle. There's a much bigger issue to consider – should it be consistent for different locations – but leaving that aside for now (it's covered later), there will be a need to put in place a strict process of production, translation, validation, publishing for every shared piece.

26.2.5 Tricky issues

I'll start by mentioning a notorious gotcha – different languages need more or less space to say the same thing[169]. Typically the most awkward spot is website top-navigation. Reducing your top-level categories is *not* an easy challenge to tackle.

A different issue, but one which also affects site navigation, is that of sizes. Local size-schemes don't necessarily translate naturally into size-schemes for other countries. For example there isn't a one-to-one match between UK or US and European shoe-sizes, and although sizes are gender-uniform in Europe, they are gender-specific in the US and many Asian countries.

In fact this raises another challenge – it isn't just translation, there's also a potential (big!) data maintenance challenge. Do you, for example, quote measurements in metric, US or UK imperial? If so, you might need multiple

---

[169] For example various sources suggest that Spanish typically needs 25% more space than English on average. An estimate for German is left as an exercise for the reader.

different versions of the product specification: American consumers tend not to love millimetres for example.

As a final point, maybe you aren't going to list your whole product range, for various reasons (logistics, cultural, licenses...). Does this have navigational and taxonomy implications? Is there any danger of a site with empty branches or dead ends on it?

Even if you do list most of your products: do you need to translate them all to start with? You probably need to translate their navigational features, otherwise your site navigation will end up with a linguistic mess – colour-filters in two languages for example. But most product ranges follow the 80/20 rule when it comes to sales. Why not take the same approach to translation?

26.3   Market entry

26.3.1 Introduction

If your ecommerce exposure has mainly been to the UK, US, Western Europe or Australia, then your instinctive picture of an online presence is probably 'your' website (www.mysite.co.uk). Logically enough, your first picture of your presence in a new overseas market is probably the same – www.mysite.overthere. If so, you're probably picturing a translated version of your local site as a starting point. As we established in the previous section, deciding to produce a translated version of your website can be a major undertaking, potentially requiring some pretty big changes to overall business processes.

However ecommerce is most definitely NOT the same everywhere in the world, and this isn't just a question of dealing with some of the more difficult localisation challenges such as payment methods (see below). Rather, it's a bigger question – the structure of online retailing.

26.3.2 Marketplaces & platforms

One of the bigger differences is the relative importance of marketplaces and platforms. In many countries, eBay (or its equivalents) is often used only as a clearance channel, or dismissed as 'not for serious retailers' (especially considering its charges). Elsewhere in the world, including some very interesting countries for brands and retailers, marketplaces and platforms are where the main action happens (*Figure 117*):

Figure 117 - Marketplaces & platforms as a % of online retail[170,171]

In the UK, for example, many big retailers mostly saw ecommerce coming early, got started with it in good time, and so managed to hold on to their share of consumers; in fact that's exactly what this Handbook is encouraging you to do if you're still fortunate enough to be based in a country where online shopping is still in the earlier development phase! Not so elsewhere in the world, where marketplace and platform sites are where serious shoppers go to do serious shopping, not just to hunt around for bargains. And therefore they're also where serious brands want to be.

Nowhere is this more true than China. Alibaba has recognised that it wants to follow two potentially incompatible strategies – maintain a stranglehold on online retail; and be a comfortable place for top brands and retailers. Its solution is to split its offer into C2C TaoBao and B2C TMall. TMall is almost certainly where you want to be seen, and the recognised way to be seen is to create a Flagship Store, which showcases your products and brands. Try entering the URL *brandname*.tmall.com for any reasonably well-known brand, and you'll soon get the idea. (A hint, just in case you haven't already come across this trick – if you want to look easily at foreign-language websites, use Google Chrome. In the top RH corner of

---

[170] Data source (except UK): Nyenrode Business University et al, 2015.
[171] The corresponding figure for the US is believed to be around 20% - primarily eBay and Amazon marketplace – but it's surprisingly difficult to verify

the URL area, there's a translate icon which lets you flip between original source and – an approximation of – your own language).

One other consideration is vertical integration. At the time of writing there's an ongoing divorce of PayPal from eBay. The opposite is true elsewhere. For example Alibaba's great rival in China, Tencent, owns WeChat, which is the local mobile/social network *combined* equivalent of Facebook, Twitter, Pinterest, Instagram, any other social platforms you like using for any reason… and claims 700m active users accessing it at least four times per day. Tencent also has a major stake in JD.com, Alibaba's upcoming rival, 58.com the top classified ads site, dianping.com the top local info site, etc etc. Meanwhile Alibaba owns Alipay, the top online/mobile payment method, and many more. By entering via a platform you're likely to get access to a lot more local services and support.

In summary, a marketplace/platform approach might be a great way to dip your toe in the water in many countries. In some countries, such as China, it might be the best way to proceed to scale too.

26.3.3 Domain names and hosting

Suppose the marketplace route doesn't appeal to you. Obviously the first thing you can do is just permit international shipping from your local site. To go beyond that, you're going to want a local online presence, and that means a website. This raises an interesting question – what should you call it?

A few years ago, this question would have had one sensible answer: separate domains e.g. www.mysite.de, www.mysite.com.au, etc. The obvious benchmarks for this approach are Amazon and especially Google, who you might expect to know what they are doing with this issue. However as sites have increasingly sought a global presence, alternative approaches are more prominent, which are now much better supported, especially by Google. The three options are shown in *Figure 118*:

Option	Structure	Examples
Multiple Domains	www.mysite.co.uk www.mysite.de etc	Amazon, Google, Zalando
Subdomains	fr.mysite.com de.mysite.com	Wikipedia
Folders	www.mysite.com/de www.mysite.com/fr-be	Apple, IKEA

Figure 118 - Three domain structure options

Google around the topic, and you'll find a great deal of confusing and conflicting advice in this area, mostly focussed on the potential impact on SEO. Unless you are very large organisation, however, the reality is that SEO is probably not your primary consideration here (even if maybe it should be) – manageability will tend to trump other considerations every time.

There are two key questions to ask.

"How structurally similar are my different country sites (apart from language), and how much resource do I have to manage the differences?"

If your sites are essentially clones, and are going to be managed by a single central team, take the folders option.

On the other hand, if your sites will be quite different, with significant de-centralised/local site administration and content, and maybe structural differences in critical areas such as taxonomy, then take the different domains option.

"Where are we (or who is) hosting my different country sites?"

There may be specific legal or technical reasons to host sites locally in certain countries (see below). If not, then this is once again a question of manageability – are you comfortable working with multiple partners in different countries?

One consideration to remove from this decision-frame early is that of performance. As soon as you leave your home shores, the digital media on your site belongs on a content distribution network. This is especially true if you are targeting another continent; simple intercontinental latency issues can make an otherwise good site feel clunky and slow.

If you want central control, or a single partner, then once again folders is probably your best option.

26.3.4 Getting found

It's not just about Google.

OK, just kidding, it is mostly about Google, almost everywhere (*Figure 119*).

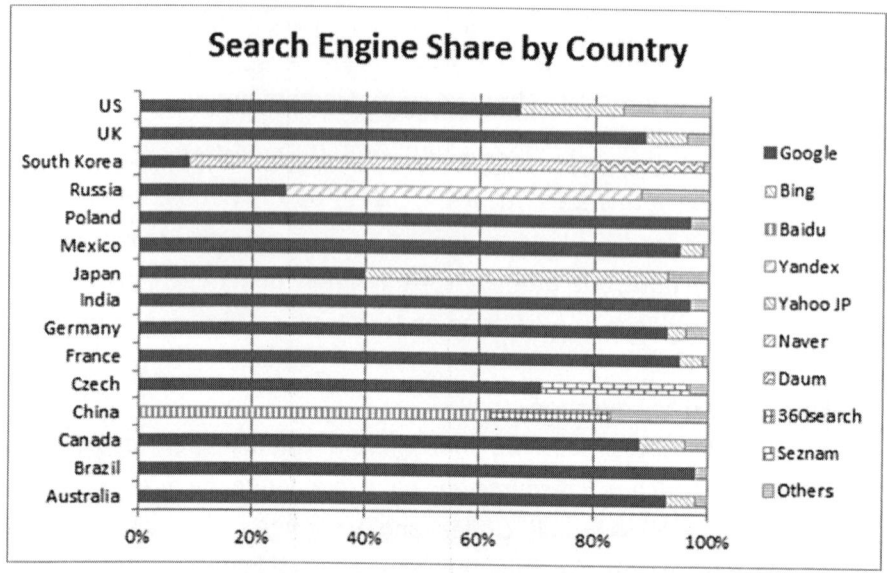

Figure 119 – Search engine share by country[172]

Moreover, the general trend for many countries – with the exception of China – is that Google's market share is increasing, in some cases (e.g. South Korea) quite strongly. An interesting related statistic – sorry Microsoft - is that both Baidu and Yandex have a greater share of global search than Bing.

Just for a change, then, something to make your life easier when planning international ecommerce – the techniques you've mastered for SEO and SEM are likely to be the same techniques that will work in other countries. You might decide to use a local agency – probably recommended, optimisation relies to a significant extent on local knowledge – but the reports and proposals they produce should look familiar and you'll largely able to evaluate their effectiveness using your existence 'home' experience.

---

[172] Webcertain Global Search Report, 2013

In some ways, with the possible exception of Japan, the outliers are very clear cut – China, Russia, South Korea. You'll need specialist support for these, otherwise Google is the obvious starting place.

However… in marketplace-dominated countries, not all retail search starts from a search engine. In China or Japan, for example, the local primary search engines, Baidu and Yahoo respectively, are simply not where shoppers begin their searches. They start from within the platform itself. Again you'll need specialist support: SEO considerations within marketplaces are *very* different, strongly driven by the profitability for the marketplace.

26.3.5 Getting loved

Another trend which makes life easier for marketeers planning the entry into new countries is the consolidation of social networking. At home it might seem that there's always another channel popping up (before it gets acquired by one of the big players anxious to protect its position…). Globally the macro-trend, once again with the exceptions of China and Russia - oh yes and Iran – is towards Facebook dominance, with Twitter generally the runner-up (*Figure 120*).

Countries	Non-Facebook dominant social networks
Russia, Kazakhstan	1: VKontakt; 2: Facebook; 3: Odnoklassniki
China	QZone / Wechat And definitely **not** Facebook or Twitter which are blocked by the Great Firewall!
Japan	1: Twitter; 2: Facebook
Uzbekistan, Turkmenistan	1: Odnoklassniki; 2: VKontakt; 3: Facebook
Iran	Facenama

Figure 120 - Where Facebook is not the dominant social network[173]

What is also helpful here is that a lot of dying or mythical social networks can be reduced in priority, especially Orkut, which used to be dominant in countries such as India and Brazil, but has now been

---

[173] Data source: wearesocial.net plus www.vincos.it mentioned in the next note

eclipsed[174] (remember MySpace?). This makes it very easy to make a recommendation for this guide: apart from China and maybe Russia, start with Facebook and worry about the others later, maybe beginning with Twitter.

There's quite a high probability that this is what you're already doing! Where the catch comes is similar to the issues with domain naming – are you going to be doing it with your existing team, or will you be devolving the responsibility? With this comes an important question – one Facebook page or many?

Localising to multiple pages, especially if this involves multiple languages, is almost certainly the better option, *if* you can afford the time to do it, otherwise your page risks ending up a confusing Tower of Babel, potentially limiting interaction. Before you opt for the multi-page direction, however, evaluate the effort that currently goes into your (single) current page – do you have the resources to do this many times over?

A last point to conclude this section – key opinion leaders are almost invariably local. If microsites, blogs, endorsements etc are part of your marketing mix, you are probably going to need to do that locally. That may in turn mean following the set by many cross-border retailers and setting up a small local marketing team as your first baby step towards full internationalisation.

26.4   Legal, payment & finance

26.4.1 Introduction

If you are entering a country via a marketplace or platform, then the rules of engagement with the platform will pretty much ensure that you are fully compliant in all these areas. *Don't* assume that they are the same rules as eBay or Amazon or your other local favourite – take the time to wade through all the small print (this is another major factor in favour of using marketplaces as an entry-strategy.)

If you're not going through the tightly controlled environment of a marketplace, then you should assume that legal, finance and most

---

[174] The apparently meticulously researched blog, vincos.it, contains some beautiful maps showing the consolidation of social networking globally over the last 5 years. Goodbye Orkut, Friendster, Zing, Wretch, Maktoob, and many more...

especially payment issues are going to be any implementation project's critical path, at least until proven otherwise.

26.4.2 Legal issues

There are a lot of myths and rumours surrounding the legal issues involved in international ecommerce. Legal issues are not a good area for myths, so here are three starting pointers.

If it walks like a duck and talks like a duck, it is a duck

If international customers believe they are shopping from a local site that just happens to ship overseas, then you can reasonably apply local law/consumer protection etc to the site and the transaction. Within the EU this principle is (partially) endorsed by EU law.

If, on the other hand, the site 'looks like' a local site – local language, currency etc – then you should assume that local law applies to the transaction. Putting small print in the T&Cs on the site about your preferred jurisdiction is not going to help. You *must* assume that localisation means local law unless explicitly professionally advised otherwise.

When in Rome, do as the Romans do

Take a look at what the top local players put in their policies. Every website has T&Cs, returns policies, and so forth. It's easy to find out who the top sites are in any country (ignore Amazon and any marketplaces and concentrate on local pure-players). With the exception of free delivery, it's rare for any of these policies to be there as marketing ploys – they are almost certainly in place for local compliance reasons.

Never take legal advice from the internet, or from Handbooks such as this one

Include a provision in your budget for some local, professional advice. Spend that budget. (For avoidance of doubt, this is a disclaimer: your author is NOT a legal professional and what's written here is just guidance about where to start and should not be regarded in any way as legal advice.)

26.4.3 A basic legal issues checklist

Taking careful note of the previous point, here is a suggested checklist of areas you may need to consider for compliance purposes. It's a starting point, not a comprehensive list (*Figure 121*):

Key Area	Comments
T&Cs	Self-explanatory. You'll need local language T&C. Pay particular attention to any policies around site usage by under-18s
Distance selling	Especially cooling off periods (e.g. 7-days to change your mind) and permitted exceptions (like ear-rings)
Consumer protection	Especially the reasons and the length of time permitted to return goods (30 or 90 days is NOT standard worldwide)
Returns	In some countries, it is not accepted, or even in some cases permitted, to charge postage for returns. Germany is a particularly well known example; the effect is higher returns rates and costs
Cookies	All of Europe requires an explicit statement to the customer if your site uses cookies. Most require an opt-out option (although this can just be, "OK, the site won't work for me then"). A few countries require the customer to explicitly opt-in.
Data protection	An area with more than its share of myths. The main issues are typically around *retaining* information (not capturing it for transient use such as in checkout or shipping). All likely target countries have applicable law, and some are more stringent than you may be used to (Germany for example).
Promotion & sales	In many countries, retailers are not free to promote as they fancy. France, for example, restricts clearance sale periods, and Boxing Day is not one of the permitted ones. Other countries restrict items being sold for less than cost-price other than via approved clearance processes

Price display	Check rules on displaying values such as MRP, inc/ex-VAT etc
Distribution rights	If you're not the brand or manufacturer, check you have the rights to sell their range into the country you are targeting
Permitted imports	Some countries have bizarre restrictions: no umbrellas to Brazil, sewing machines to China, or leather to Sri Lanka, for example[175]
Labelling	Once you are selling locally, your product labelling needs to be locally compliant. Some of this is regulatory; other areas are good presentation practice. For example US consumers like to know country-of-origin even if this is not legally mandated

Figure 121 - Some legal issues

26.4.4 Payment

Payment methods are probably the nastiest "technical" issue to be tackled in order to access overseas customers. Preferred online payment methods vary quite widely by country, and not being able to pay the way you are comfortable is a big barrier to customers (*Figure 122*).

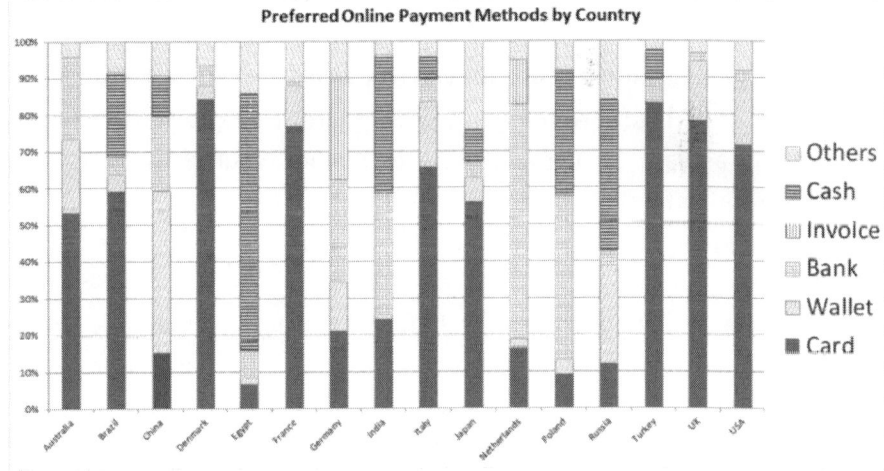

Figure 122 – Preferred payment methods in various countries[176]

---

[175] Source: Retail Touchpoints, Global E-Commerce Roadmap (Pitney Bowes 2013)

Be warned that even countries that appear sympathetic to "standard" methods such as Visa/Mastercard in theory may not be so in practice – Brazilian cards, for example, often don't support international transactions.

In practice, payment method support can be broken down into a fairly straightforward hierarchy of difficulty versus reward.

First, you're almost certainly supporting Visa and MasterCard. Extending such support to international transactions is usually simply a matter of configuration. What isn't quite so easy is tuning your fraud-screening, where specialist advice may be required (often this is available via your payment gateway).

Second, in countries where e-wallets have significant share, it's most likely to be Paypal (except China where it's Alipay). If you aren't already offering it at home, do so in advance to get used to working with it. Many companies find the additional transaction costs offset by additional sales, often significantly.

Third, check if there are local card schemes which operate in a transaction flow more-or-less consistent with Visa/MasterCard. JCB-card in Japan is a reasonably example. Implementation can require a lot of elapsed time, due to registration and certification requirements, but technically it isn't particularly difficult, and more importantly won't impact on the normal transaction and accounting flow on your site. (Unipay in China is an exception).

Fourth, there are some countries where specialist local methods have to be tackled. iDeal in the Netherlands (59% share) is an obvious example. There aren't actually so many of these as rumour would have it, it's just that they're in otherwise very attractive markets (especially Netherlands and Germany). As with the previous point, allow *plenty* of time in any project plan.

Fifth, take a very deep breath before tackling any methods which involve you in a significant variation to your normal transaction flow. The main such is likely to be cash-on-delivery if you don't already offer it in your local markets. Typically it isn't actually very hard to do on the ground – the main parcel-delivery companies in such countries offer doorstep payment handling and settlement as a standard add-on service. Where it really

---

[176] Data source (mainly):Worldpay Alternative Payments 2nd Edition, 2014

messes you up is in transaction flow and accounting policy. See **Chapter 15** for more information.

26.4.5 Finance

Many key issues are easy to demonstrate, by using IKEA's ubiquitous Billy Bookcase (**Figure 123**).

France	Poland	Sweden	Spain	Singapore	USA	Czech	UK
£46.09	£43.97	£45.83	£48.93	£58.90	£50.94	£46.57	£55

> IKEA furniture has suddenly became a scarce good in Russia. The Swedish furniture maker has followed Apple (AAPL, Tech30) and suspended sales after a dramatic fall in the ruble.

Figure 123 - IKEA Billy Bookcase[177]

Any company trading internationally is exposed to exchange-rate risks. How much risk obviously depends on your chosen operating model, especially logistics – if you decide to send significant quantities of stock into another country to have local availability then clearly you're exposed to it changing in local value. Similarly, technical issues such as transfer pricing need to be checked out. The Russian headlines quoted in **Figure 123** are obviously an extreme case, but even more "normal" markets can be exposed to quite big variations:

"Rest of the world growth was also impacted by adverse currency movements in the first half, when revenues declined by 11%, but recovered in the second half after implementation of a re-pricing strategy in Australia" [subsequently indicated as being reductions in the 15%-20% range].[178]

IKEA is trading via localised websites, and so is obliged to include local VAT or sales tax in its prices. This is another area to take professional

---

[177] Pricing from IKEA's global website in June 2015. The quotation is from CNN on 18th Dec 2014

[178] Boohoo.com, FY15 annual report and subsequent Q1 update

advice about, but a reasonable starting assumption for planning purposes is similar to the legal one above – if your website purports to be local, then so is its sales tax.

(If you are a non-US reader planning to localise for the US, then this is a horribly complex area that will require connecting your checkout to a sales-tax and/or DDP (see below) calculating service. These in turn require you to classify every product on your site with an extra product-type code, adding to the burden of product master data maintenance and translation; US sales tax rates vary by state and product type. This often requires an even more unpleasant change – your checkout flow may have to be amended because the final price isn't known until *after* the delivery address is nominated).

And then there's the customer perception issue. How happy are you that a French customer can buy the same IKEA book-case 16% cheaper than a British one? Just because you might redirect your customers based on IP-address geo-location doesn't stop them being able to look at the sites for other countries (IKEA is a case in point – I've easily been able to check their pricing globally to make that graphic) and compare prices... and complain, and write unpleasant posts about the difference on social media. You can't realistically flex prices up-and-down as the exchange rate varies day-to-day, some stability is required for customers, and therefore discrepancies will occur.

How serious this is may in turn depend on an issue covered later in this chapter – is your international ecommerce competing with local distributors of the same products?

26.5   Logistics and shipping

26.5.1 Sending your parcels

Pretty obviously the first thing you need is a shipping partner who will take parcels outside your home country. Most of the usual suspects do so, but don't just assume you should use your current partners, for several reasons.

The most basic reason is cost. The most cost-effective partner for delivering your particular products overseas may not be the partner you use locally. Incidentally cross-border orders tend to be higher value and for more articles per order, because customers want to consolidate the (presumably) higher delivery charges, which may in turn affect the delivery-cost-profile of your orders (**Figure 124**):

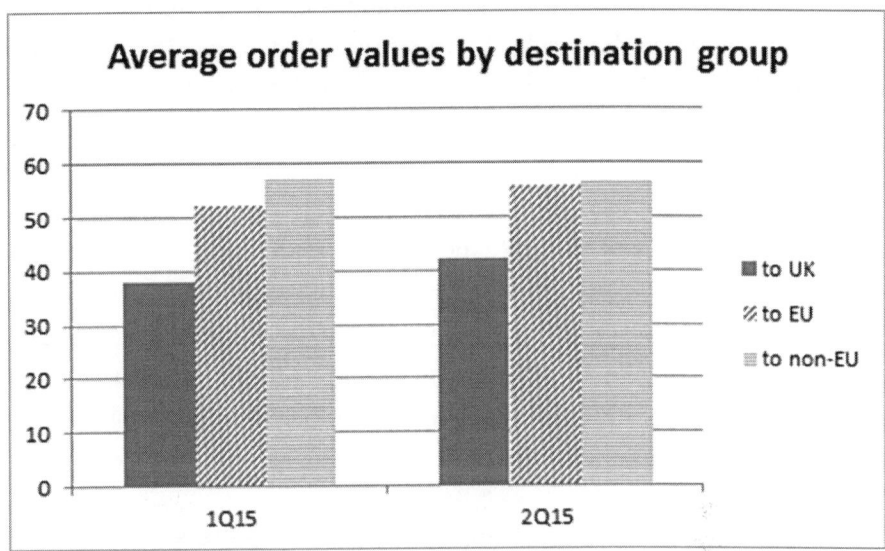

Figure 124 – Average 1-man non-food order values for UK retailers[179]

(Delivery fees on the order themselves only really become an issue if you localise the site. Customers then have a reasonable expectation of receiving local delivery pricing. Since even domestic delivery is often subsidised by retailers to help conversion, competing with the offer from local players could be quite expensive.)

Of course introducing another delivery partner increases the complexity in your fulfilment centre. On the other hand, you are unlikely to be flooded with overseas orders on the day you launch, and so babysitting such a change is practical: remember the happy days when you launched your first transactional site and watched the orders start to trickle in.

Next up on the list is track-and-trace. Your delivery company may be using a partner network for some or all countries on your list. For any countries to which you hope to ship significant volumes, you need to be sure you can trace the parcels with the same confidence and granularity you are used to back home... or possibly even more confidence if cash-on-delivery is involved. Preferably your international customers should be able to track themselves – experience suggests that international customers are

[179] IMRG Metapack UK Delivery Index Report July 2015

even more neurotic than domestic ones if the delivery looks to them like it might have fallen behind schedule.

As we all know from experience, track-and-trace is less necessary if you can be sure you have the right address in the first place. There are two stages to this. The first is simple – ensure your checkout doesn't actually reject address details from overseas customers. International phone numbers routinely include the characters '+()-.' and so a checkout that rejects non-digits just lost you a conversion and a new customers. Similarly postcode checkers need to relax when dealing with foreign addresses. Or not. The second stage is to add international address-checking, which many existing solutions will support in theory. It has to be said that this varies in effectiveness, especially for parts of Asia or Latin America, so you may still be forced to adopt a more laid-back approach than would be appropriate for domestic addresses (this in turn of course has an impact on fraud-screening).

Set realistic expectations around delivery times and the process, and display these clearly in the help pages of your website. What delivery times and process you can expect to be displaying ultimately depends on how you decide to solve all these challenges. Fundamentally you have three possible approaches (*Figure 125*):

Postal	Pretty much as it sounds: you give it to the parcel company in at home, and they send it on.
	Essentially 'unmanaged' and therefore cheapest, although increasing numbers of destinations have services offering some tracking
Express point-to-point	The big global carriers will undoubtedly get it there, quickly, and you'll be able to track it the whole way through
	Premium cost for premium service
Managed direct access	An emerging mid-tier class of solution, which uses local partners at both ends of the process, manages the hand-off between the two and the associated issues which arise at this hand-off, especially duties (see below) and connecting up track-and-trace

Figure 125 - approaches to cross-border shipping

26.5.2 The call of duties

Once you step outside a trade-zone such as the EU the complexities of customs duties are fairly bewildering. *Every* country has different rules applying to different categories of products. Best practice is to offer the customer to pre-pay the import duty where this is possible, known as DDP (delivery and duty paid) (**Figure 126**). Online footwear retailer Planet Shoes saw international conversions rates almost double when this option was introduced.[180]

Figure 126 – Turning Japanese[181]

Some customer might prefer to have the option of taking their chances by not paying the duty, but in practice most do so, and you might find it simpler – and less likely to lose you a customer later – to simply make it

---

[180] A Nation of Shopkeepers, IMRG, July 2015
[181] Collage from Harrods checkout

mandatory. Some sample opt-in rates for shipments to various countries (*Figure 127*):

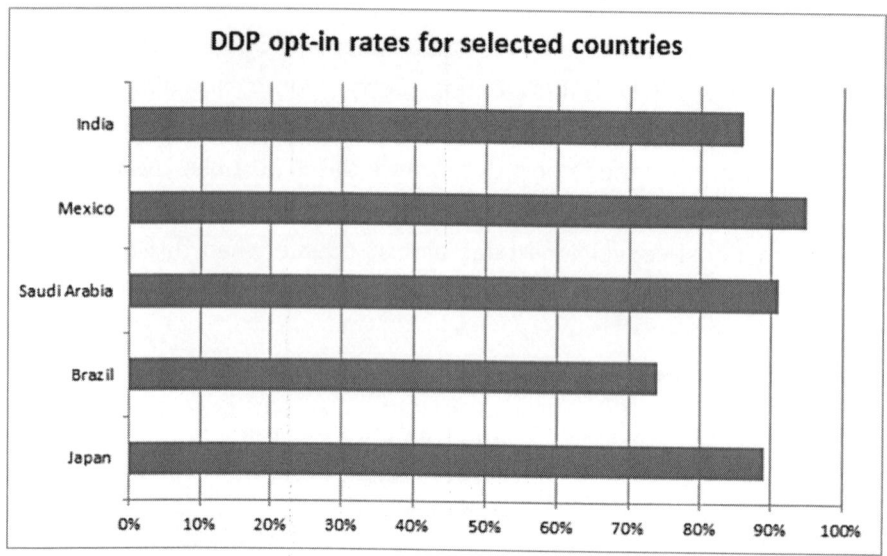

Figure 127 – country DDP opt-in rates for shipments[182]

26.5.3 Returns

The practicality of returns is the single biggest reason that makes customers nervous about purchasing from overseas websites (*Figure 128*), far more important than language for example:

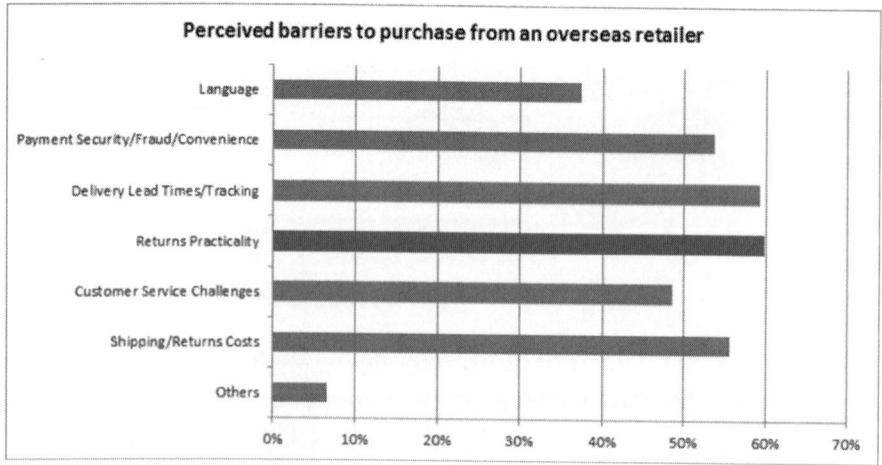

Figure 128 – Reasons for not shopping from overseas sites[183]

---

[182] A Nation of Shopkeepers, IMRG, July 2015

What is perhaps surprising about these answers is how many of them are fairly easily avoidable in ways we have already discussed above, often by absolute basics such as clearly setting expectations, displaying quality marks (specific to the target local market, not domestic), offering duty-paid shipping etc. Returns, and the associated customer service is more operationally challenging is. Here's a view from a couple of experts (**Figure 129**):

What the opinion former blogged	*"What I found was that ASOS has an Australian returns address, meaning I didn't have to pay for international shipping to send the clothes back. Bonus!* *I was in big trouble. The clothes were my kind of style, they offered free international shipping, and refunds were allowed; a lethal combination, in short, I said farewell to $1,000 that day."*
What the retailer said in its annual accounts	*"A key part of retaining customers is ensuring that the returns process is as smooth as possible. We process returns locally in the USA and Australia (our biggest markets outside the UK): this ensures that customers receive their refund as quickly as possible and the service is as cheap as possible"*

Figure 129 – International returns: expert opinions[184]

Notice the emphasis on customer retention in the retailer quote, and on conversion in the customer quote. It could be argued that the former is even more important – if that's possible – than when serving domestic customers. An international customer who already justified the perceived risk of making an overseas purchase may be more likely to stay hooked, and equally more likely to depart for good if exposed to a very long delay before getting credited. In short, a good returns policy and process is a sales-driver.

---

[183] IMRG Blackbay Consumer Home Delivery Review, 2015

[184] Corporate quote from ASOS annual accounts 2012. Blog written by someone who describes herself as "I'm Nikki and I'm hooked on online shopping"

As always, there are some potential steps-up in complexity available. Providing an overseas returns address, but then consolidating returns periodically into a single shipment back home, is one way to start.

The same step-by-step-up approach applies to customer service activities. A full multilingual 24x7 telephone support line is a major step for all except the most committed, but intermediate options are available, and email is likely to be an easier option anyway – customers who don't speak your native language are probably just as scared of calling as you are of answering!

Whatever you finally decide to do, spell the process out very clearly to customers, both on the website and preferably in the parcel documentation too. This is an area where the payback on the costs of translation such as documentation and instructions, at least into the languages of your top handful of target countries, may well be rapid. While doing so, check your packaging complies with local law and customs – it's no good using a wine-bottle pictogram to represent "fragile" when shipping to Islamic destinations.

26.5.4 Overseas fulfilment

A fully-fledged overseas fulfilment centre is likely to be the last link in the chain, although it is worth noting that several IMRG survey respondents already had one. Do be very aware of the local competition and benchmarks before you attempt this – the "delivery 3 hours after your order is placed" offer from JD.com in China, for example, is not one you are going to be competing with

However, this is not necessarily an all-or-nothing type decision. Every retailer and brand typically has a strong 80/20 element to their range. The business-case for locating that 20% of top-sellers nearer to its customers in a local mini-fulfilment centre can look compelling. Be aware, however, that the IT, finance and order management challenges in managing split fulfilment orders (products shipped from different fulfilment centres for a single order) are fairly formidable even domestically; getting this all to work cross-border may leave the logistics elements of the project looking like the easy part.

One other possibility to explore for brands is that of using their local distributor to fulfil orders from the centrally managed website. This question – a classic channel conflict problem - leads us nicely on to some of the thornier strategic challenges to be faced in becoming international.

26.6 Strategic Issues

26.6.1 Introduction

Most of the previous sections of this paper have a common theme – they are a lengthy liturgy of systematically overcoming negatives, about lowering the barriers to international shoppers purchasing from what, to them, is a foreign retailer.

It's surprising how often the other side of the coin gets overlooked[185]. Even if you have overcome all possible negatives, there still need to be some positive reasons for international consumers to purchase from your site. Once you've identified what these might be, it becomes practical to start to estimate the size of the prize and hence to decide where to focus your energies.

26.6.2 Finding the motivators/differentiation

Once again, we can use the P.R.I.C.E. framework (see **Chapter 5**) as a way to consider what might motivate an overseas shopper to buy from you.

Price	Realistically speaking, it's pretty difficult for a retailer to sustain a price advantage when trading internationally, at least without making the major step-change investments needed to effectively operate fully from another country.
	Exchange rates, duties, shipping costs etc all make a price-based strategy generally challenging to execute. In many countries this is exacerbated by the presence of local pure-players interested only in (tiny) cash margins or with

---

[185] I recall a number of discussions with retailers who had fixed a few basic cross-border hygiene factors on their site (e.g. checkout), and then spent PPC money bringing international customers to it. Conversion was non-existent. On closer inspection, there was simply no reason for an overseas customer to buy there instead of domestically.

	access to thriving grey-markets
Range	The top reason customers give for shopping from an overseas site is that they couldn't buy what they wanted at home.[186]
	Having something unique to sell is by far the most compelling proposition to a prospective overseas customer. Typically this means being the brand or manufacturer, or just possibly owning the regional rights
	Conversely being a generic seller is likely to be tough going, although let's not forget Amazon(!), ASOS or Zalando.
Information	It's always tough to use this as a sustainable differentiator, especially if you have to translate it all too
	Niche players, however, stand a better chance, playing on that same "couldn't get it at home" theme.
Convenience	Obviously this is very difficult to do, given the logistics challenges involved. On the other hand it has evidently been a fundamental pillar for the success of ASOS for example – see the quotes above – and of course for Amazon.
Experience	An interesting one. The development of online retail does still vary a lot from country-to-country, and so the opportunity to offer a superior experience still exists. In general don't try this in any country where Amazon has got going in strength, nor in China.
	There's also a question about whether any such advantage is sustainable in the long-term, as local players 'catch up'.

In summary, four main strategic options seem to have proven track-records:

1. Be the brand or manufacturer

2. Be a strongly defined niche player in particular categories

3. Target niche countries and try to stay ahead

---

[186] For example, see eDigital Research survey for IMRG, July 2014

4. Have a successful proposition at home, and really go for replicating it big time abroad (Amazon springs to mind!)

26.6.3 Estimating the opportunity

There are two stages to this. The first is to look at the generic opportunity a country represents. This used to be rather difficult to do, due to the paucity of helpful statistics. This in turn was partly due to the need to estimate the *future* potential of a country, based on underlying factors such as broadband penetration, payment card penetration, parcel-shipping infrastructure, and general internet take-up. By far the most important of these, by the way, is broadband penetration – online purchasing is a relatively complex transaction and needs reasonable network speed as a general enabler; the difference in 2015 is that this could be either landline or, in many countries such as India or China, mobile.

Such an approach is increasingly obsolete. Internet retailing is maturing in most interesting markets, to the point where it becomes more realistic to look at *now*, not the speculative future. Lots of detailed studies, based on experience, are available to help with this. Just Google a bit and you'll soon find (a lot) of them.

There are also various published indices which attempt to rank the ecommerce attractiveness of potential countries in various ways. A bit of common-sense needs to be applied when reading them (unless you plan to really go hard for that niche market strategy proposed above) – the top 20 fastest growing markets include Albania, Azerbaijan, Macedonia, and Ecuador, while the fourth highest penetration of online retail (theoretically) is in Suriname – and then they generally tell you what you would expect.

These generic overviews provide the essential starting inputs to the second stage of the process – drilling down to the much more critical question "what opportunity does this country represent for us?" We can consider a 4-stage approach to evaluating the answer to this (*Figure 130*):

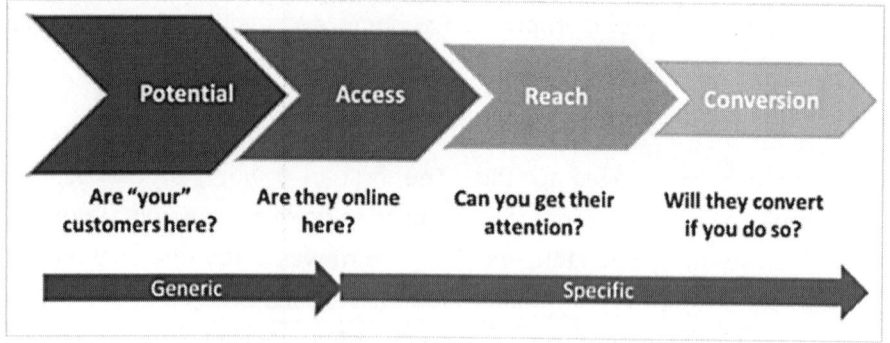

Figure 130 – Drilling down to country size of prize

Potential: are "your" customers here?

This is largely a sense check. If you are selling deer-stalker hats, does anybody in this country stalk deer? If so, how many of them? Can they afford your hats?

Similarly, the generic inputs and reports about ecommerce activity and potential in this country can be applied – is this a realistic country to target right now?

One other obvious point: you'll be used to the competitor landscape at home. It might be rather different elsewhere, with local category killers.

Access: are they online here?

In most highly developed countries, internet access and usage is very broad-based. If your products target a particular consumer segment, you can reasonably assume they are online shoppers. This is emphatically not the case in other countries, even quite developed ones.

Firstly, access, and especially the broadband access that is a necessary enabler for online retail, is heavily concentrated in big cities in many countries. 60% of online retail in Russia, for example, takes place in the Moscow and St Petersburg regions[187] despite only 15% of the population living there.

Secondly, consumer some segments, especially older demographics, have not (yet) seen internet take-up to the same extent. Only 4% of Russian

---

[187] Morgan Stanley, Russian eCommerce, January 2013

internet users are retired[188], for example, although 15% of the population are over 65[189].

So if your target consumer is an affluent pensioner who retired to the countryside, it's probably best to forget about Russia!

Reach: can you get their attention?

Many brands will be familiar with the experience that the majority of their visits are in some way based on brand-terms. In turn the activity on brand-terms is driven by the profile of the brand itself – there's usually a straightforward correlation. This isn't going to be any different elsewhere. If your brand has no profile, your international presence will get no traffic.

Various inputs can help you get colour on this including (obviously) visitor numbers to your existing site from overseas, and Google Trends (or Baidu Index for China, which needs registration), or relevant marketplace searches.

Ultimately you are going to have to invest in building brand awareness. Even harnessing all the power of social media, this is still potentially expensive, which in turn helps with focus: there's little point in spreading too thinly or else *nobody* will notice you!

If you are selling generic products, there's typically a lot more data to go on, but then there's typically a lot more competition too.

Conversion: will they actually buy?

"Yes", is the short answer, but the trouble is that in many countries this can be enlarged to "yes, but only if you are on promotion." There is a perception that stores are where you buy at normal prices, and the internet is where you get deals.

Nowhere is this more so than China, where a proliferation of artificial "festivals" with numerological date names such as 11.11, 6.18 and so forth, is fuelled almost entirely by promotions, and the success of a brand for a year can be determined by a single day event. Even guidance from JD.com, Alibaba's big competitor, and which has a vested interested in trying to reduce the intensity of price war, is – 10% of a range should be top-sellers (or unique) and priced around 10% under the normal store price, another

---

[188] TNS Web Index
[189] CIA World Factbook

20% should be on promotion in some way, and 70% should be at standard prices; the expected rate of sale on that long-tail is left to your imagination.

In short, consider your margins. Remembering too that you might be paying overseas shipping rates, consider your delivered-margins even more carefully.

26.6.4 Matching opportunity to difficulty

Bringing all of the previous topics together, we arrive at the 64 million dollar (OK, that would be nice wouldn't it) question – where and how? A good way to visualise the answer to that question is to plot prospective target markets into quadrants, considering size of prize versus all the operational difficulties (*Figure 131*):

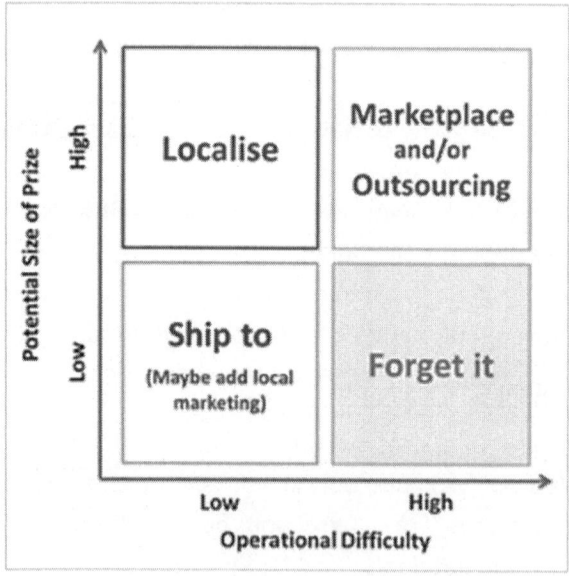

Figure 131 – Evaluating the options

Having taken the basic decision about which approach to adopt, there's no need to try and swallow the whole elephant in one gulp. A good approach is to gradually step-up the depth and complexity of international integration. This isn't a single-track road either – one might operate at different levels for different competencies, gradually moving more successful or interesting countries up the curve (*Figure 132*).

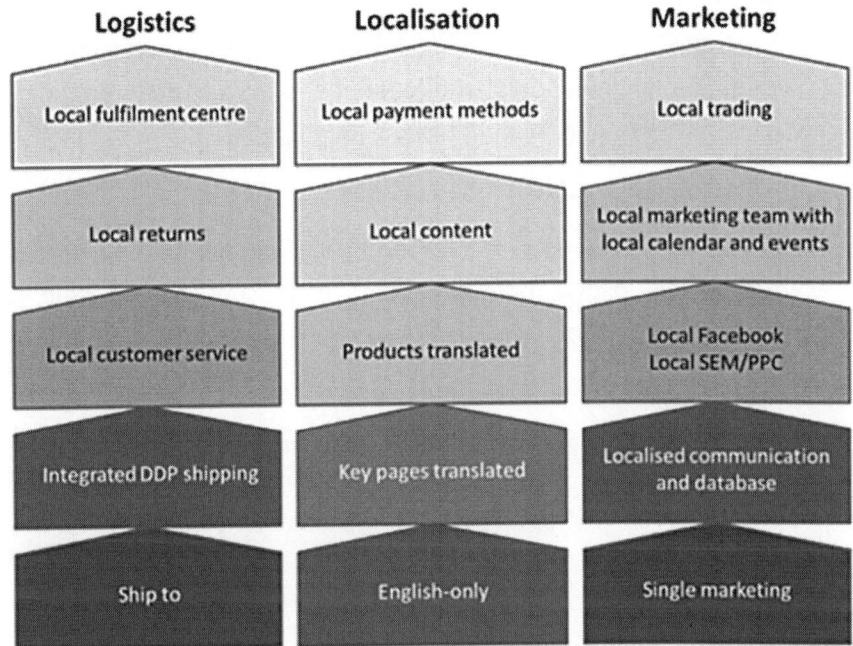

Logistics	Localisation	Marketing
Local fulfilment centre	Local payment methods	Local trading
Local returns	Local content	Local marketing team with local calendar and events
Local customer service	Products translated	Local Facebook Local SEM/PPC
Integrated DDP shipping	Key pages translated	Localised communication and database
Ship to	English-only	Single marketing

Figure 132 – Implementation paths towards internationalisation

26.6.5 Summary of Approaches

The different tiers, or approaches, to cross-border ecommerce can be summed up as:

Ship To

Typically you extend your existing offering to make it easier for international customers, offering appropriate shipping options, possibly adding payment options, and just possibly doing some translation. Customers remain fully aware that this is a "foreign" site they're buying from.

Marketplace

You localise, but do so by participating in a local marketplace or platform, rather than constructing your own customer experience. For many countries this is probably the easiest step along the journey beyond a simple ship-to approach.

Localised

You localise in the full sense: customers are left with the impression that they are interacting with a local site (even if they remain fully aware that it's an overseas brand or retailer operating it).

26.7 Implementation Checklists

This chapter has covered a lot of ground, so in addition to the usual top-takeaways (which follow), here are some basic checklists to help get started.

26.7.1 Translation checklist

Task	Ship-to	Market-place	Localised	Size of task
Help screens	Yes		Yes	Small
Checkout prompts	Yes		Yes	Small
Emails	Yes	Some	Yes	Small
Website error messages			Yes	Medium
Marketing & merchandising Comms		Some	Yes	Medium & ongoing
Top-seller products	Maybe	Yes	Yes	Medium & ongoing
Base dictionary	Maybe	Yes	Yes	Medium
Brand dictionary	Maybe	Maybe	Yes	Medium
Navigation & taxonomy	Maybe		Yes	Complex
Long tail products		Maybe	Yes	Large & ongoing

Figure 133 – Translation checklist

26.7.2 Language-related tasks

Task	Ship-to	Market-place	Localised	Size of task
Navigation & taxonomy	Maybe		Yes	Complex
Website layout adjustments	Maybe		Yes	Large
Homepage & geo-IP landing pages			Yes	Medium
Business seasonal cycle		Maybe	Yes	HUGE
Product launch critical path		Maybe	Yes	Large
Sizes & measurements	Maybe	Yes	Yes	Large

Figure 134 – Language-related tasks checklist

26.7.3 Domains & related issues

Task	Ship-to	Market-place	Localised	Size of task
Domain name structure	Maybe		Yes	Medium
Marketplace flagship store		Yes		Large
Non-Google SEO		Yes	Maybe	Medium
Non-Google PPC / local agency		Maybe	Yes	Medium
Site hosting			Yes	Large
Content distribution network		Maybe	Yes	Large
Site structure (e.g. hreflang tags)	Maybe		Yes	Medium

Figure 135 – Domains & related issue checklist

26.7.4 Other marketing

Task	Ship-to	Market-place	Localised	Size of task
Local language SEO	Maybe		Yes	Medium
Local language PPC / local agency	Maybe		Maybe	Small
Customer database segmentation	Maybe	Yes	Maybe	Medium
Facebook page structure	Maybe	Maybe	Yes	Small
Social conversation management / agency	Maybe	Maybe	Maybe	Large
Local marketing team decision		Maybe	Maybe	Large
Engage local opinion formers/bloggers etc	Maybe	Maybe	Maybe	Medium

Figure 136 – Other marketing activities setup checklist

26.7.5 Legal

Task	Ship-to	Market-place	Localised	Size of task
Terms & conditions			Yes	Small
Distance selling regulations		Maybe	Yes	Small
Consumer protection periods etc	Maybe	Maybe	Yes	Medium
Returns policies	Maybe	Yes	Yes	Medium
Cookie policies			Yes	Mostly small
Data protection	Yes	Yes	Yes	Small
Promotion rules		Yes	Yes	Medium
Price display			Yes	Usually small
Distribution rights checking	Yes	Yes	Yes	Medium

Product labelling		Yes	Yes	Could be huge

Figure 137 – Legal issues checklist

26.7.6 Payment

Task	Ship-to	Market-place	Localised	Size of task
Research local payment methods			Yes	Small
Add local pay-on-despatch methods	Maybe		Maybe	Large
Add local pay-on-delivery methods	Maybe		Maybe	Huge
Change order-flow phasing	Maybe		Maybe	Huge
Change customer services SOPs	Maybe		Maybe	Large
Additional financial reconciliations	Maybe		Maybe	Medium
New accounting processes	Maybe		Maybe	Large
New fraud screening processes	Maybe		Maybe	Large
Local sales taxes			Yes	Large
Checkout changes	Yes		Yes	Large

Figure 138 – Payment checklist

26.7.7 Other finance

Task	Ship-to	Market-place	Localised	Size of task
Local pricing policy		Yes	Yes	Medium
VAT		Maybe	Yes	Medium
Transfer pricing issues		Maybe	Maybe	Small
Exchange rate exposure		Maybe	Maybe	Medium

Figure 139 – Other finance issues checklist

26.7.8 Shipping Basics

Task	Ship-to	Market-place	Localised	Size of task
Shipping partner selection	Yes	Yes	Yes	Medium
Secondary shipping partner implement	Maybe	Maybe	Maybe	Medium
Delivery pricing to customers	Yes	Maybe	Yes	Small
Fulfilment centre SOPs	Yes	Yes	Yes	Large
Parcel labelling	Yes	Yes	Yes	Medium
Cross-border track-and-trace	Yes	Yes	Yes	Medium
Address capture format changes	Yes		Yes	Small
International address checking	Maybe		Maybe	Large
Address fraud screening	Maybe		Maybe	Medium
Delivery notes & invoices translation	Maybe	Yes	Yes	Small
Site delivery pages	Yes		Yes	Small
Cross-border returns policies	Yes	Maybe	Yes	Medium
Amended returns SOPs	Yes	Yes	Yes	Medium

Figure 140 – Shipping basics checklist

26.7.9 Other logistics issues

Task	Ship-to	Market-place	Localised	Size of task
DDP	Maybe	Maybe	Maybe	Large or outsource
Checkout integration	Yes		Yes	Large
Local returns address	Maybe	Maybe	Maybe	Large or outsource
Local fulfilment centre		Maybe	Maybe	Huge
Engaging local partners (e.g. distributor)		Maybe	Maybe	Huge
Local customer services		Maybe	Maybe	Large

Figure 141 – Other logistics issues checklist

26.7.10 Country research checklist

Task	Ship-to	Market-place	Localised	Size of task
P.R.I.C.E. differentiation research	Maybe	Yes	Yes	Medium
Brand channel conflict planning	Maybe	Maybe	Maybe	Large
Opportunity estimation – demographics		Maybe	Yes	Small
Opportunity estimation - access		Maybe	Yes	Medium
Opportunity estimation – attention		Yes	Yes	Large
Opportunity estimation – conversion	Maybe	Yes	Yes	Medium

Figure 142 – Country research checklist

26.8   Top takeaways

26.8.1 Implementation

Many customers are prepared to purchase online in a language other than their native tongue, especially English.

Translation is not localisation, it's just one part of it.

In order of priority, you might translate the following: checkout; delivery and returns information; website prompts and error messages; customer services; marketing and merchandising communication; product details.

Challenging areas for translation include specialist terms, descriptive phrases, brand terms.

Commonly used generic search terms require translation of applicable landing pages and category structures.

Do not use Google translate!

Adding a lengthy translation step into the calendar rhythm of your business is a major change.

Beware of sizes and measurements when localising.

Consider marketplaces and platforms, as well as dedicated sites, in many markets (especially China).

If opting for a dedicated site approach, a domain naming choice is required: multiple domains; sub-domains; or folders. Key criteria are structural similarity, manageability, and (maybe) SEO.

Google is the dominant search engine in many countries. Key exceptions are Chinese, Japanese, Korean and Russian languages.

Facebook is the dominant social network in almost all potentially relevant countries. Key exceptions are China, and to a lesser extent Russian-language countries (Vkontakt, Odnoklassniki).

Take professional legal advice!

Some key legal areas: Ts & Cs and other policies; distance selling regulations; consumer protection; returns; cookie legislation (especially in the EU); data protection; regulation of promotion and sale periods; price display; distribution rights; permitted imports; product labelling rules.

Preferred payment methods vary widely across the globe. Key families are: credit/debit card; e-wallet (e.g. PayPal); invoice; bank-transfer; pay-on-delivery.

Take advice on fraud protection for cross-border payments; your payment-gateway may be a good source.

Plan for exchange rate exposure, and for selling the same product at different prices in different markets in a way that's visible to customers.

Overseas orders are typically higher value.

Alternative shipping partners should be considered. Options include: postal, express point-to-point, managed direct access.

Consider a DDP solution (delivery and duty paid).

Returns are the biggest barrier to converting international customers.

26.8.2 Planning and Choosing Countries

Using e-commerce to sell internationally/cross-border could be a huge opportunity. As one example, more overseas customers bought from UK websites than did UK citizens in 2013, and 18% of orders were shipped overseas.

Apply the P.R.I.C.E framework to your overseas customers. Remember you are differentiating against the local competition in your target countries, not your usual domestic competitors.

Best candidates for international e-commerce are: brands and manufacturers; well-defined niche players; niche countries; replication of the domestic offer in a full on way.

e-Retail is mature enough in 2015 to use "actual" statistics about specific countries, not predictive models of future take-up. (If you do predict, focus on broadband penetration).

Consider a four-stage filter:

- **Potential**: are "your" customers there?
- **Access**: are then online there?

- **Reach**: can you get their attention?
- **Conversion**: will they buy if you do so? Is it only on discount or promotion?

Implementation maturity can be at different stages within the same country market; for example you could have sophisticated logistics, fully local marketing, but limited localisation of your site.

A quadrant model for size-of-prize vs difficulty can be applied: options are simple ship-to, marketplaces, full localisation.

Glossary of Terms

Every discipline has its specialist terms, not necessarily purely in order to confound the outsider. I have tried to avoid jargon other than that which I have defined in the text, but some is inevitable, especially standard "business" jargon such as B2C. Moreover some terms which I have defined in the text nevertheless crop up sufficiently frequently to make it difficult to read an individual chapter standalone if you missed the definition in another chapter, hence the glossary.

A/B testing
The process of simultaneously serving two different experiences to a random cross-section of online customers, and measuring the difference in the results. See also *analytics*. See **Chapter 16**.

Adaptive Design
Adaptive design (suggested definition): adapting the user experience to fit the capabilities of the device. For example does it support GPS, or pinch-gestures? See **Chapter 23.**

Affiliate
A website which specialises in directing traffic to retailer sites in exchange for a commission on consequently checked out orders. See **Chapter 14**.

Analytics
An aggregated statistical view of the page to page journeys taken by online customers, used to measure the effectiveness of website customer experience in delivering goals. See **Chapter 16**.

ATP
Available to Promise. A description of the stock promise to online customers. See **Chapter 15.**

B2B
Business to Business

B2C
Business to Consumer

BIN Range
The first 6 digits of a credit card number, which define the issuing scheme and country of the issuer.

Bricks'n'clicks'n'flicks
The mixture of online, brick-and-mortar and paper (e.g. catalogue) retailing.

Broadband
Has different exact meanings in different countries. Generally used to refer to fixed-line connectivity which is faster than 56K dial-up modem, or to

mobile connectivity provided by 3G or 4G networks.

C2C Consumer to Consumer – typically used to describe marketplaces such as eBay or TaoBao.

Cannibalisation One sales channel taking sales away from another; typically used to refer to the switch of sales from brick-and-mortar to online channels within a single retailer.

Channel conflict Describes a retailer whose sales channels compete not collaborate with each other, most commonly competition between online and brick-and-mortar.

Click-and-collect An order online, collect from store proposition (often also referred to as "pick-up" or "pick-up in store"). See *Chapter 21*.

Click-through-rate The percentage of clicks to displays of an element on a screen.

CNP Card Not Present or Customer Not Present. Usually in the context of credit/debit cards payments via websites.

Conversion rate The percentage of visits to a store which result in a checkout.

CRM Customer Relationship Management

Cross-channel The joining up of retail channels from checkout and afterwards. See *Chapter 10.*

CSS Cascading Style Sheet. The technology used to determine what a page on a website "looks like" to the browser viewing it.

D2C Direct to Consumer – used to describe manufacturers or brands selling direct to end consumers, bypassing the retailer.

DC Distribution Centre. Warehouse used to replenish brick-and-mortar stores. Used as a term to distinguish from an online order Fulfilment Centre.

DDP Delivery and Duty Paid. Used in reference to parcels shipped cross-border with duty pre-paid during checkout.

Delivered Margin — Margin including delivery fee income but minus shipping costs (and other order lifecycle costs). See *Chapter 18*.

DSV — Drop Ship Vendor – a supplier which accepts orders from retailer websites and sends the goods directly to the end-customer. See *Chapter 15.*

Endless aisle — A category assortment containing a much broader range of products than can fit into a brick-and-mortar store aisle, because it includes a long tail.

ERP — Enterprise Resource Management (System)

FC — Fulfilment Centre. Warehouse used to process customer orders. Used as a term to distinguish from Distribution Centre.

FTE — Full Time Equivalent – one employee working full time.

Kompetenz — A word borrowed from German to describe a good multichannel assortment, having capability, authority, competence, jurisdiction. See *Chapter 7*

KPI — Key Performance Indicator.

Localisation — The process of making a proposition (website) "feel" to overseas customers as though they are shopping from a local domestic retailer

Long tail — Products which complete a range but are by no means the best-sellers which might fit into a store.

Merchandising — Used in a narrower sense to describe *how* products are sold; includes various practices such as cross-selling, up-selling, personalisation, recommendations

Omni-channel — The joining up of the customer's experience up to and including checkout. See *Chapter 10.*

OMS — Order Management Systems

One Second Rule — See *Chapter 4.* A way to describe the rapidity of customers to assess if an online screen is worth further attention

Order Lifecycle	Everything that happens to an order from checkout onwards. See **Chapter 15**.
P.R.I.C.E.	Differentiation framework based around 5 factors: Price, Range, Information, Convenience, Experience. See **Chapter 5** and following.
Payment Gateway	A service for processing customer payments online. See Chapter 15.
Payment policy	When money for an online order is taken from the customer. Typically one of on-despatch, on-order, on-delivery. See **Chapter 15.**
Persona	A stereo-typical artificially defined customer, used for planning purposes. See **Chapter 4**
Personalisation	Varying a proposition for each customer to offer an individual customer the things like are most likely to buy. See **Chapter 22**
PPC	Pay-per-click. See also SEM.
Price Transparency	An effect of online retailing in a market or country: prices for all standard products are available for customers to research and compare
PSP	Payment Service Provider – see payment gateway
Pure-play	A retailer which sells only online, with no brick-and-mortar stores.
Range	Synonym for assortment.
Responsive Design	Ensuring each page caters for the layout of any device that might be accessing it, by changing itself to fit. See **Chapter 23.**
Searchandising	Solutions which blend merchandising and search.
SEM	Search Engine Marketing
SEO	Search Engine Optimisation
Showrooming	The customer practice of visiting brick-and-mortar stores purely to touch and feel products which they subsequently buy online.
Silver Surfer	An older internet user, typically characterised by a mixture of careful research and higher spending

power.

SKU	Stock keeping unit. Usually a synonym for product, used in a numerical sense e.g. "this retailer has 9000 SKUs in its main assortment"
TaoBao/TMall	China's answer to eBay, operated by Alibaba.
TLA	Three letter acronym!
UCD	User Centric Design
WMS	Warehouse Management System

Printed in Great Britain
by Amazon